CHILDREN
OF
THE
DEAD
END

CHILDREN OF THE DEAD END

THE AUTOBIOGRAPHY OF AN IRISH NAVVY

BY
PATRICK
MACGILL

NEW YORK
E. P. DUTTON & COMPANY
681 Fifth Avenue

THE ANCHOR PRESS, LTD., TIPTREE, ESSEX, ENGLAND.

FOREWORD

"I WISH the Kinlochleven navvies had been thrown into the loch. They would fain turn the Highlands into a cinderheap," said the late Andrew Lang, writing to me a few months before his death.

In the following pages I have endeavoured to tell of the navvy; the life he leads, the dangers he dares, and the death he often dies. Most of my story is autobiographical. Moleskin Joe and Carroty Dan are true to life; they live now, and for all I know to the contrary may be met with on some precarious job, in some evil-smelling model lodging-house, or, as suits these gipsies of labour, on the open road. Norah Ryan's painful story shows the dangers to which an innocent girl is exposed through ignorance of the fundamental facts of existence; Gourock Ellen and Annie are types of women whom I have often met. While asking a little allowance for the pen of the novelist it must be said that nearly all the incidents of the book have come under the observation of the writer: that such incidents should take place makes the tragedy of the story.

PATRICK MACGILL.

The Garden House,
   Windsor.
 January, 1914.

CONTENTS

CONTENTS

CHILDREN
OF
THE
DEAD
END

CHILDREN OF THE DEAD END

CHAPTER I

A NIGHT IN MY FATHER'S HOUSE

" The wee red-headed man is a knowing sort of fellow,
　His coat is cat's-eye green and his pantaloons are yellow,
　His brogues be made of glass and his hose be red as cherry,
　He's the lad for devilment if you only make him merry,
　He drives a flock of goats, has another flock behind him.
　The little children fear him but the old folk never mind him.
　To the frogs' house and the goats' house and the hilly land and
　　hollow,
　He will carry naughty children where the parents dare not follow.
　Oh ! little ones, beware.　If the red-haired man should catch you,
　You'll have only goats to play with and croaking frogs to watch
　　you,
　A bed between two rocks and not a fire to warm you !—
　Then, little ones, be good and the red-haired man can't harm you."

　　　　　　—From *The Song of the Red-haired Man.*

IT was night in the dead of winter, and we sat around the fire that burned in red and blue flames on the wide open hearth.　The blue flames were a sign of storm.

The snow was white on the ground that stretched away from the door of my father's house, down the dip of the brae and over the hill that rose on the other side of the glen.　I had just been standing out by the little hillock that rose near the corner of the home gable-end, watching the glen people place their lamps in the window corners. I loved to see the lights come out one by one until every house was lighted up.　Nothing looks so cheerful as a lamp seen through the darkness.

B

On the other side of the valley a mountain stream tumbled down to the river. It was always crying out at night and the wail in its voice could be heard ever so far away. It seemed to be lamenting over something which it had lost. I always thought of woman dreeing over a dead body when I listened to it. It seemed so strange to me, too, that it should keep coming down and down for ever.

The hills surrounding the glen were very high ; the old people said that there were higher hills beyond them, but this I found very hard to believe.

These were the thoughts in my mind as I entered my home and closed the door behind me. From the inside I could see the half-moon, twisted like a cow's horn, shining through the window.

" It will be a wet month this," said my father. " There are blue flames in the fire, and a hanging moon never keeps in rain."

The wind was moaning over the chimney. By staying very quiet one could hear the wail in its voice, and it was like that of the stream on the far side of the glen. A pot of potatoes hung over the fire, and as the water bubbled and sang the potatoes could be seen bursting their jackets beneath the lid. The dog lay beside the hearthstone, his nose thrust well over his forepaws, threaping to be asleep, but ready to open his eyes at the least little sound. Maybe he was listening to the song of the pot, for most dogs like to hear it. An oil lamp swung by a string from the roof-tree backwards and forwards like a willow branch when the wind of October is high. As it swung the shadows chased each other in the silence of the farther corners of the house. My mother said that if we were bad children the shadows would run away with us, but they never did, and indeed we were often full of all sorts of mischief. We felt afraid of the shadows, they even frightened mother. But father was afraid of nothing. Once he came from

Ardara fair on the Night of the Dead* and passed the graveyard at midnight.

Sometimes my mother would tell a story, and it was always about the wee red-headed man who had a herd of goats before him and a herd of goats behind him, and a salmon tied to the laces of his brogues for supper. I have now forgotten all the great things which he went through, but in those days I always thought the story of the wee red-headed man the most wonderful one in all the world. At that time I had never heard another.

For supper we had potatoes and buttermilk. The potatoes were emptied into a large wicker basket round which we children sat with a large bowl of buttermilk between us, and out of this bowl we drank in turn. Usually the milk was consumed quickly, and afterwards we ate the potatoes dry.

Nearly every second year the potatoes went bad ; then we were always hungry, although Farley McKeown, a rich merchant in the neighbouring village, let my father have a great many bags of Indian meal on credit. A bag contained sixteen stone of meal and cost a shilling a stone. On the bag of meal Farley McKeown charged sixpence a month interest ; and fourpence a month on a sack of flour which cost twelve shillings. All the people round about were very honest, and paid up their debts whenever they were able. Usually when the young went off to Scotland or England they sent home money to their fathers and mothers, and with this money the parents paid for the meal to Farley McKeown. "What doesn't go to the landlord goes to Farley McKeown," was a Glenmornan saying.

The merchant was a great friend of the parish priest, who always told the people if they did not pay their debts they would burn for ever and ever in hell. " The fires of eternity will make you sorry for the debts that you did not

* The evening of All Souls' Day.

pay," said the priest. "What is eternity?" he would ask in a solemn voice from the altar steps. "If a man tried to count the sands on the sea-shore and took a million years to count every single grain, how long would it take him to count them all? A long time, you'll say. But that time is nothing to eternity. Just think of it! Burning in hell while a man, taking a million years to count a grain of sand, counts all the sand on the sea-shore. And this because you did not pay Farley McKeown his lawful debts, his lawful debts within the letter of the law." That concluding phrase " within the letter of the law " struck terror into all who listened, and no one, maybe not even the priest himself, knew what it meant.

Farley McKeown would give no meal to those who had no children. " That kind of people, who have no children to earn for them, never pay debts," he said. " If *they* get meal and don't pay for it they'll go down—down," said the priest. " 'Tis God Himself that would be angry with Farley McKeown if he gave meal to people like that."

The merchant established a great knitting industry in West Donegal. My mother used to knit socks for him, and he paid her at the rate of one and threepence a dozen pairs, and it was said that he made a shilling of profit on a pair of these in England. My mother usually made a pair of socks daily ; but to do this she had to work sixteen hours at the task. Along with this she had her household duties to look after. " A penny farthing a day is not much to make," I once said to her. " No, indeed, if you look at it in that way," she answered. " But it is nearly two pounds a year and that is half the rent of our farm of land."

Every Christmas Farley McKeown paid two hundred and fifty pounds to the church. When the priest announced this from the altar he would say, " That's the man for you ! "

and all the members of the congregation would bow their heads, feeling very much ashamed of themselves because none of them could give more than a sixpence or a shilling to the silver collection which always took place at the chapel of Greenanore on Christmas Day.

When the night grew later my mother put her bright knitting-needles by in a bowl over the fireplace, and we all went down on our knees, praying together.   Then mother said : " See and leave the door on the latch ; maybe a poor man will need shelter on a night like this."   With these words she turned the ashes over on the live peat while we got into our beds, one by one.

There were six children in our family, three brothers and three sisters.   Of these, five slept in one room, two girls in the little bed, while Fergus and Dan slept along with me in the other, which was much larger.   Father and mother and Kate, the smallest of us all, slept in the kitchen.

When the light was out, we prayed to Mary, Brigid, and Patrick to shield us from danger until the morning.   Then we listened to the winds outside.   We could hear them gather in the dip of the valley and come sweeping over the bend of the hill, singing great lonely songs in the darkness. One wind whistled through the keyhole, another tapped on the window with an ivy leaf, while a third swept under the half-door and rustled across the hearthstone.   Then the breezes died away and there was silence.

" They're only putting their heads together now," said Dan, " making up a plan to do some other tricks."

" I see the moon through the window," said Norah.

" Who made the moon ? " asked Fergus.

" It was never made," answered Dan.   " It was there always."

" There is a man in the moon," I said.   " He was very bad and a priest put him up there for his sins."

" He has a pot of porridge in his hand."

"And a spoon."

"A wooden spoon."

"How could it shine at night if it's only a wooden spoon? It's made of white silver."

"Like a shillin'."

"Like a big shillin' with a handle to it."

"What would we do if we had a shillin'?" asked Ellen.

"I'd buy a pocket-knife," said Dan.

"Would you cut me a stick to drive bullocks to the harvest fair of Greenanore?" asked Fergus.

"And what good would be in havin' a knife if you cut sticks for other folk?"

"I'd buy a prayer-book for the shillin'," said Norah.

"A prayer-book is no good, once you get it," I said. "A knife is far and away better."

"I would buy a sheep for a shillin'," said Fergus.

"You couldn't get a sheep for a shillin'."

"Well, I could buy a young one."

"There never was a young sheep. A young one is only a lamb."

"A lamb turns into a sheep at midsummer moon."

"Why has a lamb no horns?" asked Norah.

"Because it's young," we explained.

"We'll sing a holy song," said Ellen.

"We'll sing *Holy Mary*," we all cried together, and began to sing in the darkness.

> "Oh! Holy Mary, mother mild,
> Look down on me, a little child,
> And when I sleep put near my bed
> The good Saint Joseph at my head,
> My guardian Angel at my right
> To keep me good through all the night;
> Saint Brigid give me blessings sweet;
> Saint Patrick watch beside my feet.
> Be good to me O! mother mild,
> Because I am a little child."

" Get a sleep on you," mother called from the next room.
" The wee red-headed man is comin' down the chimley
and he is goin' to take ye away if ye aren't quiet."

We fell asleep, and that was how the night passed by in
my father's house years ago.

CHAPTER II

OLD CUSTOMS

'Put a green cross beneath the roof on the eve of good Saint Bride
And you'll have luck within the house for long past Lammastide;
Put a green cross above the door—'tis hard to keep it green,
But 'twill bring good luck and happiness for long past Hallow
  E'en
The green cross holds Saint Brigid's spell, and long the spell
  endures,
And 'twill bring blessings on the head of you and all that's yours."
—From *The Song of Simple People.*

ONCE a year, on Saint Bride's Eve, my father came home from his day's work, carrying a load of green rushes on his shoulders. At the door he would stand for a moment with his feet on the threshold and say these words :

" Saint Bride sends her blessings to all within. Give her welcome."

Inside my mother would answer, " Welcome she is," and at these words my father would loosen the shoulder-knot and throw his burden on the floor. Then he made crosses from the rushes, wonderful crosses they were. It was said that my father was the best at that kind of work in all the countryside. When made, they were placed in various parts of the house and farm. They were hung up in our home, over the lintel of the door, the picture of the Holy Family, the beds, the potato pile and the fireplace. One was placed over the spring well, one in the pig-sty, and one over the roof-tree of the byre. By doing this the blessing of Saint Bride remained in the house for the whole of the following year. I liked to watch my father plaiting the crosses, but I could never make one myself.

When my mother churned milk she lifted the first butter that formed on the top of the cream and placed it against the wall outside the door. It was left there for the fairy folk when they roamed through the country at midnight. They would not harm those who gave them an offering in that manner, but the people who forgot them would have illness among their cattle through all the length of the year.

If my father met a red-haired woman when he was going to the market he would turn home. To meet a red-haired woman on the high-road is very unlucky.

It is a bad market where there are more women than men. " Two women and a goose make a market," is the saying among the Glenmornan folk.

If my mother chanced to overturn the milk which she had drawn from the cow, she would say these words: " Our loss go with it. Them that it goes to need it more than we do." One day I asked her who were the people to whom it went. " The gentle folk," she told me. These were the fairies.

You very seldom hear persons called by their surname in Glenmornan. Every second person you meet there is either a Boyle or an O'Donnell. You want to ask a question about Hugh O'Donnell. " Is it Patrick's Hugh or Mickey's Hugh or Sean's Hugh? " you will be asked. So too in the Glen you never say *Mrs.* when speaking of a married woman. It is just " Farley's Brigid " or "Patrick's Norah " or " Cormac's Ellen," as the case may be. There was one woman in Glenmornan who had a little boy of about my age, and she seldom spoke to anybody on the road to chapel or market. Everyone seemed to avoid her, and the old people called her " that woman," and they often spoke about her doings. She had never a man of her own, they said. Of course I didn't understand these things, but I knew there was a great difference in being called somebody's Mary or Norah instead of " that woman."

On St. Stephen's Day the Glenmornan boys beat the bushes and killed as many wrens as they could lay their hands on. The wren is a bad bird, for it betrayed St. Stephen to the Jews when they wanted to put him to death. The saint hid in a clump of bushes, but the wrens made such a chatter and clatter that the Jews, when passing, stopped to see what annoyed the birds, and found the saint hiding in the undergrowth. No wonder then that the Glenmornan people have a grudge against the wren !

Kissing is almost unknown in the place where I was born and bred. Judas betrayed the Son of God with a kiss, which proves beyond a doubt that kissing is of the devil's making. It is no harm to kiss the dead in Glenmornan, for no one can do any harm to the dead.

Once I got bitten by a dog. The animal snapped a piece of flesh from my leg and ate it when he got out of the way. When I came into my own house my father and mother were awfully frightened. If three hairs of the dog that bit me were not placed against the sore I would go mad before seven moons had faded. Oiney Dinchy, who owned the dog, would not give me three hairs because I was unfortunate enough to be stealing apples when the dog rushed at me. For all that it mattered to Oiney, I might go as mad as a March hare. The priest, when informed of the trouble, blessed salt which he told my father to place on the wound. My father did so, but the salt pained me so much that I rushed screaming from the house. The next door neighbours ran into their homes and closed their doors when they heard me scream. Two little girls were coming to our house for the loan of a half-bottle of holy water for a sick cow, and when they saw me rush out they fled hurriedly, shrieking that I was already mad from the bite of Oiney

Dinchy's dog. When Oiney heard this he got frightened and he gave my father three hairs of the dog with a civil hand. I placed them on my sore, the dog was hung by a rope from the branch of a tree, and the madness was kept away from me. I hear that nowadays in Glenmornan the people never apply the holy salt to the bite of a dog. Thus do old customs change.

The six-hand reel is a favourite Glenmornan dance, but in my time a new parish priest came along who did not approve of dancing. " The six-hand reel is a circle, the centre of which is the devil," said he, and called a house in which a dance was held the " Devil's Station." He told the people to cease dancing, but they would not listen to him. " When we get a new parish priest we don't want a new God," they said. " The old God who allowed dancing is good enough for us." The priest put the seven curses on the people who said these words. I only know three of the seven curses.

> May you have one leg and it to be halting.
> May you have one eye and it to be squinting
> May you have one tooth and it to be aching.

The second curse fell on one man—old Oiney Dinchy, who had a light foot on a good floor. When tying a restive cow in the byre, the animal caught Oiney in the ball of one eye with the point of its horn, and Oiney could only see through the other eye afterwards. The people when they saw this feared the new parish priest, but they never took any heed to the new God, and up to this day there are many good six-hand reelers in Glenmornan. And the priest is dead.

The parish priest who came in his place was a little pot-bellied man with white shiny false teeth, who smoked ninepenny cigars and who always travelled first-class in a railway train. Everybody feared him because he put curses on most of the people in Glenmornan ; and usually on the people whom I thought best in the world. Those whom I did not like at all became great friends of the priest. I always left the high-road when I saw him coming. His name was Father Devaney, and he was eternally looking for money from the people, who, although very poor, always paid when the priest commanded them. If they did not they would go to hell as soon as they died. So Father Devaney said.

A stranger in Glenmornan should never talk about crows. The people of the Glen are nicknamed the " Crow Chasers," because once in the bad days, the days of the potato failure, they chased for ten long hours a crow that had stolen a potato, and took back the potato at night in triumph. This has been cast up in their teeth ever since, and it is an ill day for a stranger when he talks about crows to the Glenmornan people.

Courtship is unknown in Glenmornan. When a young man takes it in his head to marry, he goes out in company with a friend and a bottle of whisky and looks for a woman. If one refuses, the young man looks for another and another until the bottle of whisky is consumed. The friend talks to the girl's father and lays great stress upon the merits of the would-be husband, who meanwhile pleads his suit with the girl. Sometimes a young man empties a dozen bottles of whisky before he can persuade a woman to marry him.

In my own house we had flesh meat to dinner four times each year, on St. Patrick's Day, Easter Sunday, Christmas Day, and New Year's Day. If the harvest had been a good one we took bacon with our potatoes at the ingathering of the hay. Ours was a hay harvest ; we grew very little corn.

Of all the seasons of the year I liked the harvest-time best. Looking from the door of my father's house I had the whole of Glenmornan under my eyes. Far down the Glen the road wound in and out, now on one side of the river and now on the other, running away to the end of Ireland, and for all that I knew, maybe to the end of the world itself.

The river came from the hills, tumbling over rocks in showers of fine white mist and forming into deep pools beneath, where it rested calmly after its mad race. Here the trout leaped all day, and turned the placid surface into millions of petulant ripples which broke like waves under the hazel bushes that shaded the banks. In the fords further along the heavy milch cows stood belly-deep in the stream, seeking relief from the madness that the heat and the gad-flies put into their blood.

The young cattle grazed on the braes, keeping well in the shadow of the cliffs, while from the hill above the mountain-sheep followed one another in single file, as is their wont, down to the lower and sweeter pastures.

The mowers were winding their scythes in long heavy sweeps through the meadow in the bottomlands, and rows of mown hay lay behind them. Even where I stood, far up, I could hear the sharp swish of their scythes as they cut through the bottom grass.

The young maidens, their legs bare well above their knees, tramped linen at the brookside and laughed merrily at every joke that passed between them.

The neighbours spoke to one another across the march ditches, and their talk was of the weather and the progress of the harvest.

The farmer boy could be seen going to the moor for a load of peat, his creel swinging in a careless way across his shoulders and his hands deep in his trousers' pockets. He was barefooted, and the brown moss was all over the calves of his legs. He was thinking of something as he walked along and he looked well in his torn shirt and old hat. Many a time I wondered what were the thoughts which filled his mind.

Now and again a traveller passed along the road, looking very tired as he dragged his legs after him. His hob-nailed boots made a rasping sound on the grey gravel, and it was hard to tell where he was going.

One day a drover passed along, driving his herd of wild-eyed, panting bullocks before him. He was a little man and he carried a heavy cudgel of a stick in his hands. I went out to the road to see him passing and also to speak to him if he took any notice of a little fellow.

" God's blessing be on every beast under your care," I said, repeating the words which my mother always said to the drovers which she met. " Is it any harm to ask you where you are going ? "

" I'm goin' to the fair of 'Derry," said he.

"Is 'Derry fair as big as the fair of Greenanore, good man?"

He laughed at my question, and I could see his teeth black with tobacco juice. " Greenanore ! " he exclaimed. " 'Derry fair is a million times bigger."

Of course I didn't believe him, for had I not been at the harvest-fair of Greenanore myself, and I thought that there could be nothing greater in all the seven corners of the world. But it was in my world and I knew more of the bigger as the years went on.

In those days the world, to me, meant something intangible, which lay beyond the farthest blue line of mountains which could be seen from Glenmornan Hill. And those mountains were ever so far away! How many snug little houses, white under their coatings of cockle lime, how many wooden bridges spanning hurrying streams, and how many grey roads crossing brown moors lay between Glenmornan Hill and the last blue line of mountain tops that looked over into the world for which I longed with all the wistfulness of youth, I did not know.

CHAPTER III

" When brown trout leap in ev'ry burn, when hares are scooting on
the brae,
When rabbits frisk where e'er you turn, 'tis sad to waste your hours
away
Within bald Learning's droning hive with pen and pencil, rod and
rule—
Oh! the unhappiest soul alive is oft a little lad at school."

—From *The Man who Met the Scholars*.

I DID not like school. My father could neither read
nor write, and he didn't trouble much about my
education.

The priest told him to send me to the village school, and
I was sent accordingly.

" The priest should know what is best," my father said.

The master was a little man with a very large stomach.
He was short of breath, and it was very funny to hear him
puffing on a very warm day, when the sweat ran down his
face and wetted his collar. The people about thought that he
was very wise, and said that he could talk a lot of wisdom
if he were not so short of breath. Whenever he sat by the
school fire he fell asleep. Everyone said that though very
wise the man was very lazy. When he got to his feet after
a sleep he went about the schoolroom grunting like a sick
cow. For the first six months at school I felt frightened
of him, after that I disliked him. He beat me about three
times a day. He cut hazel rods on his way to school, and
used them every five minutes when not asleep. Nearly
all the scholars cried whenever they were beaten, but I

never did. I think this was one of his strongest reasons for hating me more than any of the rest. I learned very slowly, and never could do my sums correctly, but I liked to read the poems in the more advanced books and could recite *Childe Harold's Farewell* when only in the second standard.

When I was ten years of age I left school, being then only in the third book. This was the way of it. One day, when pointing out places on the map of the world, the master came round, and the weather being hot the man was in a bad temper.

" Point out Corsica, Dermod Flynn," he said.

I had not the least idea as to what part of the world Corsica occupied, and I stood looking awkwardly at the master and the map in turn. I think that he enjoyed my discomfited expression, for he gazed at me in silence for a long while.

" Dermod Flynn, point out Corsica," he repeated.

" I don't know where it is," I answered sullenly.

" I'll teach you ! " he roared, getting hold of my ear and pulling it sharply. The pain annoyed me ; I got angry and hardly was aware of what I was doing. I just saw his eyes glowering into mine. I raised the pointer over my head and struck him right across the face. Then a red streak ran down the side of his nose and it frightened me to see it.

" Dermod Flynn has killed the master ! " cried a little girl whose name was Norah Ryan and who belonged to the same class as myself.

I was almost certain that I had murdered him, for he dropped down on the form by the wall without speaking a word and placed both his hands over his face. For a wee bit I stood looking at him ; then I caught up my cap and·rushed out of the school.

Next day, had it not been for the red mark on his face,

the master was as well as ever. But I never went back to school again. My father did not believe much in book learning, so he sent me out to work for the neighbours who required help at the seed-time or harvest. Sixpence a day was my wages, and the work in the fields was more to my liking than the work at the school.

Whenever I passed the scholars on the road afterwards they said to one another: " Just think of it ! Dermod Flynn struck the master across the face when he was at the school."

Always I felt very proud of my action when I heard them say that. It was a great thing for a boy of my age to stand up on his feet and strike a man who was four times his age. Even the young men spoke of my action and, what was more, they praised my courage. They had been at school themselves and they did not like the experience.

Nowadays, whenever I look at Corsica on the map, I think of old Master Diver and the days I spent under him in the little Glenmornan schoolhouse:

CHAPTER IV

THE GREAT SILENCE

" Where the people toil like beasts in the field till their bones are
strained and sore,
There the landlord waits, like the plumbless grave, calling out
for more
Money to flounce his daughters' gowns or clothe his spouse's hide,
Money so that his sons can learn to gamble, shoot, and ride ;
And for every debt of honour paid and for every dress and
frill,
The blood of the peasant's wife and child goes out to meet the
bill."

—From *The Song of the Glen People.*

I WAS nearly twelve years old when Dan, my youngest
brother, died. It was in the middle of winter, and
he was building a snow-man in front of the half-
door when he suddenly complained of a pain in his
throat. Mother put him to bed and gave him a drink of
hot milk. She did not send for the doctor because there
was no money in the house to pay the bill. Dan lay in
bed all the evening and many of the neighbours came in
to see him. Towards midnight I was sent to bed, but
before going I heard my father ask mother if she thought
that Dan would live till morning. I could not sleep, but
kept turning over in the bed and praying to the Blessed
Virgin to save my little brother. The new moon, sharp
as a scythe, was peeping through the window of my room
when my mother came to my bed and told me to rise and
kiss Dan for the last time. She turned her face away as
she spoke, and I knew that she was weeping. My brother
was lying on the bed, gazing up at the ceiling with wide-

staring eyes. A crimson flush was on his face and his breath pained him. I bent down and pressed his cheek. I was afraid, and the kiss made my lips burn like fire. The three of us then stood together and my father shook the holy water all over the room. All at once Dan sat up in the bed and gripped a tight hold of the blankets. I wanted to run out of the room but my mother would not let me.

" Are ye wantin' anything ? " asked my father, bending over the bed, but there was no answer. My brother fell back on the bed and his face got very white.

" Poor Dan is no more," said my father, the tears coming out of his eyes. 'Twas the first time I ever saw him weeping, and I thought it very strange. My mother went to the window and opened it in order to let the soul of my brother go away to heaven.

" It is all in the hands of God," she said. " He is only taking back what He sent us."

There was silence in the room for a long while. My father and mother wept, and I was afraid of something which was beyond my understanding.

" Will Dan ever come back again ? " I asked.

" Hush, dearie ! " said my mother.

" It will take a lot of money to bury the poor boy," said my father. " It costs a good penny to rear one, but it's a bad job when one is taken away."

I had once seen an old woman buried—" Old Nan," the beggarwoman. For many years she had passed up and down Glenmornan Road, collecting bottles and rags, which she paid for in blessings and afterwards sold for pence. Being wrinkled, heavy-boned, and bearded like a man, everyone said that she was a witch. One summer Old Nan died, and two days later she was carried to the little graveyard. I played truant from school and followed the sweating men who were carrying the coffin on their shoulders. They seemed to be well-pleased when they came in sight of the churchyard and the cold silent tombstones.

" The old witch was as heavy as lead," I heard the bearers say.

They set down their burden and dug a hole in the soft earth, throwing up black clay and white bones to the surface with their shovels. The bones looked like those of sheep which die on the hills and are left to rot. The air was heavy with the humming of bees, and a little brook sang a soft song of its own as it hurried past the graveyard wall. The upturned earth had a sickly smell like mildewed corn. Some of the diggers knew whose bone this was and whose that was, but they had a hard argument about a thigh-bone before Old Nan was put into the earth. Some said that the thigh-bone belonged to old Farley Kelly, who had died many years before, and others said that it belonged to Farley's wife. I thought it a curious thing that people could not know the difference between a man and a woman when dead. While the men were discussing the thigh-bone it was left lying on the black clay which fringed the mouth of the grave, and a long earth-worm crawled across it. A man struck at the worm with his spade and broke the bone into three pieces. The worm was cut in two, and it fell back into the grave while one of the diggers threw the splinters of bone on top of it. Then they buried Old Nan, and everyone seemed very light-hearted over the job. Why shouldn't they feel merry? She was only an old witch; anyhow. But I did not feel happy. The grave looked a cold cheerless place and the long crawling worms were ugly.

So our poor Dan would go down into the dark earth like Old Nan, the witch ! The thought frightened me, and I began to cry with my father and mother, and we were all three weeping still, but more quietly, when the first dim light of the lonely dawn came stealing through the window panes.

Two old sisters, Martha and Bride, lived next door. My mother asked me to go out and tell them about Dan's death. I ran out quickly, and I found both women up and at work washing dishes beside the dresser. Martha had a tin basin in her hand, and she let it drop to the floor when I delivered my message. Bride held a jug, and it seemed for a moment that she was going to follow her sister's example, but all at once she called to mind that the jug was made of delft, so she placed it on the dresser, and both followed me back to my home. Once there they asked many questions about Dan, his sickness and how he came to die. When they had heard all, they told of several herbs and charms which would have cured the illness at once. Dandelion dipped in rock water, or bogbine* boiled for two hours in the water of the marsh from which it was plucked, would have worked wonders. Also seven drops of blood from a cock that never crowed, or the boiled liver of a rabbit that never crossed a white road, were the very best things to give to a sick person. So they said, and when Bride tried to recollect some more certain cures Martha kept repeating the old ones until I was almost tired of listening to her voice.

" Why did ye not take in the docthor ? " asked Martha.

" We had no money in the house," said my mother.

" An' did ye not sell half a dozen sheep at the fair the day afore yesterday ? " asked Bride. " I'm sure that ye got a good penny for them same sheep."

" We did that," said my mother ; " but the money is for the landlord's rent and the priest's tax."

At that time the new parish priest, the little man with the pot-belly and the shiny false teeth, was building a grand new house. Farley McKeown had given five hundred

* Marsh trefoil.

pounds towards the cost of building, which up to now amounted to one thousand five hundred pounds. So the people said, but they were not quite sure. The cost of building was not their business, that was the priest's ; all the people had to do was to pay their tax, which amounted to five pounds on every family in the parish. They were allowed five years in which to pay it. On two occasions my father was a month late in paying the money and the priest put a curse on him each time. So my father said. I have only a very faint recollection of these things which took place when I was quite a little boy.

" God be good to us ! but five pounds is a heavy tax for even a priest to put on poor people," said Bride.

" It's not for us to say anything against a priest, no matter what he does," said my father, crossing himself.

" I don't care what ye say, Michael Flynn," said the old woman ; " five pounds is a big tax to pay. The priest is spending three hundred gold sovereigns in making a lava-thury (lavatory). Three hundred sovereigns ! that's a waste of money."

" Lava-thury ? " said my mother. " And what would that be at all ? "

" It's myself that does not know," answered Bride. " But old Oiney Dinchy thinks that it is a place for keeping holy water."

" Poor wee Dan," said Martha, looking at the white face in the bed. " It's the hard way that death has with it always. He was a lively boy only three days ago. Wasn't it then that he came over to our house and tied the dog's tail to the bundle of yarn that just came from Farley McKeown's. I was angry with the dear little rascal, too ; God forgive me ! "

Then Martha and Bride began to cry together, one keeping time with the other, but when my mother got ready some tea they sat down and drank a great deal of it.

A great number of neighbours came in during the day. They all said prayers by Dan's bedside, then they drank whisky and tea and smoked my father's tobacco. For two nights my dead brother was waked. Every day fresh visitors came, and for these my father had to buy extra food, snuff, and tobacco, so that the little money in his possession was sliding through his fingers like water in a sieve.

On the day of the funeral Dan went to the grave in a little deal box which my father himself fashioned. They would not let me go and see the burial.

In the evening when my parents came back their eyes were red as fire and they were still crying. We sat round the peat blaze and Dan's stool was left vacant. We expected that he would return at any moment. We children could not understand the strange silent thing called Death. The oil lamp was not lighted. There was no money in the house to pay for oil.

" There's very little left now," said my mother late that night, as I was turning in to bed. She was speaking to my father. " Wasn't there big offerings ? " she asked.

Everybody who comes to a Catholic funeral in Donegal pays a shilling to the priest who conducts the burial service, and the nearest blood relation always pays five shillings, and is asked to give more if he can afford it. Money lifted thus is known as offerings, and all goes to the priest, who takes in hand to shorten the sufferings of the souls in Purgatory.

" Eight pounds nine shillings," said my father. " It's a big penny. The priest was talking to me, and says that he wants another pound for his new house at once. I'm over three weeks behind, and if he puts a curse on me this time what am I to do at all, at all ? "

" What you said is the only thing to be done," my

mother said. I did not understand what these words meant, and I was afraid to ask a question.

" It's the only thing to be done," she remarked again, and after that there was a long silence.

" Dermod, asthor * ! " she said all at once. " Come next May, ye must go beyont the mountains to push yer fortune, pay the priest, and make up the rent for the Hallow E'en next coming."

* Darling.

CHAPTER V

THE SLAVE MARKET

" My mother's love for me is warm,
  Her house is cold and bare,
A man who wants to see the world
  Has little comfort there;
And there 'tis hard to pay the rent,
  For all you dig and delve,
But there's hope beyond the Mountains
  For a little Man of Twelve."

—From *The Man of Twelve.*

WHEN the following May came round, I had been working at the turnip-thinning with a neighbouring man, and one evening I came back to my own home in the greyness of the soft dusk. It had been a long day's work, from seven in the morning to nine of the clock at night. A boy can never have too much time to himself and too little to do, but I was kept hard at work always, and never had a moment to run about the lanes or play by the burns with other children. Indeed, I did not care very much for the company of boys of my own age. Because I was strong for my years I despised them, and in turn I was despised by the youths who were older than myself. " Too-long-for-your-trousers " they called me, and I believe that I merited the nickname, for I wished ever so much to grow up quickly and be able to carry a creel of peat like Jim Scanlon, or drive a horse and cart with Ned O'Donnel, who lived next door but one to my father's house.

Sometimes I would go out for a walk with these two

men on a Sunday afternoon, that is, if they allowed me to accompany them. I listened eagerly to every word spoken by them and used to repeat their remarks aloud to myself afterwards. Sometimes I would speak like them in my own home.

" Isn't it a shame the way Connel Diver of the hill treats his wife," I said to my father and mother one day. " He goes out in the evening and courts Widow Breslin when he should stay at home with his own woman."

" Dermod, asthor ! What puts them ideas into yer head ? " asked my mother. " What d'ye know abot Connel Diver and the Widow Breslin ? "

" It's them two vagabonds, Micky's Jim and Dinchy's Ned, that's tellin' him these things," said my father ; " but let me never catch him goin' out of the door with any of the pair of them again."

Whatever was the reason of it, I liked the company of the two youths a great deal more afterwards.

On this May evening, as I was saying, I came back from the day's work and found my mother tying all my spare clothes into a large brown handkerchief.

" Ye're goin' away beyont the mountains in the mornin', Dermod," she said. " Ye have to go out and push yer fortune. We must get some money to pay the rent come Hallow E'en, and as ye'll get a bigger penny workin' with the farmers away there, me and yer da have thought of sendin' ye to the hirin'-fair of Strabane on the morra."

I had been dreaming of this journey for months before, and I never felt happier in all my life than I did when my mother spoke these words. I clapped my hands with pure joy, danced in front of the door, and threw my cap into the air.

" Are ye not sorry at leavin' home ? " my mother asked, and from her manner of speaking I knew that she was not pleased to see me so happy.

" What would I be sorry for ? " I asked, and ran off to
tell Micky's Jim about the journey which lay before me
the next morning. Didn't I feel proud, too, when Micky's
Jim, who had spent many seasons at the potato digging
in Scotland, shook hands with me just the same as if I had
been a full-grown man. Indeed, I felt that I was a man
when I returned to my own doorstep and saw the prepara-
tions that were being made for my departure. Everyone
was hard at work, my sisters sewing buttons on my clothes,
my mother putting a new string in the *Medal of the Sacred
Heart* which I had to wear around my neck when far away
from her keeping, and my father hammering nails into my
boots so that they would last me through the whole summer
and autumn.

That night when we were on our knees at the Rosary,
I mumbled through my prayers, made a mistake in the
number of *Hail Marys*, and forgot several times to respond
to the prayers of the others. No one said a word of reproof,
and I felt that I had become a very important person. I
thought that my mother wept during the prayers, but of
this I was not quite certain.

" Rise up, Dermod," said my mother, touching me on
the shoulder next morning. " The white arm of the dawn
is stealin' over the door, and it is time ye were out on yer
journey."

I took my breakfast, but did not feel very hungry. At
the last moment my mother looked through my bundle
to see if I had everything which I needed, then, with my
father's blessings and my mother's prayers, I went out
from my people in the grey of the morning.

A pale mist was rising off the braes as I crossed the
wooden bridge that lay between my home and the leading
road to Greenanore. There was hardly a move in the wind,
and the green grass by the roadside was heavy with drops

of dew. Under the bridge a salmon jumped, all at once, breaking the pool into a million strips of glancing water. As I leant over the rails I could see, far down, a large trout waving his tail in slow easy sweeps and opening and closing his mouth rapidly as if he was out of breath. He was almost the colour of the sand on which he was lying.

I stopped for a moment at the bend of the road, and looked back at my home. My father was standing at the door waving his hand, and I saw my mother rub her eyes with the corner of her apron. I thought that she was crying, but I did not trouble myself very much about that, for I knew women are very fond of weeping. I waved my hand over my head, then I turned round the corner and went out of their sight, feeling neither sorry nor afraid.

I met Norah Ryan on the road. She had been my schoolmate, and when we were in the class together I had liked to look at her soft creamy skin and grey eyes. She always put me in mind of pictures of angels that were hung on the walls of the little chapel in the village. Her mother was going to send her into a convent when she left school—so the neighbours said.

" Where are ye for this morning, Dermod Flynn ? " she asked.

" Beyond the mountains," I told her.

" Ye'll not come back for a long while, will ye ? "

I said that I would never come back, just to see how she took it, and I was very vexed when she just laughed and walked on. I felt sorrier leaving her than leaving anyone else whom I knew, and I stood and looked back after her many, many times, but she never turned even to bid me good-bye.

On the road several boys and girls, all bound for the hiring market of Strabane, joined me. When we were all together there was none amongst us over fourteen years of age. The girls carried their boots in their hands. They were so used to running barefooted on the moors that they found themselves more comfortable walking along the gritty road in that manner. While journeying to the station they sang out bravely, all except one girl, who was crying, but no one paid very much heed to her. A boy of fourteen who was one of the party had been away before. His shoulders were very broad, his legs were twisted and his body was all awry. Some said that he was born in a frost and that he got slewed in a thaw. He smoked a short clay pipe which he drew from his mouth when the girls started singing.

" Sing away now, ye will ! " he cried. " Ye'll not sing ,much afore ye're long away." For all that he was singing louder than any three of the party himself before we arrived at the railway station.

The platform was crowded. I saw youngsters who had come a distance of twelve miles and who had been travelling all night. They looked worn out and sleepy. With some of the children fathers and mothers came.

" We are goin' to drive a hard bargain with the masters," some of the parents said.

" Some of them won't bring in a good penny because they're played out on the long tramp to the station," said others.

They meant no disrespect for their children, but their words put me in mind of the manner of speaking of drovers who sell bullocks at the harvest-fair of Greenanore.

There was a rush for seats when the train came in and nearly every carriage became crowded in an instant. There were over twenty in my compartment, some standing, a few sitting, but most of us trying to look out of the windows. Next to us was a first-class carriage, and I noticed that it contained only one single person. I had never been in a railway train before and I knew very little about things.

" Why is there only one man in there, while twenty of us are crammed in here ? " I asked the boy with the clay pipe, for he happened to be beside me.

My friend looked at me with the pride of one who knows.

" Shure, ye know nothin'," he answered. " That man's a gintleman."

" I would like to be a gintleman," I said in all simplicity.

" Ye a gintleman ! " roared the boy. " Ye haven't a white shillin' between ye an' the world an' ye talk as if ye were a king. A gintleman, indeed ! What put that funny thought into yer head, Dermod Flynn ? "

After a while the boy spoke again.

" D'ye know who that gintleman is ? " he asked.

" I don't know at all," I answered.

" That's the landlord who owns yer father's land and many a broad acre forbye."

Then I knew what a gentleman really was. He was the monster who grabbed the money from the people, who drove them out to the roadside, who took six ears of every seven ears of corn produced by the peasantry ; the man who was hated by all men, yet saluted on the highways by most of the people when they met him. He had taken the money which might have saved my brother's life, and it was on account of him that I had now to set out to the Calvary of mid-Tyrone. I went out on the platform again and stole a glance at the man. He was small, thin-lipped, and ugly-looking. I did not think much of him, and I wondered why the Glenmornan people feared him so much.

We stood huddled together like sheep for sale in the market-place of Strabane. Over our heads the town clock rang out every passing quarter of an hour. I had never in my life before seen a clock so big. I felt tired and placed my bundle on the kerbstone and sat down upon it. A girl, one of my own country-people, looked at me.

"Sure, ye'll never get a man to hire ye if ye're seen sitting there," she said.

I got up quickly, feeling very much ashamed to know that a girl was able to teach me things. It wouldn't have mattered so much if a boy had told me.

There was great talk going on about the Omagh train. The boys who had been sold at the fair before said that the best masters came from near the town of Omagh, and so everyone waited eagerly until eleven o'clock, the hour at which the train was due.

It was easy to know when the Omagh men came, for they overcrowded an already big market. Most of them were fat, angry-looking fellows, who kept moving up and down examining us after the manner of men who seek out the good and bad points of horses which they intend to buy.

Sometimes they would speak to each other, saying that they never saw such a lousy and ragged crowd of servants in the market-place in all their life before, and they did not seem to care even if we overheard them say these things. On the whole I had no great liking for the Omagh men.

A big man with a heavy stomach came up to me.

"How much do ye want for the six months?" he asked.

"Six pounds," I told him.

"Shoulders too narrow for the money," he said, more to himself than to me, and walked on.

Standing beside me was an old father, who had a son and daughter for sale. The girl looked pale and sickly. She had a cough that would split a rock.

"Arrah, an' will ye whisth that coughin'!" said her brother, time and again. "Sure, ye know that no wan will give ye wages if ye go on in that way."

The father never spoke. I suppose he felt that there was nothing to be said. During one of these fits of coughing an evil-faced farmer who was looking for a female servant came around and asked the old man what wages did he want for his daughter.

" Five pounds," said the old man, and there was a tremble in his voice when he spoke.

" And maybe the cost of buryin' her," said the farmer with a white laugh as he passed on his way.

High noon had just passed when a youngish man, curiously old in appearance, stood in front of me. His shoulders were very broad, and one of them was far higher than the other. His waist was slender like a girl's, but his buttocks were heavy out of all proportion to his thin waist and slim slivers of shanks.

" Six pounds ! " he repeated when I told him what wages I desired. " It's a big penny to give a wee man. I'll give ye a five-pound note for the six months and not one white sixpence more."

He struck me on the back while he spoke as if to test the strength of my spine, then ran his fingers over my shoulder and squeezed the thick of my arm so tightly that I almost roared in his face with the pain of it. After a long wrangle I wrung an offer of five pounds ten shillings for my wages and I was his for six months to come.

" Now gi' me your bundle and come along," he said.

I handed him my parcel of clothes and followed him through the streets, leaving the crowd of wrangling masters and obdurate boys fighting over final sixpences behind me. My master kept talking most of the time, and this was how he kept going on.

" What is yer name ? Dermod Flynn ? A Papist ?— all Donegals are Papists. That doesn't matter to me, for if ye're a good willin' worker me and ye 'ill get on grand. I suppose ye'll have a big belly. It'll be hard to fill. Are ye hungry now ? I suppose yer teeth will be growin' long with starvation, so I'll see if I can get ye anything to ate."

We turned up a little side street, passed under a low archway and went into an inn kitchen, where a young woman with a very red face was bending over a frying-pan on which she was turning many thick slices of bacon. The odour caused my stomach to feel empty.

" This is a new cub that I got, Mary," said the man to the servant. " He's a Donegal like yerself and he's hungry. Give him some tay and bread."

" And some butter," added Mary, looking at me.

" How much is the butter extra ? " asked my master.

" Tuppence," said Mary.

" I don't think that this cub cares for butter. D'ye ? " he asked, turning to me.

" I like butter," I said.

" Who'd have thought of that, now ? " he said, and he did not look at all pleased. " Ye can wait here," he con tinued, " and I'll come back for ye in a wee while and the two of us can go along to my farm together."

He went out and left me alone with the servant. As he passed the window, on his way to the street, Mary put her thumb to her nose and spread her fingers out towards him.

" I hate Orangemen," she said to me ; " and that pig of a Bennet is wan of the worst of the breedin'. Ah, the old slobber-chops ! See and keep up yer own end of the house with him, anyhow, and never let the vermint tramp over you."

She made ready a pot of tea, gave me some bread and butter and two rashers of bacon.

" Ate yer hearty fill now, Dermod," said the good-natured girl ; " for ye'll not get a dacent male for the next six months."

And I didn't.

D

CHAPTER VI

BOYNE WATER AND HOLY WATER

" Since two can't gain in the bargain,
    Then who shall bear the loss
When little children are auctioned
    As slaves at the Market Cross?
Come to the Cross and the Market,
    Where the wares of the world are sold,
And the wares are little children,
    Traded for pieces of gold."

—From *Good Bargains.*

MY master's name was Bennet—Joe Bennet. He owned a farm of some eighty acres and kept ten milch cows, two cart-horses, and twenty sheep. He possessed a spring-cart, but he seldom used it. It had been procured at one time for taking the family to church, but they were ashamed to put any of the cart-horses between the shafts, and no wonder. One of the horses was spavined and the other was covered with angleberries.

He brought me home from Strabane on the old cart drawn by the spavined horse, and though it was well past midnight when we returned I had to wash the vehicle before I turned into bed. My supper consisted of butter-milk and potatoes, which were served up on the table in the kitchen. The first object that encountered my eye was a large picture of *King William Crossing the Boyne,* hung from a nail over the fireplace and almost brown with age. I hated the picture from the moment I set eyes on it, and though my dislikes are short-lived they are intense while they last. This picture almost assumed an orange tint before I left, and many a time I used to spit at it out of pure spite when left alone in the kitchen.

The household consisted of five persons, Bennet, his father and mother, and two sisters. He was always quarrelling with his two sisters, who, in addition to being wasp-waisted and spider-shanked, were peppery-tongued and salt-tempered, but he never got the best of the argument. The two hussies could talk the head off a drum. The old father was half-doting, and he never spoke to anybody but me. He sat all day in the chimney-corner, rubbing one skinny hand over the other, and kicking the dog if ever it happened to draw near the fire. When he spoke to me it was to point out some fault which I had committed at my work.

The woman of the house was bent like the rim of a dish from constant stooping over her work. She got up in the morning before anyone else and trudged about in the yard all day, feeding the hens, washing the linen, weeding the walk or seeing after the cows. I think that she had a liking for me. One day when I was working beside her in the cabbage patch she said these words to me:

" It's a pity you're a Papist, Dermod."

I suppose she meant it in good part, but her talk made me angry.

My bedroom was placed on the second floor, and a rickety flight of stairs connected the apartment with the kitchen. My room was comfortable enough when the weather was good, but when it was wet the rain often came in by the roof and soaked through my blankets. But the hard work on Bennet's farm made me so tired that a wet blanket could not keep me from sleeping. In the morning I was called at five o'clock and sent out to wash potatoes in a pond near the house. Afterwards they were boiled in a pot over the kitchen fire, and when cooked they were eaten by the pigs and me. I must say that I was allowed to pick the best potatoes for myself, and I got a bowl of buttermilk to wash them down. The pigs got buttermilk also. This was my breakfast during the six months. For dinner I had potatoes and buttermilk, for supper buttermilk and potatoes. I never got tea in the afternoon. The Bennets took tea themselves, but I suppose they thought that such a luxury was unnecessary for me.

I always went down on my knees at the bedside to say my prayers. I knew that young Bennet did not like this, so I always left my door wide open that he might see me praying as he passed by on the way to his own bedroom.

From the moment of my arrival I began to realise that the Country beyond the Mountains, as the people at home call Tyrone, was not the best place in the world for a man of twelve. Sadder than that it was for me to learn that I was not worthy of the name of man at all. Many and many a time did Bennet say that he was paying me a man's wages while I was only fit for a child's work. Sometimes when carrying burdens with him I would fall under the weight, and upon seeing this he would discard his own, run forward, and with arms on hips, wait until I rose from the ground again.

" Whoever saw such a thing ! " he would say and shake his head. " I thought that I got a man at the hirin'-fair." He drawled out his words slowly as if each one gave him pleasure in pronouncing it. He affected a certain weariness in his tones to me by which he meant to imply that he might, as a wise man, have been prepared for such incompetency on my part. " I thought that I had a man ! I thought that I· had a man ! " he would keep repeating until I rose to my feet. Then he would return to his own burden and wait until my next stumble, when he would repeat the same performance all over again.

Being a Glenmornan man, I held my tongue between my teeth, but the eternal persecution was wearing me down. By nature being generous and impulsive, I looked with kindly wonder on everything and everybody. I loved my brothers and sisters, honoured my father and mother, liked the neighbours in my own townland, and they always had a kind word for me, even when working for them at so much a day. But Bennet was a man whom I did not understand. To him I was not a human being, a boy with an appetite and a soul. I was merely a ware purchased in the market-place, something less valuable than a plough, and of no more account than a barrow. I felt my position from the first. I, to Bennet, represented five pounds ten shillings' worth of goods bought at the market-place, and the buyer wanted, as a business man, to have his money's worth. The man was, of course, within his rights ; everybody wants the worth of their money, and who was I, a boy bought for less than a spavined horse, to rail against the little sorrows which Destiny imposed upon me ? I was only an article of exchange, something which represented so much amidst the implements and beasts of the farm ; but having a heart and soul I felt the position acutely.

I worked hard whenever Bennet remained close by me, but I must admit that I idled a lot of the time when he was away from my side. Somehow I could not help it.

Perhaps I was working all alone on the Dooish Mountain, making rikkles of peat. There were rag-nails on my fingers, I was hungry and my feet were sore. I seemed to be always hungry. Potatoes and buttermilk do not make the best meal in the world, and for six of every seven days they gave me the heartburn. Sometimes I would stand up and bite a rag-nail off my finger while watching a hare scooting across the brown of the moor. Afterwards a fox might come into view, showing clear on the horizon against the blue of the sky. The pain that came into the small of my back when stooping over the turf-pile would go away. There was great relief in standing straight, although Bennet said that a man should never stand at his work. And there was I, who believed myself a man, standing over my work like a child and watching foxes and hares while I was biting the rag-nails off my fingers. No sensible man would be seen doing such things.

At one moment a pack of moor-fowl would rise and chatter wildly over my head, then drop into the heather again. At another a wisp of snipe would suddenly shoot across the sky, skimming the whole stretch of bogland almost as quickly as the eye that followed it. Just when I was on the point of restarting my work, a cast of hawks might come down from the highest reach of the mountain and rest immovable for hours in the air over my head. It strains the neck to gaze up when standing. Naturally I would lie down on my back and watch the hawks for just one little while longer. Minutes would slip into hours, and still I would lie there watching the kindred of the wild as they worked out the problems of their lives in their several different ways. Meanwhile I kept rubbing the cold moss over my hacked hands in order to drive the pain out of them. When Bennet came round in the evening to see my day's work he would stand for a moment regarding the rikkles of peat with a critical stare. Then he would look at me with pity in his eyes.

" If yer hands were as eager for work as yer stomach is for food I'd be a happy master this day," he would say, in a low weary voice. " I once thought that ye were a man, but such a mistake, such a mistake ! "

Ofttime when working by the stream in the bottom-lands, I would lay down my hay-rake or shearing hook and spend an hour or two looking at the brown trout as they darted over the white sand at the bottom of the

quiet pools. Sometimes I would turn a pin, put a berry
on it and throw it into the water. I have caught trout in
that fashion many a time. Bennet came across me fishing
one day and he gave me a blow on the cheek. I did not
hit him back ; I felt afraid of him. Although twelve
years of age, I don't think that I was much of a man after
all. If anybody struck Micky's Jim in such a manner
he would strike back as quickly as he could raise his fist.
But I could not find courage to tighten my knuckles and
go for my man. When he turned away from me, my eyes
followed his ungainly figure till it was well out of sight.
Then I raised my fist and shook it in his direction.

" I'll give you one yet, my fine fellow, that will do for
you ! " I cried.

Although I idled when alone in the fields I always kept
up my own end of the stick when working with others.
I was a Glenmornan man, and I couldn't have it said
that any man left me behind in the work of the fields.
When I fell under a burden no person felt the pain as much
as myself. A man from my town should never let anything beat him. When he cannot carry his burden like
other men, and better than other men, it cuts him to the
heart, and on almost every occasion when I stumbled and
fell I almost wished that I could die on the bare ground
whereon I stumbled. But every day I felt that I was
growing stronger, and when Lammastide went by I thought
that I was almost as strong even as my master. When
alone I would examine the muscles of my arms, press
them, rub them, contract them and wonder if I was really
as strong of arm as Joe Bennet himself. When I worked
along with him in the meadowlands and corn-fields he
tried to go ahead of me at the toil ; but for all he tried
he could not leave me behind. I was a Glenmornan man,
proud of my own townland, and for its sake and for the
sake of my own people and for the sake of my own name

I was unwilling to be left behind by any human being. "A Glenmornan man can always handspike his own burden," was a word with the men at home, and as a Glenmornan man I was jealous of my own town's honour.

'Twas good to be a Glenmornan man. The pride of it pulled me through my toil when my bleeding hands, my aching back and sore feet well nigh refused to do their labour, and that same pride put the strength of twenty-one into the spine of the twelve-year-old man. But God knows that the labour was hard! The journey upstairs to bed after the day's work was a monstrous futility, and often I had hard work to restrain from weeping as I crawled weakly into bed with maybe boots and trousers still on. Although I had not energy enough remaining to take off my clothes I always went on my knees and prayed before entering the bed, and once or twice I read books in my room even. Let me tell you of the book which interested me. It was a red-covered volume which I picked up from some rubbish that lay in the corner of the room, and was called the *History of the Heavens*. I liked the story of the stars, the earth, the sun and planets, and I sat by the window for three nights reading the book by the light of the moon, for I never was allowed the use of a candle. In those nights I often said to myself: "Dermod Flynn, the heavens are sending you light to read their story."

CHAPTER VII

A MAN OF TWELVE

" ' Why d'ye slouch beside yer work when I am out o' sight ? '
' I'm hungry, an' an empty sack can never stand upright.' "

*   *   *   *   *

" ' Stoop to yer work, ye idle cub ; ye slack for hours on end.'
' I've eaten far too much the day. A full sack cannot bend.' "

—From *Farmyard Folly.*

ABOUT a week after, on the stroke of eleven at
night, I was washing potatoes for breakfast in
a pond near the farmhouse. They were now
washed always on the evening before, so that the pigs
might get their meals a little earlier in the morning.
Those same pigs were getting fattened for the Omagh pork
market, and they were never refused food. When they
grunted in the sty I was sent out to feed them, when they
slept too long I was sent out to waken them for another
meal. Although I am almost ashamed to say it, I envied
those pigs.

Potato-washing being the last job of the day, I always
thought it the hardest. I sat down beside the basket of
potatoes which I had just washed, and felt very much
out of sorts. I was in a far house and a strange man was
my master. I felt a bit homesick and I had a great longing
for my own people. The bodily pain was even worse. My
feet were all blistered ; one of my boots pinched my toes
and gave me great hurt when I moved. Both my hands

were hacked, and when I placed them in the water sharp stitches ran up my arms as far as my shoulders.

I looked up at the stars above me, and I thought of the wonderful things which I had read about them in the book picked up by me in my bedroom. There they were shining, thousands upon thousands of them, above my head, each looking colder and more distant than the other. And nearly all of them were larger than our world, larger even than our sun. It was so very hard to believe it. Then my thoughts turned to the God who fashioned them, and I wondered in the way that a man of twelve wonders what was the purpose behind it all. Ever since I could remember I had prayed to God nightly, and now I suddenly thought that all my prayers were very weak and feeble. Behind His million worlds what thought would He have for a ragged dirty plodder like me? Were there men and women on those worlds, and little boys also who were very unhappy? Had the Son of God come down and died for men on every world of all His worlds? These thoughts left me strangely disturbed as I sat there on the brink of the pond beside my basket. Things were coming into my mind, new thoughts that almost frightened me, and which I could not thrust away.

As I sat the voice of Bennet came to me.

" Hi! man, are ye goin' to sit there all night? " he shouted. " Ye're like the rest of the Donegal cubs, ye were born lazy."

I carried the potatoes in, placed them beside the hearth, then dragged myself slowly upstairs to bed.

" Ye go upstairs like a dog paralysed in the hind-quarters," shouted my boss from the kitchen.

" Can ye not let the cub a-be? " his mother reproved him, in the aimless way that mothers reprove grown-up children.

At the head of the stairs I sat down to take off my

boots, for a nail had passed through the leather and was entering the sole of my right foot. I was so very tired that I fell asleep when untying the laces. A kick on the ankle delivered by my master as he came up to bed wakened me.

"Hook it," he roared, and I slunk into my room, too weary to resent the insult. I slid into bed, and when falling asleep I suddenly remembered that I had not said my prayers. I sat up in my bed, but stopped short when on the point of getting out. Every night since I could remember I had knelt by my bedside and prayed, but as I sat there in the bed I thought that I had very little to pray for. I looked at the stars that shone through the window, and felt defiant and unafraid and very, very tired.

"No one cares for me," I said, "not even the God who made me." I bent down and touched my ankle. It was raw and bleeding where Bennet's nailed boot had ripped the flesh. I was too tired to be even angry, and I lay back on the pillows and fell asleep.

Morning came so suddenly! I thought that I had barely fallen into the first sleep when I again heard Bennet calling to me to get up and start work. I did not answer, and he was silent for a moment. I must have fallen asleep again, for the next thing that I was aware of was my master's presence in the room. He pulled me out of bed and threw me on the floor, and kicked me again with his heavy boots. I rose to my feet, and, mad with anger, for passion seizes me quickly, I hit him on the belly with my knee. I put all my strength into the blow, and he got very white and left the room, holding his two hands to his stomach. He never struck me afterwards, for I believe that he knew I was always waiting and ready for him. If he hit me again I would stand up to him until he knocked me stupid; my little victory in the bedroom had given me so much more courage and belief in my own powers.

In a fight I never know when I am beaten ; even as a child I did not know the meaning of defeat, and I have had many a hard fight since I left Glenmornan, every one of which went to prove what I have said. Anyhow, why should a Glenmornan man, and a man of twelve to boot, know when he is beaten ?

The bat I gave Bennet did not lessen my heavy toil in the fields. On the contrary, the man kept closer watch over me and saw that I never had an idle moment. Even my supply of potatoes was placed under restriction.

Bennet caused me to feed the pigs before I took my own breakfast, and if a pig grunted while I was eating he would look at me with the eternal eyes of reproach.

" Go out and give that pig something more to eat," he would say. " Don't eat all yerself. I never saw such a greedy-gut as ye are."

One day I had a good feed; I never enjoyed anything so much in all my life, I think. A sort of Orange gathering took place in Omagh, and all the Bennets went. Even the old grizzled man left his seat by the chimney-corner, and took his place on the spring-cart drawn by the spavined mare. They told me to work in the fields until they came back, but no sooner were their backs turned than I made for the house, intending to have at least one good feed in the six months. I made myself a cup of tea, opened the pantry door, and discovered a delightful chunk of currant cake. I took a second cup of tea along with the cake. I opened the pantry door by inserting a crooked nail in the lock, but I found that I could not close the door again. This did not deter me from drinking more tea, and I believe that I took upwards of a dozen cups of the liquid.

I divided part of the cake with the dog. I could not resist the soft look in the eyes which the animal fixed on me while I was eating. Before I became a man, and when

I lived in Glenmornan, I wept often over the trouble of
the poor soft-eyed dogs. They have troubles of their own,
and I can understand their little worries. Bennet's dog
gave me great help in disposing of the cake, and when he
had finished the meal he nuzzled up against my leg, which
was as much as to say that he was very thankful for my
kindness to him. I got into trouble when the people of
the house returned. They were angry, but what could
they do ? Bread eaten is like fallen rain ; it can never be
put back in its former place.

Never for a moment did I dream seriously of going
home again for a long, long while. Now and again I wished
that I was back for just one moment, but being a man,
independent and unafraid, such a foolish thought never
held me long. I was working on my own without anyone
to cheer me, and this caused me to feel proud of myself
and of the work I was doing.

Once every month I got a letter from home, telling me
about the doings in my own place, and I was always glad
to hear the Glenmornan news. Such and such a person had
died, one neighbour had bought two young steers at the
harvest-fair of Greenanore, another had been fined a couple
of pounds before the bench for fishing with a float on
Lough Meenarna, and hundreds of other little items were
all told in faithful detail.

My thoughts went often back, and daily, when dragging
through the turnip drills or wet hay streaks, I built up great
hopes of the manner in which I would go home to my own
people in the years to come. I would be very rich. That
was one essential point in the dreams of my return. I would
be big and very strong, afraid of no man and liked by all
men. I would pay a surprise visit to Glenmornan in the
night-time when all the lamps were lit on both sides of
the valley. At the end of the boreen I would stand for a
moment and look through the window of my home, and see

my father plaiting baskets by the light of the hanging lamp. My mother would be seated on the hearthstone, telling stories to my little sisters. (Not for a moment could I dream of them other than what they were when I saw them last.) Maybe she would speak of Dermod, who was pushing his fortune away in foreign parts.

And while they were talking the latch of the door would rise, and I would stand in the middle of the floor.

" It's Dermod himself that's in it ! " they would all cry in one voice. " Dermod that's just come back, and we were talking about him this very minute."

Dreams like these made up a great part of my life in those days. Sometimes I would find myself with a job finished, failing to remember how it was completed. During the whole time I was buried deep in some dream while I worked mechanically, and at the end of the job I was usually surprised to find such a large amount of work done.

I was glad when the end of the term drew near. I hated Bennet and he hated me, and I would not stop in his service another six months for all the stock on his farm. I would look for a new master in Strabane hiring-mart, and maybe my luck would be better next time. I left the farmhouse with a dislike for all forms of mastery, and that dislike is firmly engrained in my heart even to this day. The covert sneers, the insulting jibes, the kicks and curses were good, because they moulded my character in the way that is best. To-day I assert that no man is good enough to be another man's master. I hate all forms of tyranny ; and the kicks of Joe Bennet and the weary hours spent in earning the first rent which I ever paid for my people's croft, were responsible for instilling that hatred into my being.

I sent four pounds fifteen shillings home to my parents, and this was given to the landlord and priest, the man I had met six months before on Greenanore platform and the pot-bellied man with the shiny false teeth, who smoked ninepenny cigars and paid three hundred pounds for his lavatory. Years later, when tramping through Scotland, I saw the landlord motoring along the road, accompanied by his two daughters, who were about my age. When I saw those two girls I wondered how far the four pounds fifteen which I earned in blood and sweat in mid-Tyrone went to decorate their bodies and flounce their hides. I wondered, too, how many dinners they procured from the money that might have saved the life of my little brother.

And as far as I can ascertain the priest lives yet ; always imposing new taxes ; shortening the torments of souls in Purgatory at so much a soul ; forgiving sins which have never caused him any inconvenience, and at word of his mouth sending the peasantry to heaven or to hell.

CHAPTER VIII

OLD MARY SORLEY

" Do that ? I would as soon think of robbing a corpse ! "

—As is said in Glenmornan.

I DEVOTED the fifteen shillings which remained from my wages to my own use. My boots were well-nigh worn, and my trousers were getting thin at the knees, but the latter I patched as well as I was able and paid half a crown to get my boots newly soled. For the remainder of the money I bought a shirt and some under-clothing to restock my bundle, and when I went out to look for a new master in the slave market of Strabane I had only one and sevenpence in my pockets.

I never for a moment thought of keeping all my wages for myself. Such a wild idea never entered my head. I was born and bred merely to support my parents, and great care had been taken to drive this fact into my mind from infancy. I was merely brought into the world to support those who were responsible for my existence. Often when my parents were speaking of such and such a young man I heard them say : " He'll never have a day's luck in all his life. He didn't give every penny he earned to his father and mother."

I thought it would be so fine to have all my wages to myself to spend in the shops, to buy candy just like a little boy or to take a ride on the swing-boats or merry-go-rounds at the far corner of the market-place. I would like to do those things, but the voice of conscience reproved me for even thinking of them. If once I started to spend it was hard to tell when I might stop. Perhaps I would spend the whole one and sevenpence. I had never in all my life spent a penny on candy or a toy, and seeing that I was a man I could not begin now. It was my duty to send my money home, and I knew that if I even spent as much as one penny I would never have a day's luck in all my life

I had grown bigger and stronger, and I was a different man altogether from the boy who had come up from Donegal six months before. I had a fight with a youngster at the fair, and I gave him two black eyes while he only gave me one.

A man named Sorley, a big loose-limbed rung of a fellow who came from near Omagh, hired me for the winter term. Together the two of us walked home at the close of the evening, and it was near midnight when we came to the house, the distance from Strabane being eight miles. The house was in the middle of a moor, and a path ran across the heather to the very door. The path was soggy and miry, and the water squelched under our boots as we walked along. The night was dark, the country around looked bleak and miserable, and very few words passed between us on the long tramp. Once he said that I should like his place, again, that he kept a lot of grazing cattle and jobbed them about from one market to another. He also alluded to another road across the moor, one better than the one taken by us ; but it was very roundabout, unless a man came in from the Omagh side of the country.

There was an old wrinkled woman sitting at the fire having a shin heat when we entered the house. She was dry and withered, and kept turning the live peats over and over on the fire, which is one of the signs of a doting person. Her flesh resembled the cover of a rabbit-skin purse that is left drying in the chimney-corner.

E

" Have ye got a cub ? " she asked my master without as much as a look at me.

" I have a young colt of a thing," he answered.

" They've been at it again," went on the old woman. " It's the brannat cow this time."

" We'll have to get away, that's all," said the man. " They'll soon not be after leavin' a single tail in the byre."

" Is it me that would be leavin' now ? " asked the old woman, rising to her feet, and the look on her face was frightful to see. " They'll niver put Mary Sorley out of her house when she put it in her mind to stay. May the seven curses rest on their heads, them with their Home Rule and rack-rint and what not ! It's me that would stand barefoot on the red-hot hob of hell before I'd give in to the likes of them."

Her anger died out suddenly, and she sat down and began to turn the turf over on the fire as she had been doing when I entered.

" Maybe ye'd go out and wash their tails a bit," she went on. " And take the cub with ye to hould the candle. He's a thin cub that, surely," she said, looking at me for the first time. " He'll be a light horse for a heavy burden."

The man carried a pail of water out to the byre, while I followed holding a candle which I sheltered from the wind with my cap.

The cattle were kept in a long dirty building, and it looked as if it had not been cleaned for weeks. There were a number of young bullocks tied to the stakes along the wall, and most of these had their tails cut off short and close to the body. A brindled cow stood at one end, and the blood dripped from her into the sink. The whole tail had been recently cut away.

" Why do you cut the tails off the cattle ? " I asked Sorley, as he proceeded to wash the wound on the brindled cow.

" Just to keep them short," he said, stealing a furtive glance at me as he spoke. I did not ask any further questions, but I could see that he was telling an untruth. At once I guessed that the farm was boycotted, and that the peasantry were showing their disapproval of some action of Sorley's by cutting the tails off his cattle. I wished that moment that I had gotten another master who was on a more friendly footing with his neighbours.

When we returned to the house the old woman was sitting still by the fire mumbling away to herself at the one thing over and over again.

" Old Mary Sorley won't be hounded out of her house and home if all the cattle in me byre was without tails," she said in rambling tones, which now and again rose to a shriek almost. " What would an old woman like me be carin' for the band of them ? Am I not as good as the tenant that was here before me, him with his talk of rackrint and Home Rule ? Old Mary Sorley is goin' to stay here till she leaves the house in a coffin."

The man and I sat down at a pot of porridge and ate our suppers.

" Don't take any heed of me mother," he said to me. " It's only dramin' and dotin' that she is."

Early next morning I was sent out to the further end of the moor, there to gather up some sheep and take them back to the farmyard. I met three men on the way, three rough-looking, angry sort of men. One of them caught hold of me by the neck and threw me into a bog-hole. I was nearly drowned in the slush. When I tried to drag myself out, the other two threw sods on top of me. The moment I pulled myself clear I ran off as hard as I could.

" This will teach ye not to work for a boycotted bastard," one of them called after me, but none of them made any attempt to follow. I ran as hard as I could until I got to the house. When I arrived there I informed Sorley of all that had taken place, and said that I was going to stop no longer in his service.

" I had work enough lookin' for a cub," he said ; " and I'm no goin' to let ye run away now."

" I'm going anyway," I said.

" Now and will ye ? " answered the man, and he took my spare clothes and hid them somewhere in the house. My bits of clothes were all that I had between me and the world, and they meant a lot to me. Without them I would not go away, and Sorley knew that. I had to wait for three days more, then I got my clothes and left.

That happened when old Mary Sorley died.

It was late in the evening. She was left sitting on the hearthstone, turning the fire over, while Sorley and I went to wash the tails of the wounded cattle in the byre. My master had forgotten the soap, and he sent me back to the kitchen for it. I asked the old woman to give it to me. She did not answer when I spoke, and I went up close to her and repeated my question. But she never moved. I turned out again and took my way to the byre.

" Have ye got it ? " asked my master.

" Your mother has fainted," I answered.

He ran into the house, and I followed. Between us we lifted the woman into the bed which was placed in one corner of the kitchen. Her body felt very stiff, and it was very light. The man crossed her hands over her breast.

" Me poor mother's dead," he told me.

" Is she ? " I asked, and went down on my knees by the bedside to say a prayer for her soul. When on my knees I noticed where my spare clothes were hidden. They were under the straw of the bed on which the corpse was lying. I hurried over my prayers, as I did not take much pleasure in praying for the soul of a boycotted person.

" I must go to Omagh and get me married sister to come here and help me for a couple of days," said Sorley when I got to my feet again. " Ye can sit here and keep watch until I come back."

He went out, saddled the pony, and in a couple of minutes I heard the clatter of hoofs echoing on the road across the moor. In a little while the sounds died away, and there I was, all alone with the corpse of old Mary Sorley.

I edged my chair into the corner where the two walls met, and kept my eye on the woman in the bed. I was afraid to turn round, thinking that she might get up when I was not looking at her. Out on the moor a restless dog commenced to voice some ancient wrong, and its mournful howl caused a chill to run down my backbone. Once or twice I thought that someone was tapping at the window-pane behind me, and feared to look round lest a horrible face might be peering in. But all the time I kept looking at the white features of the dead woman, and I would not turn round for the world. The cat slept beside the fire and never moved.

The hour of midnight struck on the creaky old wag-of-the-wall, and I made up my mind to leave the place for good. I wanted my clothes which I had seen under the straw of the kitchen bed. It was an eerie job to turn over a corpse at the hour of midnight. The fire was almost out, for I had placed no peat on it since Sorley left for Omagh. A little wind came under the door and whirled the pale-grey ashes over the hearthstone.

I went to the bed and turned the woman over on her side, keeping one hand against the body to prevent it falling back on me. With the other hand I drew out my clothes, counting each garment until I had them all. As soon as I let the corpse go it nearly rolled out on the ground. I could hardly remove my gaze from the cold quiet thing. The eyes were wide open all the time, and they looked like icy pools seen on a dark night. I wrapped my garments up in a handkerchief which was hanging from a nail in the bedstock. The handkerchief was not mine. It belonged to the dead woman, but she would not need it any more. I took it because I wanted it, and it was the only wages which I should get for my three days' work on the farm. While I was busy tying my clothes together the cat rose from the fireplace and jumped into the bed. I suppose it felt cold by the dying fire. I thought at the time that it would not be much warmer beside a dead body. From the back of the corpse the animal watched me for a few minutes, then it fell asleep.

I took my bundle in my hand, opened the door, and went out into the darkness, leaving the sleeping cat and the dead woman alone in the boycotted house. The night was fine and frosty and a smother of cold stars lay on the face of the heavens. A cow moaned in the byre as I passed, while the stray dog kept howling miserably away on the middle of the moor. I took the path that twisted and turned across the bogland, and I ran. I was almost certain that the corpse was following me, but I would not turn and look behind for the world. If you turn and look at the ghost that follows you, it is certain to get in front, and not let you proceed any further. So they said in Glenmornan.

After a while I walked slowly. I had already left a good stretch of ground between me and the house. I could hear the brown grass sighing on the verge of the black ponds of water. The wind was running along the ground and it made strange sounds. Far away the pale cold flames of the will-of-the-wisp flitted backwards and forwards, but never came near the fringe of the road on which I travelled.

I heard the rattle of horse's hoofs coming towards me, and I hid in a clump of bracken until the rider passed by. I knew that it was Sorley on his way back from Omagh. There was a woman sitting behind him on the saddle, and when both went out of sight I ran until I came out on the high-road. Maybe I walked three miles after that, and maybe I walked more, but at last I came to a haystack by the roadside. I crept over the dyke, lay down in the hay and fell asleep, my head resting on my little bundle of clothes.

CHAPTER IX

A GOOD TIME

" There's a good time comin', though we may never live to see it."
—MOLESKIN JOE.

A WATERY mid-November sun was peering through a leafless birch tree that rose near my sleeping-place when I awoke to find a young healthy slip of a woman looking at me with a pair of large laughing eyes.

" The top o' the morn to ye, me boy," she said. " Ye're a young cub to be a beggar already."

" I'm not a beggar," I answered, getting up to my feet.

" Ye might be worse now," she replied, making a sort of excuse for her former remark. " And anyway, it's not a dacent man's bed ye've been lyin' on all be yerself, me boy." I knew that she was making fun of me, but for all that I liked the look of her face.

" Now, where would ye be a-goin' at this time o' the morn ? " she asked.

" That's more than I know myself, good woman," I said. " I have been working with a man named Sorley, but I left him last night."

" Matt Sorley, the boycotted man ? "

" The same."

" Ye'll be a Donegal cub ? "

" That I am," I replied.

" Ye're a comely lookin' fellow," said the woman. " An' what age may ye be ? "

" I'll be thirteen come Christmas," I said proudly.

" Poor child ! " said the woman. " Ye should be in yer own home yet. Was old Mary Sorley good to ye ? "

" She's dead."

" Under God the day and the night, and d'ye tell me so ! " cried the woman, and she said a short prayer to herself for the soul of Mary Sorley.

" She was a bad woman, indeed, but it's wrong to speak an ill word of the dead," my new friend went on when she had finished her prayer. " Now where would ye be makin' for next ? "

" That's it," I answered.

For a moment the woman was deep in thought. " I suppose ye'll be lookin' for a new place ? " she asked suddenly.

" I am that," I said.

" I have a half-brother on the leadin' road to Strabane, and he wants a cub for the winter term," said the woman. " I live in the same house meself and if ye care ye can come and see him, and I meself will put in a word in yer favour. His name in James MaCrossan, and he's a good man to his servants."

That very minute we set out together. We came to the house of James MaCrossan, and found the man working in the farmyard. He had a good, strong, kindly face that was pleasant to look upon. His shirt was open at the front, and a great hairy chest was visible. His arms, bare almost to the shoulders, were as hairy as the limbs of a beast, and much dirtier. His shoes were covered with cow-dung, and he stood stroking a horse as tenderly as if it had been a young child in the centre of the yard. His half-sister spoke to him about me, while I stood aside with my little bundle dangling from my arm. When the woman had finished her story MaCrossan looked at me with good humour in his eyes

" And how much wages would ye be wantin' ? " he asked.

" Six pounds from now till May-day," I said.

The man was no stickler over a few shillings. He took me as a servant there and then at the wages I asked.

His farm was a good easy one to work on, he and his sister were very kind to me, and treated me more like one of themselves than a servant. I lay abed every morning until seven, and on rising I got porridge and milk, followed by tea, bread and butter, for breakfast. There was no lack of food, and I grew fatter and happier. I finished my day's work at eight o'clock in the evening, and could then turn into bed when I liked. The cows, sheep, and pigs were under my care, MaCrossan worked with the horses, while Bridgid, his half-sister, did the house-work and milked the cows. I did not learn to milk, for that is a woman's job. At least, I thought so in those days. Pulling the soft udder of a cow was not the proper job for a man like me.

One day my master came into the byre and asked me if I could milk.

" No," I answered. " And what is more I don't want to learn. It is not a manly job."

MaCrossan merely laughed, and by way of giving me a lesson in manliness, he lifted me over his head with one wrench of his arm, holding me there for at least a minute. When he replaced me on the ground I felt very much ashamed, but the man on seeing this laughed louder than ever. That night he told the story to his half-sister.

" Calls milkin' a job for a woman, indeed ! " she exclaimed. " The little rogue of a cub! if I get hold of him."

With these words she ran laughing after me, and I ran out of the house into the darkness. Although I knew she was not in earnest I felt a bit afraid of her. Three times she followed me round the farmyard, but I managed to keep out of her reach each time. In the end she returned to the house.

"Dermod, come back," she called. "No one will harm ye."

I would not be caught in such an easy manner, and above all I did not want the woman to grip me. For an hour I stood in the darkness, then I slipped through the open window of my bedroom, which was on the ground floor, and turned into my bed. A few moments afterwards Bridgid came into the room carrying a lighted candle, and found me under the blankets. I watched her through the fringe of my eyelashes while pretending that I was fast asleep.

"Ha, ye rogue!" she cried. "I have ye now."

She ran towards me, but still I pretended to be in a deep slumber. I closed my eyes tightly, but I felt awfully afraid. She drew closer, and at last I could feel her breath warm on my cheek. But she did not grip me. Instead, she kissed me on the lips three times, and I was so surprised that I opened my eyes.

"Ye little shamer! d'ye think that *that* is a woman's job too?" she asked, and with these words she ran out of the room.

I stayed on the farm for nineteen months, and then, though MaCrossan was a very good master, I set my mind on leaving him. Day and night the outside world was calling to me, and something lay awaiting for me in other lands. Maybe I could make more money in foreign parts, and earn a big pile for myself and my people. Some day, when I had enough and to spare, I would do great things. There was a waste piece of land lying near my father's house in Glenmornan, and my people had set their eyes on it. I would buy that piece of land when I was rolling in money. Oh! what would I not do when I got rich?

About once a month I had a letter from mother. She

was not much of a hand at the pen, and her letters were always short. Most of the time she wanted money, and I always sent home every penny that I could spare.

Sometimes I longed to go back again. In a boy's longing way I wanted to see Norah Ryan, for I liked her well. Her, too, I would remember when I got rich, and I would make her a great lady. These were some of my dreams, and they made me hate the look of MaCrossan's farm. Daily I grew to hate it more, its dirty lanes, the filthy byre, the low-thatched house, the pigs, cows, horses, and everything about the place. Everything was always the same, and I was sick of looking at the same things day after day for all the days of the year.

My mind was set on leaving MaCrossan, though his half-sister and himself liked me better than ever a servant was liked before in mid Tyrone. The thought of leaving them made me uncomfortable, but the voice that called me was stronger than that which urged me to stay. I had a longing for a new place, and the longing grew within me day after day. Over the hills, over the sea, and miles along some dusty road which I had never seen, some great adventure was awaiting me. Nothing would keep me back, and I wrote home to my own mother, asking if Micky's Jim wanted any new men to accompany him to Scotland. Jim was the boss of a potato-digging squad, and each year a number of Donegal men and women worked with him across the water.

Then one fine morning, a week later, and towards the end of June, this letter came from Micky's Jim himself:

" DEAR DERMID,

"i am riting you these few lines to say that i am very well at present, hoping this leter finds you in the same state of health. Well, dear Dermid i am gathering up a squad of men and women to come and work with me beyont the water to dig potatoes in Scotland. there is a great lot of the Glenmornan people coming, Tom of the hill, Neds hugh, Red mick and Norah ryan, Biddy flannery and five or six more. Well this is to say that if you woud care to come i will keep a job open for you. Norah ryan, her father was drounded fishing in Trienna Bay so she is not going to be a nun after all. If you will come with me rite back and say so. your wages is going to be sixteen shillings a week accordingley. Steel away from your master and come to derry peer and meet me there. its on the twenty ninth of the month that we leave Glenmornan.

" Yours respectfuly,
" JIM SCANLON."

CHAPTER X

THE LEADING ROAD TO STRABANE

" No more the valley charms me and no more the torrents glisten,
My love is plain and homely and my thoughts are far away ;
The great world voice is calling and with throbbing heart I listen,
And I cannot but obey ; I cannot but obey."
—From *Songs of the Dead End.*

ON the morning of the twenty-ninth of June, 1905, I left Jim MaCrossan's, and went out to hoe turnips in a field that lay nearly half a mile away from the farmhouse. I had taken a hoe from a peg on the wall of the barn, and had thrown it across my shoulder, when MaCrossan came up to me.

" See an' don't be late comin' in for yer dinner, Dermod," he said. " Ye'll know the time be the sun."

That was his last speech to me, and I was sorry at leaving him, but for the life of me I could not tell him of my intended departure. There is no happiness in leaving those with whom we are happy. I liked MaCrossan more because of his strength than his kindness. Once he carried an anvil on his back from Lisnacreight smithy to his own farmhouse, a distance of four miles. When he brought it home I could not lift it off the ground. He was a wonderful man, powerful as a giant, good and kindly-spoken. I liked him so much that I determined to steal away from him. I was more afraid of his regret than I would be of another man's anger.

I slung the hoe over my shoulder and whistled a wee tune that came into my head as I plodded down the cart-

road that led to the field where the turnips were. The
young bullocks gazed at me over the hedge by the wayside,
and snorted in make-believe anger when I tried to touch
their cold nostrils with my finger-tips. The crows on the
sycamore branches seemed to be very friendly and merry.
I could almost have sworn that they cried, " Good morning,
Dermod Flynn," as I passed by.

The lane was alive with rabbits at every turn. I could
see them peering out from their holes under the blossomed
hedgerows with wide anxious eyes. Sometimes they ran
across in front of me, their ears acock and their white tufts
of tails stuck up in the air. I never thought once of
flinging a stone at them that morning ; I was out on a
bigger adventure than rabbit-chasing.

A little way down I met MaCrossan's half-sister, Bridgid.
She had just taken out the cows and was returning to the
house after having fastened the slip rails on the gap of the
pasture field.

" The top o' the mornin' to ye, Dermod," she cried.

" The same to you," I answered.

She walked on, but after she had gone a little way, she
called back to me.

" Will ye be goin' to the dance in McKirdy's barn on
Monday come a week ? "

" I will, surely," I replied across my shoulder. I did
not look around, but I could hear the soles of her shoes
rustling across the dry clabber as she continued on her
journey.

The moment I entered the field I flung the hoe into the
ditch, and crossed to the other side of the turnip drills.
I put my hand into the decayed trunk of a fallen tree, and
took out a little bundle of clothes which was concealed
there. I had hidden the clothes when I received Jim
Scanlon's letter. I hung the bundle over my arm, and made
for the high-road leading to Strabane. It was nearly three

hours' walk to the town, and the morning was grand. I cut a hazel rod to keep me company, and swung it round in my hand after the manner of cattle-drovers. I went on my way with long swinging strides, thinking all the time, not of Micky's Jim and the Land Beyond the Water, but of Norah Ryan whom I would see on 'Derry Pier with the rest of the potato squad.

I could have shouted with pure joy to the people who passed me on the road. Most of them bade me the time of day with the good-natured courtesy of the Irish people. The red-faced farmer's boy, who sat on the jolting cart, stopped his sleepy horse for a minute to ask me where I was bound for.

" Just to Strabane to buy a new rake," I told him, for grown-up men never tell their private affairs to other people.

" Troth, it's for an early harvest that same rake will be," he said, and flicked his horse on the withers with his whip. Then, having satisfied his curiosity, he passed beyond the call of my voice for ever.

A girl who stood with her back to the roses of a roadside cottage gave me a bowl of milk when I asked for a drink of water. She was a taking slip of a girl, with soft dreamy eyes and red cherry lips.

" Where would ye be goin' now ? " she asked.

" I'm goin' to Strabane."

" And what would ye be doin' there ? "

" My people live there," I said.

" It's ye that has the Donegal tongue, and be the same token ye're a great liar," said the girl, and I hurried off.

A man gave me a lift on the milk-cart for a mile of the way. " Where are ye goin' ? " he asked me.

" To Strabane to buy a new spade," I told him.

" It's a long distance to go for a spade," he said with a laugh. " D'ye know what I think ye are ? "

" What ? " I asked.

" Ye're a cub that has run away from his master," said the man. " If the pleece get ye ye'll go to jail for brekin' a contract."

I slid out of the cart, pulling my bundle after me, and took to my heels along the dry road. " Wan cannot see yer back for dust," the man shouted after me, and he kept roaring aloud for a long while. Soon, however, I got out of the sound of his voice, and I slowed down and recovered my wind. About fifteen minutes later I overtook an old withered woman, lean as a rake, who was talking to herself. I walked with her for a long distance, but she was so taken up with her own troubles that she had not a word for me.

" Is it on a day like this," the old body was saying aloud to herself, " that the birds sing loud on the trees, and the sun shines for all he is worth in the hollow of the sky, a day when the cruel hand of God strikes heavy on me heart, and starves the blood in me veins ? Who at all would think that me little Bridgid would go so soon from her own door, and the fire on her own hearthstone, into the land where the cold of death is and the darkness ? Mother of God ! be good to a poor old woman, but it's bitter that I am, bekase she was tuk away from me, lavin' me alone in me old age with no wan sib to meself, to sleep under me own roof. Well do I mind the day when little Bridgid came. That day, my good man Fergus himself was tuk away from me, but I wasn't as sorry as an old woman might be for her man, for she was there with the black eyes of her lookin' into me own and never speakin' a word at all, at all. Then she grew big, with the gold on her hair, and the redness on her mouth, and the whiteness of the snow on her teeth. 'Tis often meself would watch her across the half-door, when she was a-chasin' the geese in the yard, or pullin' the feathers from the wings of the ducks in the puddle.

F

And I would say to meself : ' What man will take her away from her old mother some fine mornin' and lave me lonely be the fire in the evenin' ? ' And no man came at all, at all, to take her, and now she's gone. The singin' birds are in the bushes, and the sun is laughin', the latch of me door is left loose, but she'll not come back, no matter what I do. So I do be trampin' about the roads with the sweat on me, and the shivers of cold on me at the same time, gettin' a handful of meal here, and a goupin of pratees there, and never at all able to forget that I am lonely without her."

I left the woman and her talk behind me on the road, and I thought it a strange thing that anyone could be sorry when I was so happy. In a little while I forgot all about her, for my eyes caught the chimneys of Strabane sending up their black smoke into the air, and I heard some church clock striking out the hour of noon.

It was well on in the day when I got the 'Derry train, but on the moment I set my foot on the pier by the water-side I found Micky's Jim sitting on a capstan waiting for me. He was chewing a plug of tobacco, and spitting into the water.

" Work hasn't done ye much harm, Dermod Flynn, for ye've grown to be a big, soncy man," was Jim's greeting, and I felt very proud of myself when he said these words.

CHAPTER XI

THE 'DERRY BOAT

" Bad cess to the boats ! for it's few they take back of the many they take away."—A GLENMORNAN SAYING.

JIM and I had a long talk together, and I asked him about the people at home, my father and mother, the neighbours, their doings, their talk, and all the rest of the little things that went to make up the world of the Glenmornan folk. In return for his information I told Jim about my life in Tyrone, the hardships of Bennet's place, the poor feeding, the hard work, the loneliness, and, above all, the fight in the bedroom where I gave Joe Bennet one in the stomach that made him sick for two hours afterwards.

" That's the only thing that a Glenmornan man could do," said Micky's Jim, when I told him of the fight.

Afterwards we sauntered along the wharf together, waiting for the other members of the party, who had gone to the Catholic chapel in 'Derry to say their prayers before leaving their own country. Everything I saw was a source of wonder to me. I lived many miles from the sea at home, and only once did I even see a fishing-boat. That was years before, when I passed Doon Ferry on my way to the Holy Well of Iniskeel. There did I see the fishing-boats of Trienna lying by the beach while the fishermen mended their nets on the foreshore. Out by the rim of the deep-sea water the bar was roaring, and a line of restless creamy froth stretched across the throat of the bay, like the bare white arms of a girl who bathes in a darksome pool. I asked one of the fishers if he would let me go with him across the bar. He only laughed at me and said that it would suit me far better to say my prayers.

For the whole of the evening I could not take my eyes off the boats that lay by 'Derry Pier. Micky's Jim took no notice of them, because he had seen them often enough before.

" Ye'll not wonder much at ships when ye've seen them as much as I've seen them," he said.

We sought out our own boat, and Jim said that she was a rotten tub when he had examined her critically with his eyes for a moment.

" It'll make ye as sick as a dog goin' roun' the Moils o' Kentire," he said. " Ye'll know what it is to be sea-sick this night, Dermod."

We went on board, and waited for the rest of the party to come along. While waiting Jim prowled into the cook's galley and procured two cups of strong black tea, which we drank together on deck.

It was, " Under God, the day an' the night, ye've grown to be a big man, Dermod," and " Ye're a soncy rung o' a fellow this minute, Dermod Flynn," when the people from my own arm of the Glen came up the deck and saw me there along with Micky's Jim. Many of the squad were old stagers who had been in the country across the water before. They planted their patch of potatoes and corn in their little croft at home, then went to Scotland for five or six months in the middle of the year to earn money for the rent of their holding. The land of Donegal is bare and hungry, and nobody can make a decent livelihood there except landlords.

The one for whom I longed most was the last to come, and when I saw her my heart almost stopped beating. She was the same as ever with her soft tender eyes and sweet face, that put me in mind of the angels pictured over the altar of the little chapel at home. Her hair fell over her shawl like a cascade of brown waters, her forehead was white and pure as marble, her cheeks seemed made of rose-leaf, of a pale carnation hue, and her fair light body, slender as a young poplar, seemed too holy for the contact of the cold world. She stepped up the gang-plank, slowly and timidly, for she was afraid of the noise and shouting of the place.

The boat's derricks creaked angrily on their pivots, the gangways clattered loudly as they were shifted here and there by noisy and dirty men, and the droves of bullocks, fresh from the country fairs, bellowed unceasingly as they were hammered into the darkness of the hold. On these things I looked with wonder, Norah looked with fright.

All evening I had been thinking about her, and the words of welcome which I would say to her when we met. When she came on deck I put out my hand, but couldn't for the life of me say a word of greeting. She was the first to speak.

" Dermod Flynn, I hardly knew ye at all," she said with a half-smile on her lips. " Ye got very big these last two years."

" So did you, Norah," I answered, feeling very glad because she had kept count of the time I was gone. " You are almost as tall as I am."

" Why wouldn't I be as tall as ye are," she answered with a full smile. " Sure am I not a year and two months older ? "

Some of the other women began to talk to Norah, and I turned to look at the scene around me. The sun was setting, and showed like a red bladder in the pink haze that lay over the western horizon. The Foyle was a sheet of wavy molten gold which the boat cut through as she sped out from the pier. The upper deck was crowded with people who were going to Scotland to work for the summer and autumn. They were all very ragged, both women and men ; most of the men were drunk, and they discussed, quarrelled, argued, and swore until the din was deafening. Little heed was taken by them of the beauty of the evening, and all alone I watched the vessel turn up a furrow of gold at the bow until my brain was reeling with the motion of the water that sobbed past the sides of the steamer, and swept far astern where the line of white churned foam fell into rank with the sombre expanse of sea that we were leaving behind.

Many of the passengers were singing songs of harvest-men, lovers, cattle-drovers, and sailors. One man, a hairy, villainous-looking fellow, stood swaying unsteadily on the deck with a bottle of whisky in one hand, and roaring out " Judy Brannigan."

> " Oh ! Judy Brannigan, ye are me darlin',
> Ye are me lookin' glass from night till mornin'—
> I'd rather have ye without wan farden,
> Than Shusan Gallagheer with her house and garden."

Others joined in mixing up half a dozen songs in one musical outpouring, and the result was laughable in the extreme.

> " If all the young maidens were ducks in the water,
> 'Tis then the young men would jump out and swim after . . "
> " I'm Barney O'Hare from the County Clare
> I'm an Irish cattle drover,
> I'm not as green as ye may think
> Although I'm just new-over . . "
> " For a sailor courted a farmer's daughter
> That lived convainint to the Isle of Man . . ."
> " As beautiful Kitty one mornin' was trippin'
> With a pitcher of milk to the fair of Coleraine
> And her right fol the dol right fol the doddy,
> Right fol the dol, right fol the dee."

I could not understand what " right fol the dol," etc., meant, but I joined in the chorus when I found Micky's

Jim roaring out for all he was worth along with the rest.

There were many on board who were full of drink and fight, men who were ready for quarrels and all sorts of mischief. One of these, a man called O'Donnel, paraded up and down the deck with an open clasp-knife in his hand, speaking of himself in the third person, and inviting everybody on board to fistic encounter.

" This is young O'Donnel from the County Donegal," he shouted, alluding to himself, and lifting his knife which shone red with the blood hues of the sinking sun. " And young O'Donnel doesn't care a damn for a man on this bloody boat. I can fight like a two-year-old bullock. A blow of me fist is like a kick from a young colt, and I don't care a damn for a man on this boat. Not for a man on this boat ! I'm a Rosses man, and I don't care a damn for a man on this boat ! "

He looked terrible as he shouted out his threats. One eyebrow was cut open and the flesh hung down even as far as his cheekbone. I could not take my eyes away from him, and he suddenly noticed me watching his antics. Then he slouched forward and hit me on the face, knocking me down. The next instant Micky's Jim was on top of him, and I saw as if in a dream the knife flying over the side of the vessel into the sea. Then I heard my mate shouting, " Take that, you damned brat—and that—and that ! " He hammered O'Donnel into insensibility, and by the time I regained my feet they were carrying the insensible man below. I felt weak and dizzy. Jim took me to a seat, and Norah Ryan bathed my cheek, which was swollen and bleeding.

" It was a shame to hit ye, Dermod," she said more than once as she rubbed her soft fingers on the wound. Somehow I was glad of the wound, because it won such attention from Norah.

The row between O'Donnel and Jim was only the

beginning of a wild night's fighting. All over the deck and down in the steerage the harvestmen and labourers fought one with another for hours on end. Over the bodies of the women who were asleep in every corner, over coils of ropes, trunks and boxes of clothes, the drunken men struggled like demons. God knows what they had to quarrel about! When I could not see them I could hear them falling heavily as cattle fall amid a jumble of twisted hurdles, until the drink and exertion overpowered them at last. One by one they fell asleep, just where they had dropped or on the spot where they were knocked down.

Towards midnight, when, save for the thresh of the propellers and the pulsing of the engines, all was silent, I walked towards the stern of the boat. There I found Norah Ryan asleep, her shawl drawn over her brown hair, and the rising moon shining softly on her gentle face. For a moment I kept looking at her; then she opened her eyes and saw me.

"Sit beside me, Dermod," she said. "It will be warmer for two."

I sat down, and the girl nestled close to me in the darkness. The sickle moon drifted up the sky, furrowing the pearl-powdered floor with its silver front. Far away on the Irish coast I could see the lights in the houses alongshore. When seated a while I found Norah's hand resting in mine, and then, lulled with the throb of the engine and the weeping song of the sea, I fell into a deep sleep, forgetting the horror of the night and the red wound on my face where O'Donnel had struck me with his fist.

Dawn was breaking when I awoke. Norah still slept, her head close against my arm, and her face, beautiful in repose, turned towards mine. Her cherry-red lips lay apart, and I could see the two rows of pearly white teeth between. The pink tips of her ears peeped from amid the coils of her hair, and I placed my hand on her head and stroked her brown tresses ever so softly. She woke so quietly that the change from sleeping to waking was hardly noticeable. The traces of dim dreams were yet in her eyes, and as I watched her my mind was full of unspoken thoughts.

"Have ye seen Scotland yet, Dermod?" she asked.

"That's it, I think," I said, as I pointed at the shore-line visible many miles away.

"Isn't it like Ireland." Norah nestled closer to me as she spoke. "I would like to be goin' back again," she said after a long silence.

"I'm going to make a great fortune in Scotland, Norah," I said. "And I'm going to make you a great lady."

"Why are ye goin' to do that?" she asked.

"I don't know," I confessed, and the two of us laughed together.

CHAPTER XII

" ' Tell the truth and shame the devil,' they say. Well, to tell
you the truth, there are some truths which would indeed shame
the devil ! "—MOLESKIN JOE.

THE potato merchant met us on Greenock quay
next morning, and here Micky's Jim marshalled
his squad, which consisted in all of twenty-one
persons. Seventeen of these came from Ireland, and the
remainder were picked up from the back streets of Greenock
and Glasgow. With the exception of two, all the Irish
women were very young, none of them being over nineteen
years of age, but the two extra women needed for the squad
were withered and wrinkled harridans picked from the
city slums. These women met us on the quay.

" D'ye see them ? " Micky's Jim whispered to me.
" They cannot make a livin' on the streets, so they have to
come and work with us. What d'ye think of them ? "

" I don't like the look of them," I said.

The potato merchant hurried us off to Buteshire the
moment we arrived, and we started work on a farm at mid-
day. The way we had to work was this. Nine of the
older men dug the potatoes from the ground with short
three-pronged graips. The women followed behind, crawling on their knees and dragging two baskets a-piece along
with them. Into these baskets they lifted the potatoes
thrown out by the men. When the baskets were filled
I emptied the contents into barrels set in the field for that

purpose.   These barrels were in turn sent off to the markets and big towns which we had never seen.

The first day was very wet, and the rain fell in torrents, but as the demand for potatoes was urgent we had to work through it all.   The job, bad enough for men, was killing for women.   All day long, on their hands and knees, they dragged through the slush and rubble of the field.   The baskets which they hauled after them were cased in clay to the depth of several inches, and sometimes when emptied of potatoes a basket weighed over two stone.   The strain on the women's arms must have been terrible.   But they never complained.   Pools of water gathered in the hollows of the dress that covered the calves of their legs.   Sometimes they rose and shook the water from their clothes, then went down on their knees again.   The Glasgow women sang an obscene song, "just by way o' passing the time," one of them explained, and Micky's Jim joined in the chorus.   Two little ruts, not at all unlike the furrows left by a coulter of a skidding plough, lay behind the women in the black earth.   These were made by their knees.

We left off work at six o'clock in the evening, and turned in to look up our quarters for the night.   We had not seen them yet, for we started work in the fields immediately on arriving.   A byre was being prepared for our use, and a farm servant was busily engaged in cleaning it out when we came in from the fields.   He was shoving the cow-dung through a trap-door into a vault below.   The smell of the place was awful.   There were ten cattle stalls in the building, five on each side of the raised concrete walk that ran down the middle between two sinks.   These stalls were our sleeping quarters.

The byre was built on the shoulder of a hillock and the midden was situated in a grotto hollowed underneath; its floor was on a level with the cart-road outside, and in the corner of this vault we had to build a fire for cooking our food. A large dung-hill blocked the entrance, and we had to cross this to get to the fire which sparkled brightly behind. Around the blaze we dried our sodden clothes, and the steam of the drying garments rose like a mist around us.

One of the strange women was named Gourock Ellen, which goes to show that she had a certain fame in the town of that name. The day's drag had hacked and gashed her knees so that they looked like minced flesh in a butcher's shop window. She showed her bare knees, and was not in the least ashamed. I turned my head away hurriedly, not that the sight of the wounds frightened me, but I felt that I was doing something wrong in gazing at the bare leg of a woman. I looked at Norah Ryan, and the both of us blushed as if we had been guilty of some shameful action. Gourock Ellen saw us, and began to sing a little song aloud:

"When I was a wee thing and lived wi' my granny,
Oh ! it's many a caution my granny gi'ed me,
She said : ' Now be wise and beware o' the boys,
And don't let the petticoats over your knee.' "

When she finished her verse she winked knowingly at Micky's Jim, and, strange to say, Jim winked back.

We boiled a pot of potatoes, and poured the contents into a wicker basket which was placed on the floor of the vault. Then all of us sat down together and ate our supper like one large family, and because we were very hungry did not mind the reeking midden behind us.

During our meal an old bent and wrinkled man came hobbling across the dung-heap towards the fire. His clothing was streaming wet and only held together by strings, patches, and threads. He looked greedily towards the fire, and Gourock Ellen handed him three hot potatoes.

"God bless ye," said the man in a thin piping voice. "It's yerself that has the kindly heart, good woman."

He ate hurriedly like a dog, as if afraid somebody would snatch the bread from between his jaws. He must have been very hungry, and I felt sorry for the man. I handed him the can of milk which I had procured at the farmhouse, and he drank the whole lot at one gulp.

" It's yerself that is the dacent youngster, God bless ye ! " he said, and there were tears in his eyes. " And isn't this a fine warm place ye are inside of this wet night."

The smell of the midden was heavy in my nostrils, and the smoke of the fire was paining my eyes.

" It's a rotten place," I said.

" Sure and it's not at all," said the man in a pleading voice. " It's better than lyin' out under a wet hedge with the rain spat-spatterin' on yer face."

" Why do you lie under a hedge ? " I asked.

" Sure, no one wants me at all, at all, because of the pain in me back that won't let me stoop over me work," said the man. " In the farms they say to me, ' Go away, we don't want ye ' ; in the village they say, ' Go away, we're sick of lookin' at ye,' and what am I to do ? Away in me own country, that is Mayo, it's always the welcome hand and a bit and sup when a man is hungry, but here it's the scowling face and the ill word that is always afore an old man like me."

One by one the women went away from the fire, for they were tired from their day's work and wanted to turn into bed as early as possible. The old man sat by the fire looking into the flames without taking any heed of those around him. Jim and I were the last two to leave the fire, and my friend shook the old man by the shoulder before he went out.

" What are ye goin' to do now ? " asked Jim.

" Maybe ye'd let me sleep beside the fire till the morra mornin'," said the man.

" Ye must go out of here," said Jim.

" Let him stay," I said, for I felt sorry for the poor old chap.

Jim thought for a minute. " Well, I'll let him stay, cute old cadger though he is," he said, and the both of us went into the byre leaving the old man staring dreamily into the flames.

One blanket apiece was supplied to us by the potato merchant, and by sleeping two in a bed the extra blanket was made to serve the purpose of a sheet. We managed to make ourselves comfortable by sewing bags together in the form of a coverlet and placing the make-shift quilts over our bodies.

" Where is Norah Ryan ? " asked Micky's Jim, as he finished using his pack-needle on the quilts which he was preparing for our use. Jim and I were to sleep in the one stall.

Norah Ryan was not to be seen, and I went out to the fire to find if she was there. From across the black midden I looked into the vault which was still dimly lighted up by the dying flames, and there I saw Norah speaking to the old man. She was on the point of leaving the place, and I saw some money pass from her hand to that of the stranger.

" God be good to ye, decent girl," I heard the man say, as Norah took her way out. I hid in the darkness and allowed her to pass without seeing me. Afterwards I went in and gave a coin to the old man. He still held the one given by Norah between his fingers, and it was a two-shilling piece. Probably she had not another in her possession. What surprised me most was the furtive way in which she did a kindness. For myself, when doing a good action, I like everybody to notice it.

In the byre there was no screen between the women and the men. The modesty of the young girls, when the hour for retiring came around, was unable to bear this. The strange women did not care in the least.

The Irish girls sat by their bedsides and made no sign of undressing. I slid into bed quietly with my trousers still on ; most of the men stripped with evident unconcern, nakedly and shamelessly.

" The darkness is a good curtain if the women want to take off their clothes," said Micky's Jim, as he extinguished the only candle in the place. He re-lit a match the next moment, and there was a hurried scampering under the blankets in the stalls on the other side of the passage.

" That's a mortal sin, Micky's Jim, that ye're doin'," said Norah Ryan, and the two strange women laughed loudly as if very much amused at persons who were more modest than themselves.

" Who are ye lyin' with, Norah Ryan ? Is it Gourock Ellen ? " asked my bedmate.

" It is," came the answer.

" D'ye hear that, Dermod—a nun and a harridan in one bed ? " said Jim under his breath to me.

Outside the raindrops were sounding on the roof like whip-lashes. Jim spoke again in a drowsy voice.

" We're keepin' some poor cows from their warm beds to-night," he said.

I kept awake for a long while, turning thoughts over in my mind. The scenes on the 'Derry boat, and my recent experience in the soggy fields, had taken the edge off the joy that winged me along the leading road to Strabane. I was now far out into the heart of the world, and life loomed darkly before me. The wet day went to crush my dreams and the ardour of my spirits. Hitherto I had great belief in women, their purity, virtue, and gentleness. But now my grand dreams of pure womanhood had collapsed. The foul words, the loose jokes and obscene songs of the two women who were strangers, the hard, black, bleeding and scabby knees that Gourock Ellen showed to us at the fire had turned my young visions into nightmares. The sight of the girls ploughing through the mucky clay, and the wolfish stare of the old man who envied those who fed beside a dungheap were repellent to me. I looked on life in all its primordial brutishness and found it loathsome to my soul.

Only that morning coming up the Clyde, when Norah and I looked across the water to a country new to both of us, my mind was full of dreams of the future. But the rosy-tinted boyish dreams of morning were shattered before the fall of night. Maybe the old man who lay by the dungheap came to Scotland full of dreams like mine. Now the spirit was crushed out of him ; he was broken on the wheel of life, and he had neither courage to rob, sin, nor die. He could only beg his bit and apologise for begging. The first day in Scotland disgusted me, made me sick of life, and if it were not that Norah Ryan was in the squad I would go back to Jim MaCrossan's farm again.

That night, as for many nights before, I turned into bed without saying my prayers, and I determined to pray no more. I had been brought up a Catholic, and to believe in a just God, and the eternal fire of torments, but daily newer and stranger thoughts were coming into my mind. Even when working with MaCrossan in the meadowlands my mind reverted to the little book in which I read the story of the heavens. God behind His million worlds had no time to pay any particular attention to me. This thought I tried to drive away, for the Church had still a strong hold on me, and anything out of keeping with my childish creed entered my mind like a nail driven into the flesh. The new thoughts, however, persisted, they took form and became part of my being. The change was gradual, for I tried desperately to reject the new idea of the universe and God. But the sight of the women in the fields, the story of the old man with the pain in his back who slept under a wet hedge was to me conclusive proof that God took no interest in the personal welfare of men. And when I gripped the new idea as incontestable truth it did not destroy my belief in God. Only the God of my early days, the God who took a personal interest in my welfare, was gone.

Sometimes the rest of the Catholic members of the squad went to chapel, when the farm on which we wrought was near a suitable place of worship, but I never went. Their visits were few and far between, for we were distant from the big towns most of the time.

We seldom stopped longer than one fortnight at a time on any farm. We shifted about here and there, digging twenty acres for one farmer, ten for another, living in byres, pig-stys and barns, and taking life as we found it. Daily we laboured together, the men bent almost double over their graips, throwing out the potatoes to the girls who followed after, dragging their bodies through the mire and muck like wounded animals, and I lifted the baskets of potatoes and filled the barrels for market. Still, for all the disadvantages, life was happy enough to me, because Norah Ryan was near me working in the fields.

But the life was brutal, and almost unfit for animals. One night when we were asleep in a barn the rain came through the roof and flooded the earthen floor to a depth of several inches. Our beds being wet through, we had to rise and stand for the remainder of the night knee-deep in the cold water.

When morning came we went out to work in the wet fields.

Once when living in a pig-sty we were bothered by rats. When we were at work they entered our habitation, ransacked the packets of food, gnawed our clothes, and upset everything in the place. They could only get in by one entrance, a hole in the wall above my bed, and by that same way they had to go out. After a little while the rats became bolder and came in by night when we were

G

asleep. One night I awoke to find them jumping down from the aperture, landing on my body in their descent. Then they scampered away and commenced prowling around for food. I counted twenty thuds on my breast, then stuck my trousers in the throat of the opening above my bed and wakened Jim, who snored like a hog through it all. We got up and lit a candle. When the rats saw the light they hurried back to their hole, but we were ready and waiting for them, Micky's Jim with a shovel shaft, and I with a graip shank. We killed them as they came, all except one, which ran under the bed-clothes of Norah Ryan's bed. There was great noise of screaming for a while, but somehow or another Gourock Ellen got hold of the animal and squeezed it to death under the blankets. I left my trousers in the aperture all night, and they were nibbled almost to pieces in the morning. They were the only ones in my possession, and I had to borrow a pair from Jim for the next day.

The farmer gave us a halfpenny for every rat's tail handed in, as he wanted to get rid of the pests, and from that time forward Jim and I killed several, and during the remainder of the season we earned three pounds between us by hunting and killing rats. Gourock Ellen sometimes joined in the hunt, by way of amusement, but her principal relaxation was getting drunk on every pay-day.

The other woman, whose name was Annie, usually accompanied her on Saturday to the nearest village, and the two of them got full together. They also shared their food in common, but often quarrelled among themselves over one thing and another. They fought like cats and swore awfully, using the most vile language, but the next moment they were the best of friends again. One Saturday night they returned from a neighbouring village with two tramp men. Micky's Jim chased the two men away from the byre in which we were living at the time.

" I'll have no whorin' about this place," he said.

" You're a damned religious beast to be livin' in a cow-shed," said one of the tramps.

One day Gourock Ellen asked me who did my washing, though I believe that she knew I washed my own clothes with my own hands.

" Myself," I said in reply to Ellen's inquiry.

" Will yer own country girls not do it for you ? "

" I can do it myself," I replied.

When I looked for my soiled under-garments a week later I could not find them. I made inquiries and found that Gourock Ellen had washed them for me.

" It's a woman's work," she said, when I talked to her, and she washed my clothes to the end of the season and would not accept payment for the work.

Nearly everyone in the squad looked upon the two women with contempt and disgust, and I must confess that I shared in the general feeling. In my sight they were loathsome and unclean. They were repulsive in appearance, loose in language, and seemingly devoid of any moral restraint or female decency. It was hard to believe that they were young children once, and that there was still unlimited goodness in their natures. Why had Gourock Ellen handed the potatoes to the old Mayo man who was hungry, and why had she undertaken to do my washing without asking for payment ? I could not explain these impulses of the woman, and sometimes, indeed, I cannot explain my own. I cannot explain why I then disliked Gourock Ellen, despite what she had done for me, and to-day I regret that ignorance of youth which caused me to despise a human being who was (as after events proved) infinitely better than myself.

CHAPTER XIII

THE MAN WITH THE DEVIL'S PRAYER BOOK

" He would gamble on his father's tombstone and play banker with the corpse."—A KINLOCHLEVEN PROVERB.

THE middle of September was at hand, and a slight tinge of brown was already showing on the leaves. We were now working on a farm where the River Clyde broadens out to the waters of the deep ocean. One evening, when supper was over, I went out alone to the fields and sat down on the green sod and looked outwards to the grey horizon of the sea. Beside me ran a long avenue of hazel bushes, and a thrush was singing on a near bough, his amber and speckled bosom quivering with the passion of his song. The sun had already disappeared, trailing its robe of carmine from off the surface of the far water, and an early star was already keeping its watch overhead. All at once the bushes of the hazel copse parted and Norah Ryan stood before me.

" Is it here that ye are, Dermod, lookin' at the sea ? "

" I was looking at the star above me," I replied.

Norah had discarded her working clothes, and now wore a soft grey tweed dress that suited her well. Together we looked up at the star, and then my eyes fell on the sweet face of my companion. In the shadow of her hair I could see the white of her brow and the delicate and graceful curve of her neck. Her brown tresses hung down her back even as far as her waist, and the wind ruffled them ever so slightly. Somehow my thoughts went back to the June

seaweed rising and falling on the long heaving waves of
Trienna Bay. She noticed me looking at her, and she
sat down on the sod beside me.

"Why d'ye keep watchin' me?" she asked.

"I don't know," I answered in a lame sort of way, for
I am not good at making excuses. I was afraid to tell her
that I liked the whiteness of her brow, the softness of her
hair, and the wonderful glance of her eyes. No doubt she
would have laughed at me if I did.

"Do you mind the night on the 'Derry boat?" I asked.
"All that night when you were asleep, I had your hand in
mine."

"I mind it very well."

As she spoke she closed her fingers over mine and looked
at me in the eyes. The glance was one of a moment;
our gaze met and the next instant Norah's long lashes
dropped slowly and modestly over the grey depths of her
eyes. There was something strange in that look of hers;
it was the glance of a soul which did not yet know itself,
full of radiant awakening and wonderful promise. In it
was all the innocence of the present and passion of the
future; it was the glance both of a virgin and a woman.
We both trembled and looked up at the stars that came out
one by one into the broad expanse of heaven. The thrush had
gone away, and a little wind played amongst the branches
of the trees. In the distance we could hear the water
breaking on the foreshore with a murmurous plaint that
was full of longing. We kept silence, for the spell of the
night was too holy to be broken by words. How long we
remained there I do not know, but when we returned to
the byre all the rest of the party were in bed. Next night
I waited for her in the same place and she came again, and
for many nights afterwards we watched the stars coming
out while listening to the heart song of the sea.

One wet evening, early in October, when Norah and I

were sitting by the fire in the cart-shed that belonged to a farmer near Greenock, talking to Micky's Jim about Glenmornan and the people at home, a strange man came to the farmyard. Although a stranger to me, Micky's Jim knew the fellow very well, for he belonged to a neighbouring village, was a noted gambler, and visited the squad every year. He sat down and warmed his hands at the fire while he looked critically at the members of the squad who had come in to see him.

" Have ye the devil's prayer book with ye ? " asked Jim.

" That I have," answered the man, drawing a pack of cards from his pocket. " Will we have a bit o' the Gospel o' Chance ? "

The body of a disused cart was turned upside down, and six or seven men belonging to the squad sat around it and commenced to gamble for money with the stranger. For a long while I watched the play, and at last put a penny on a card and won. I put on another penny and another and won again and again, for my luck was good. It was very interesting. We gambled until five o'clock in the morning and at the finish of the game I had profited to the extent of twenty-five shillings. During the game I had eyes for nothing else ; the women had gone to bed, but I never noticed their departure, for my whole mind was given up to the play. All day following I looked forward to the evening and the return of the man with the devil's prayer book, and when he came I was one of the first to give a hand to turn the disused cart upside down. The farmer's son, Alec Morrison, a strong, well-knit youth, barely out of his teens, came in to see the play and entered into conversation with Norah Ryan. He worked as a bank clerk in Paisley, but spent every week-end at his father's farm. He was a well-dressed youth ; wore boots which were always clean, and a gold ring with a blue stone in the centre of it shone on one of his fingers. I took little heed of him, for my whole being was centred on the game and my luck was good.

" Come Hallow E'en I'll have plenty of money to take home to Glenmornan," I said to myself, more than once, for on the second night I won over thirty shillings.

The third night was against me—the third time, the gambler's own !—and afterwards I lost money every night. But I could not resist the call of the cards, the school fascinated me, and the sight of a winner's upturned " flush " or " run " set my veins on fire. So I played night after night and discussed the chances of the game day after day, until every penny in my possession was in the hands of the man with the devil's prayer book. Before I put my first penny on a card I had seven pounds in gold, which I intended to take home to my people in Glenmornan. Now it was all gone. Gourock Ellen offered me ten shillings to start afresh, but I would not accept her money. Norah Ryan took no interest in the game, her whole attention was now given up to the farmer's son, and it was only when I had spent my last penny that I became aware of the fact. He came in to see her every evening and passed hour after hour in her company. I did not like this ; I felt angry with her and with myself, and I hated the farmer's son. I had many dreams of a future in which Norah would play a prominent part, but now all my dreams were dashed to pieces. Although outwardly I showed no trace of my feelings I felt very miserable. Norah took no delight in my company any more, all her spare time was given up to Alec Morrison. The cards did not interest me any longer. I hated them, and considered that they were the cause of my present misfortune. If I had left them alone and paid more attention to Norah she would not have taken so much pleasure in the other man's company.

I nursed my mood for a fortnight, then I turned to the cards again and lost all the money in my possession. On the first week of November, when the squad broke up, I had the sum of twopence in my pocket. On the evening prior to the day of the squad's departure, I came suddenly round the corner of the hayshed by the farmhouse and saw a very curious thing. Norah was standing there with the farmer's son and he was kissing her. I came on the two of them suddenly, and when Norah saw me she ran away from the man.

I had never thought of kissing Norah when she was alone with me. It was a very curious thing to do, and it never entered into my mind. Perhaps if I had kissed her when we were together she would like me the more for it. Why I should kiss her was beyond my reasoning. All I knew was that I longed for Norah with a great longing. I was now discouraged and despondent. I felt that I had nothing to live for in the world. To-morrow the rest of the party would go away to their homes with their earnings and I would be left alone. I could not think for a moment of going home penniless. I would stay in Scotland until I earned plenty of money, and go home a rich man. I had not given up thoughts of becoming rich. A hundred pounds to me was a fortune, fifty pounds was a large amount, and twenty pounds was a sum which I might yet possess. If I lived long enough I might earn a whole twenty, or maybe fifty pounds. I had heard of workers who had earned as much. For the whole season I had only sent two pounds home to my own people, while I spent seven on the cards. I played cards because I wanted to make a bigger pile. Now I had but twopence left in my possession !

The squad broke up next day, and Norah Ryan had hardly a word to say to me when bidding good-bye, but she had two hours to spare for leave-taking with Morrison, who, although it was now the middle of the week, a time when he should be at business in the bank, had come to spend a day on the farm. No doubt he had come to bid Norah good-bye. Micky's Jim was going home to Ireland, and Gourock Ellen and Annie said that they were going to Glasgow to get drunk on their last week's pay.

It was afternoon when the party broke up and set out for the railway station, and a heavy snow was lying on the ground. I got turned out of the byre by the farmer when the rest went off, and I found myself in a strange country, houseless, friendless, and alone.

The road lay behind me and before me, and where was I to turn ? This was the question that confronted me as I went out, ragged and shivering, into the cold snow with nothing, save twopence, between me and the cold chance charity of the world. A man can't get much foi twopence. While working there was byre or pig-sty for shelter ; when idle I was not worth the shelter of the meanest roof in the whole country. I walked along, my mind confused with various thoughts, and certain only of one thing. I must look for work. But God alone knew how long it would be until I got a job ! I was only a boy who thought that he was a man, and it was now well into early winter. There was very little work to be done at that season of the year on farms or, indeed, anywhere. A man might get a job ; a boy had very little chance of finding employment. My clothes were threadbare, my boots were leaking, and the snow was on the ground. I felt cold and lonely and a little bit tired of life.

Suddenly I met Gourock Ellen, and it came to me that I was travelling towards the station. I thought that the woman was returning for something which she had for-gotten, but I was mistaken.

" I came back tae see you, Dermod," she said.

" Why ? " I asked in surprise.

" I thought up tae the very last minute that you were goin' hame till Ireland, but Jim Scanlon has tellt me at the station that you are goin' tae stop here. He says that you have ower a pound in siller. Is that so? "

" That's so," I lied, for I disliked to be questioned in such a manner. I told Jim that I had a pound in my possession. Otherwise he would have prevailed upon me to accept money from himself. But I am too proud to accept a favour of that kind.

" I've been watchin' you at the cards, Dermod, and I know the kin' o' luck you had," said Gourock Ellen. " Ye'll hardly have yin penny left at this very minute. Six shillin's, half of my last week's pay, would d'you no harm, if you'd care to take it."

" I don't want it," I said.

" Then you don't know what it is to fast for hours on end, to get turned away from every door with kicks and curses, and to have the dogs of the country put after your heels."

" I don't want your money," I said, for I could not accept money from such a woman.

" I liked you from the first time I saw you, gin that I am a bad woman itself," she said, as if divining my thoughts. " And I dinna like to see you goin' out on the cauld roads with not a copper in your pockets. I'm auld enough to be your——"

Her cheeks gave the faintest suspicion of a blush, and she stopped speaking for just a second, leaving the last word, which no doubt she intended to speak, unuttered on her tongue.

" You can have half of my money if you want it, and if you like you can come with me tae Glesga, and I'll find you a bed and bite until you get a job."

" I'm not going to Glasgow," I said, for it was not in my heart to go into the one house with that woman. I could not explain my dislike for her company, but I preferred the cold night and the snow to the bed and bite which she promised me.

" Well, you can take the couple o' shillin's anyway,"
she persisted ; " they'll do you no ill."

" I don't want your money," I said for the third time.

" 'Twas earned decently, anyway," she said.   " I canna
see why you'll no take it. Will you bid me good-bye,
Dermod ? "

She put out her hand to me as she spoke, and I pressed
it warmly, for in truth I was glad to get rid of her. Suddenly she reached forward and kissed me on the cheek ;
then hurried away, leaving me alone on the roadway. The
woman's kiss disconcerted me, and I suddenly felt ashamed
of my coldness towards her. She was kind-hearted and
considerate, and I was a brute. I looked after her. When
she would turn round I would call to her to stop, and I would
go with her to Glasgow. The thought of spending the
night homeless on the bleak road frightened me. She
reached the corner of the road and went out of my sight
without ever turning round. I looked at the two coppers
which I possessed, and wondered why I hadn't taken the
money which Gourock Ellen offered me. I also wondered
why she had kissed me.

CHAPTER XIV

PADDING IT

" A nail in the sole of your bluchers jagging your foot like a pin,
And every step of the journey driving it further in ;
Then out on the great long roadway, you'll find when you go
abroad,
The nearer you go to nature, the further you go from God."

—*A Song of the Dead End.*

OUT on tramp, homeless in a strange country, with twopence in my pocket ! The darkness lay around me and the snow was white on the ground. Whenever I took my hands out of my pockets the chill air nipped them like pincers. One knee was out through my trousers, and my boots were leaking. The snow melted as it came through the torn uppers, and I could hear the water gurgling between my toes as I walked. When I passed a lighted house I felt a hunger that was not of the belly kind. I came to the village of Bishopton, and went into a little shop, where I asked for a pennyworth of biscuits. The man weighed them in scales that shone like gold, and broke one in halves to make the exact weight.

" There's nothin' like fair measure, laddie," he said.

" Is there any chance of a man getting a job about this district ? " I asked.

" What man ? " said the shopkeeper.

" Me," I said.

" Get out, ye scamp ! " roared the man. " It would be better for you to go to bed instead of tryin' to take a rise out of yer betters."

" You are an old pig ! " I shouted at the man, for I did not like his way of speaking, and disappeared into the darkness. I ate the biscuits, but felt hungrier after my meal than I was before it.

The night was calm and deadly cold. Overhead a very pale moon forged its way through a heaven of stars. On such a night it is a pleasure to sit before a nice warm fire on a well-swept hearth. I had no fire, no home, no friends ; nothing but the bleak road and the coldness. I kept walking, walking. I knew that it would be unwise to sit down : perhaps I would fall asleep and die. I did not want to die. It was so much better to walk about on the roads of a strange country in which there was nobody to care what became of me ; no one except an old harridan, and she was far away from me now. The love of life was strong within me, for I was very young, and never did I cling closer to life than I did at that moment when it was blackest. My thoughts went to the future and the good things which might lie before me.

" I'll get a job yet," I said to myself. " I'll walk about until I meet somebody who needs me. Then I'll grow up in years and work among men, maybe getting a whole pound a week as my pay. A pound a week is a big wage, and it will amount to a lot in a year. I will pay ten shillings a week for my keep in some lodging-house, as Micky's Jim had done when he worked on Greenock pier, and I will save the other half-sovereign. Ten shillings a week amounts to twenty-six pounds a year. In ten years I shall save two hundred and sixty pounds. Such a big lump-sum of money ! Two hundred and sixty pounds !

" It will be hard to keep a wife on a pound a week, but I will always remain single, and send my money home to my own people. If I don't, I'll never have any luck. I will never gamble again. Neither will I marry, for women are no earthly use, anyway. They get old, wrinkled, and fat very quickly. They are all alike, every one of them."

I found my thoughts wandering from one subject to another like those of a person who is falling asleep. Anyhow, I had something to live for, so I kept walking, walking on.

I was in the open country, and I did not know where the road was leading to, but that did not matter. I was as near home in one place as in another.

From one point of the sky, probably the north, I saw the clouds rising, covering up the stars, and at last blotting the moon off the sky as a picture is wiped off a slate. It was more dismal than ever when the moon and stars were gone, for now I was alone with the night and the darkness. I could hear the wind as it passed through the telegraph wires by the roadside. It was a weeping wind, and put me in mind of the breeze calling down the chimney far away at home in Glenmornan.

A low bent man came out of the darkness and shuffled by. " It looks like snow," he said, in passing.

" It does," I replied. I could not see his face, but his voice was kindly. He shuffled along. Perhaps he was going home to a warm supper and bed. I did not know, and I wondered who the man was.

Suddenly the snow from the darkness above drifted down and my clothes were white in an instant. My bare knee became very cold, for the flakes melted on it as they fell. The snow ran down my legs and made me shiver. I took off my muffler and tied it around the hole in my trousers to prevent the snowflakes from getting in. I felt wearied and cold, but after a while I got very angry. I got angry, not with myself, but with the wind, the snow, my leaky boots and ragged clothes. I was angry with the man who carried the devil's prayer book, and also with the man who broke a biscuit in two because he was an honest

body and a believer in fair measure. Perhaps I ought to
have been angry with myself, for did I not spend all my
money at the card school, and was it not my own fault that
now I had only one penny in my possession ? If I had saved
my money like Micky's Jim I would have now eight or
nine pounds in my pocket.

Suddenly the snow cleared, and my eyes fell on a farmhouse hardly a stone's-throw away from the road. Thinking that I might get a shed to lie in I went towards it.
There was no light showing in the house and it must have
been long after midnight. As I approached a dog ran at
me yelping. I turned and fled, but the dog caught my
trousers and hung on, trying to fasten his teeth in my leg.
I twisted round and swung him clear, then lifted my boot
and aimed a blow at the animal which took him on the jaw.
His teeth snapped together like a trap, and he ran back
squealing. I took to my heels and returned to the road.
From there I saw a light in the farmhouse, so I ran quicker
than ever. I was frightened at what I had done ; I had
committed a crime in looking for a night's shelter along
with the beasts of the byre. I could not get sleeping with
men ; I was not a man. I could not get sleeping in a shed ;
I was not even a brute beast. I was merely a little boy
who was very hungry, ragged, and tired.

I ran for a long distance, and was sweating all over when
I stopped. I stood until I got cool, then continued my
walking, walking through the darkness. I was still walking
when the day broke cold and cheerless. I met a navvy
going to his work and I asked him for a penny. He had
no money, but he gave me half of the food which he had
brought from home for his daily meal.

On the outskirts of Paisley I went to the door of a
mansion to ask for a penny. A man opened the door.
He was a fat and comfortable-looking, round-paunched
fellow. He told me to get off before the dog was put

after me. I hurried off, and forsook the big houses afterwards.

Once in Paisley I sat down on a kerbstone under the Caledonian Railway Bridge in Moss Street. I fell asleep, and slept until a policeman woke me up.

" Go away from here ! " he roared at me. I got away.

A gang of men were laying down tramway rails on the street and I went forward and asked the overseer for a job. He laughed at me for a minute, then drew his gang around to examine me.

" He's a fine bit o' a man," said one.

" He's shouthered like a rake," said another.

Discomfited and disgusted I hurried away from the grinning circle of men, and all day long I travelled through the town. I soon got tired of looking for work, and instead I looked for food. I was very unsuccessful, and youth is the time for a healthy appetite. I spent my last penny on a bun, and when it was dark I got a crust from a night watchman who sat in a little hut by the tram-lines. About midnight I left the town and went into the country. The snow was no longer falling, but a hard frost had set in. About two o'clock in the morning I lay down on the cold ground utterly exhausted, and fell asleep. When dawn came I rose, and shivering in every limb I struck out once more on my journey. I looked for work on the farms along the road, but at every place I was turned away.

" Go back to the puirs' house," said every second or third farmer.

I went to one farmhouse when the men were coming out from dinner.

" Are you lookin' for a job ? " asked a man, whom I took to be master.

" I am," I answered.

" Then give us a hand in the shed for a while," he said.

I followed the party into a large building where implements were stored, and the men gathered round a broken reaper which had to be taken out into the open.

" Help us out with this," said the farmer to me.

There were six of us altogether, and three went to each side of the machine and caught hold of it.

" Now, lift ! " shouted the farmer.

The men at the other side lifted their end, but ours remained on the ground despite all efforts to raise it.

" Damn you, lift ! " said my two mates angrily to me.

I put all my energy into the work, but the cold and hunger had taken the half of my strength away. We could not lift the machine clear of the ground. The farmer got angry.

" Get out of my sight, you spineless brat ! " he roared to me, and I left the farmyard. When I came to the high-road again there were tears in my eyes. They were tears of shame ; I was ashamed of my own weakness.

For a whole week afterwards I tramped through the country, hating all men, despised by everyone, and angry with my own plight. A few gave me food, some cursed me from their doors, and a great number mocked me as I passed. " Auld ragged breeks ! " the children of the villages cried after me. " We're sick o' lookin' at the likes o' you ! " the fat tubs of women, who stood by their cottage doors, said when I asked them for something to eat. Others would say : " Get out o' our sight, or we'll tell the policeman about you. Then you'll go to the lock-up, where you'll only get bread and water and a bed on a plank."

Such a dreadful thing ! It shocked me to think of it, and for a while I always hurried away when women spoke in such a manner. However, in the end, suffering caused me to change my opinions. A man with an empty stomach may well prefer bread and water to water, a bed on a plank to a bed on the snow, and the roof of a prison to

H

the cold sky over him. So it was that I came into Paisley again at the end of the week and asked a policeman to arrest me. I told him that I was hungry and wanted something to eat. The man was highly amused.

" You must break the law before the king feeds you," he said.

" But I have been begging," I persisted.

" If you want me to arrest you, break a window," said the man. " Then I'll take you before a bailie and he'll put you into a reformatory, where they'll give you a jail-bird's education. You'll come out worse than you went in, and it's ten to one in favour of your life ending with a hempen cravat round your neck."

The man put his hand in his pocket and took out a sixpence, which he handed to me.

" Run away now and get something to eat," he shouted in an angry voice, and I hurried away hugging the silver coin in my hand. That night I got twopence more, and fed well for the first time in a whole week.

I met the policeman once again in later years. He was a Socialist, and happened to have the unhealthy job of protecting blacklegs from a crowd of strikers when I met him for the second time. While pretending to keep the strikers back he was urging them to rush by him and set upon the blacklegs—the men who had not the back-bone to fight for justice and right. Not being, as a Socialist, a believer in charity, he feigned to be annoyed when I reminded him of his generous action of years before.

CHAPTER XV

MOLESKIN JOE

" Soft words may win a woman's love, or soothe a maiden's fears,
But hungry stomachs heed them not—the belly hasn't ears."
—From *The Maxims of Moleskin Joe.*

THAT night I slept in a watchman's hut on the streets, and in the morning I obtained a slice of bread from a religious lady, who gave me a long harangue on the necessity of leading a holy life. Afterwards I went away from Paisley, and out on the road I came upon a man who was walking along by himself. He was whistling a tune, and his hands were deep in his trousers' pockets. He had knee-straps around his knees, and a long skiver of tin wedged between one of the straps and the legs of his trousers, which were heavy with red muck frozen on the cloth. The cloth itself was hard, and rattled like wood against the necks of his boots. He was very curiously dressed. He wore a pea-jacket, which bore marks of the earth of many strange sleeping-places. A grey cap covered a heavy cluster of thick dark hair. But the man's waistcoat was the most noticeable article of apparel. It was made of velvet, ornamented with large ivory buttons which ran down the front in parallel rows. Each of his boots was of different colour ; one was deep brown, the other dark chrome ; and they were also different in size and shape.

In later years I often wore similar boots myself. We navvies call them " subs." and they can be bought very cheaply in rag-stores and second-hand clothes-shops. One boot has always the knack of wearing better than its fellow. The odd good boot is usually picked up by a rag-picker, and in course of time it finds its way into a rag-store, where it is thrown amongst hundreds of others, which are always ready for further use at their old trade. A pair of odd boots may be got for a shilling or less, and most navvies wear them.

The man's face was strongly boned and fierce of expression. He had not shaved for weeks. His shoulders were broad, and he stood well over six feet in height. At once I guessed that he was very strong, so I liked the man even before I spoke to him.

" Where are you for ? " he asked when I overtook him.

" God knows," I answered. " Where are you for ? "

" Christ knows," he replied, and went on with the tune which he had left off to question me.

When he had finished whistling he turned to me again.

" Are you down and out ? " he asked.

" I slept out last night," I answered.

" The first time ? " he enquired.

" I slept out for a whole week."

" There's a good time comin', though we may never live to see it," he said, by way of consolation. " Had you anything to eat this mornin' ? "

" A slice of bread," I said ; then added, " and a lot of advice along with it from an old lady."

" Damn her advice ! " cried the man angrily. " The belly hasn't ears. A slice of bread is danged mealy grub for a youngster."

He stuck his hand in the pocket of his pea-jacket and drew out a chunk of currant bread, which he handed to me.

" Try that, cully," he said.

I ate it ravenously, for I was feeling very hungry.

" By cripes ! you've a stomach," said my companion, when I had finished eating. " Where are you for, any-how ? "

" I don't know. I'm looking for work."

" It's not work you need ; it's rest," said the stranger.

" You've been working," I replied, looking at his covering of muck. " Why don't you clean your trousers and shoes ? "

" If you were well fed you'd be as impudent as myself," said the man. " And clean my trousers and shoes ! What's the good of being clean ? "

" It puts the dirt away."

" It does not ; it only shifts it from one place to another. And as to work—well, I work now and again, I'm sorry to say, although I done all the work that a man is put into the world to do before I was twenty-one. What's your name ? "

" Dermod Flynn. What's yours ? "

" Joe—Moleskin Joe, my mates calls me. Have you any tin ? "

" Twopence," I replied, showing the man the remainder of the eightpence which I had picked up the night before.

" You're savin' up your fortune," he said with fine irony. " I haven't a penny itself."

" Where did you get the currant cake ? " I asked.

" Stole it."

" And the waistcoat ? "

" Stole it," said the man, and then continued with thinly-veiled sarcasm in his voice. " My name's Moleskin Joe, as I've told you already. I don't mind havin' seen my father or mother, and I was bred in a workhouse. I'm forty years of age—more or less—and I started work when I was seven. I've been in workhouse, reformatory, prison, and church. I went to prison of my own free will when the times were bad and I couldn't get a mouthful of food outside, but it was always against my will that I went to church. I can fight like hell and drink like blazes, and now that you know as much about my life as I know myself you'll maybe be satisfied. You're the most impudent brat that I have ever met."

The man made the last assertion in a quiet voice, as if stating a fact which could not be contradicted. I did not feel angry or annoyed with the man who made sarcastic remarks so frankly and good-humouredly. For a long while I kept silence and the two of us plodded on together.

" Why do you drink ? " I asked at last.

" Why do I drink ? " repeated the man in a voice of wonder. " Such a funny question ! If God causes a man to thirst He'll allow him to drink, for He's not as bad a chap as some of the parsons make Him out to be. Drink draws a man nearer to heaven and multiplies the stars ; and ' Drink when you can, the drouth will come ' is my motto. Do you smoke or chew ? "

He pulled a plug of tobacco from his pocket, bit a piece from the end of it, and handed the plug to me. Now and again I had taken a whiff at Micky's Jim's pipe, and I liked a chew of tobacco. Without answering Moleskin's question I took the proffered tobacco and bit a piece off it.

" There's some hope for you yet," was all he said.

We walked along together, and my mate asked a farmer who was standing by the roadside for a few coppers to help us on our way.

" Go to the devil ! " said the farmer.

" Never mind," Moleskin remarked to me when we got out of hearing. " There's a good time comin', though we may never live to see it in this world."

Afterwards we talked of many things, and Joe told me of many adventures with women who were not good and men who were evil. When money was plentiful he lived large and drank between drinks as long as he was able to stand on his feet.

The man impressed me, and, what was most wonderful, he seemed to enjoy life. Nights spent out in the cold, days when hardly a crust of food was obtainable, were looked upon as a matter of course by him.

"Let us live to-day, if we can, and the morrow can go be damned!" he said, and this summed up the whole of his philosophy as far as I could see. It would be fine to live such a life as his, I thought, but such a life was not for me I had my own people depending on my earnings, and I must make money to send home to Glenmornan. If I had a free foot I would live like Joe, and at that moment I envied the man who was born in a workhouse and who had never seen a father or mother.

A lot of events took place on the road. Passing along we overtook a dour-faced man who carried a spade over his shoulder.

"He's goin' to dig his own grave," said Moleskin to me.

"How do you know?" I asked.

"Well, I'd like to know how a man is goin' to live long if he works on a day like this!"

Just as we came up to him a young woman passed by and gave us an impudent glance, as Moleskin called it. She was good to look at and had a taking way with her. As she went by the man with the spade turned and looked after her.

"Did ye see that woman?" he asked Moleskin when we came abreast.

"By God, I'm not blind!" said my friend.

"Dinna sweer," said the man with the spade. "'Tis an evil habit."

"'Tisn't a habit," said Joe. "'Tis a gift."

"'Tis a gift frae the deevil," replied the other man.

" A gift frae the deevil, that's what it is. 'Tis along with that woman that ye should be, though God forgi'e me for callin' her a woman, for her house is on the way tae Sheol goin' doon tae the chambers of death. I wadna talk tae her wi' muckle mooth sine she be a scarlet woman with a wily heart."

" What are you jawin' about ? " asked Moleskin, who seemed at a loss what to make of the man with the spade, while for myself I did not in the least understand him.

" Have you a sixpence ? " asked Joe suddenly.

" A sixpence ? " queried the man. " Gin that I hae, what is it tae ye ? "

" If you have a sixpence you should have given it to that woman when she was passin'. She's a lusty wench."

" Gi'e a sixpence to that woman ! " replied the stranger. " I wadna do it, mon, if she was lyin' for death by the roadside. I'm a Chreestian."

" I would give up your company in heaven for hers in hell any day," said Moleskin, as the man with the spade turned into a turnip field by the roadside. " And never look too much into other people's faults or you're apt to forget your own ! " roared Joe, by way of a parting shot.

" Don't you think that I had the best of that argument ? " Joe asked me five minutes later.

" What was it all about ? " I asked.

" I don't know what he was jawin' at half of the time," said Joe. " But his talk about the Christian was a damned good hit against me. However, I got in two good hits myself ! The one about her company in hell and the one about lookin' too much into other people's faults were a pair up for me. I think that I did win, Flynn, and between me and you I never like to get the worst of either an argument or a fight."

CHAPTER XVI

MOLESKIN JOE AS MY FATHER

'The opinions of a man who argues with his fist are always respected.'—MOLESKIN JOE.

ABOUT midday we met a red-faced farmer driving a spring-cart along the road.

"Where are you bound for?" he called to me as he reined up his pony.

"What the hell is it to you?" asked Moleskin, assuming a pugilistic pose all of a sudden. Love of fighting was my mate's great trait, and I found it out in later years. He would fight his own shadow for the very fun of the thing. "The man who argues with his fist is always respected," he often told me.

"I'm lookin' for a young lad who can milk and take care of beasts in a byre," replied the man nervously, for Joe's remark seemed to have frightened him. "Can the youngster milk?"

"I can," I answered gleefully. I had never caught hold of a cow's teat in my life, but I wanted work at all costs, and did not mind telling a lie. A moment before I was in a despondent mood, seeing nothing in front of me but the life of the road for years to come, but now, with the prospect of work and wages before me, I felt happy. Already I was forming dreams of the future, and my mind was once more turning to the homecoming to Glenmornan when I became a rich man. A lot of my dreams had been dashed to pieces already, but I was easily captured and

made the slave of new ones. Also, there was a great deal
of my old pride slipping away. There was a time when
I would not touch a cow's teat, but the Glenmornan
pride that looked down upon such work was already
gone.

" Milk ! " cried Moleskin in answer to the last remark
of the farmer. " You should see my son under a cow !
He's the boy for a job like that, you'll find. What wages
are you goin' to offer him ? "

" Ten pounds from now till May-day, if he suits," replied
the farmer.

" He'll suit you all right," said Joe. " But he'll not go
with you for one penny less than eleven pounds."

" I'll take ten pounds, Moleskin," I cried. I did not
want to sleep another night on the cold ground.

" Hold your blessed jaw," growled my mate. Then he
turned to the farmer again and went on :

" Eleven pounds and not one penny less. Forbye, you
must give me something for lettin' him go with you, as
I do not like to lose the child."

After a great deal of haggling, during which no notice
was taken of me, a bargain was struck, the outcome of
which was that I should receive the sum of ten guineas
at the end of six months spent in the employ of the farmer.
My " father " received five shillings, paid on the nail, because
he allowed me to go to work.

" There's a good time comin', though we may never
live to see it," said Joe, as he shoved the silver into his
pocket and cast a farewell glance at me as I climbed into
the cart. I caught my mate's square look for a minute.
In the left eye a faint glimmer appeared and the eyelid
slowly descended. Then he bit a piece off the end of his
plug, started whistling a tune and went on his way.

The farmer set the young cob at a gallop, and in about
a quarter of an hour we arrived at his place, which was

called Braxey Farm. When evening came round my master found that I could not milk.

"You'll learn," he said, not at all unkindly, and proceeded to teach me the correct way in which to coax a cow's udder. In a fortnight's time I was one of the best milkers in the byre.

Just off the stable I had a room to sleep in, an evil-smelling and dirty little place crammed with horses' harness and agricultural implements But after the nights spent on the snow I thought the little room and the bed the most cosy room and bed in the world. I slept there all alone, and by night I could hear the horses pawing the floor of the stable, and sometimes I was wakened by the noise they made and thought that somebody had gotten into my room.

I started work at five o'clock in the morning and finished at seven in the evening, and when Sunday came round I had to feed the ploughman's horses in addition to my ordinary work.

I liked the place in a negative sort of way ; it was dull and depressing, but it was better than the life of the road. Now and again I got a letter from home, and my people were very angry because I had sent so little money to them during the summer months. For all that, I liked to get a letter from home, and I loved to hear what the people whom I had known since childhood were doing. On the farm there was no one to speak to me or call me friend. The two red-cheeked servant girls who helped me at the milking hardly ever took any notice of me, a kid lifted from the toll-road. They were decent ploughmen's daughters, and they let me know as much whenever I tried to become familiar. After all, I think they liked me to speak to them, for they could thus get an excuse to dwell on their own superior merits.

"Workin' wi' a lad picked off the roads, indeed !

Whoever heard of such a thing for respectable lassies ! " they exclaimed.

Even the ploughman who worked on the farm ignored me when he was out of temper. When in a good humour he insulted me by way of pastime.

" You're an Eerish pig ! " he roared at me one evening.

I am impulsive, and my temper, never the best, was becoming worse daily. When angry I am blind to everything but my own grievance, and the ploughman's taunt made me angrier than ever I had been in my life before. He had just come into the byre where the girls and I were milking. He was a married man, but he loved to pass loose jokes with the two young respectable lassies, and his filthy utterances amused them.

Although the ploughman was a big hardy fellow, his taunt angered me, and made me blind to his physical advantages. I rushed at him head down and butted him in the stomach. He flattened out in the sink amidst the cow-dung, and once I got him down I jumped on him and rained a shower of blows on his face and body. The girls screamed, the cows jumped wildly in the stalls, and we were in imminent danger of getting kicked to death. So I heard later, but at that moment I saw nothing but the face which was bleeding under my blows. The ploughman was much stronger than I, and gripping me round the waist he turned me over, thus placing me under himself. I struggled gamely, but the man suddenly hit my head against the flagged walk and I went off in a swoon. When I came to myself, the farmer, the two girls, and the ploughman were standing over me.

I struggled to my feet, rushed at the man again, and taking him by surprise I was able to shove him against one of the cows in the stall nearest him. The animal kicked him in the leg, and, mad with rage, he reached forward and gripped me by the throat with the intention of strangling me. But I was not afraid; the outside world was non-existent to me at that moment, and I wanted to fight until I fell again.

The farmer interposed. We were separated and the ploughman left the byre. That night I did not sleep; my anger burned like a fire until dawn. The next day I felt dizzy and unwell, but that was the only evil result of the fight. The ploughman never spoke to me again, civilly or otherwise, and I was left in peace.

From start to finish the work on Braxey Farm was very wearisome, and the surroundings were soul-killing and spiritless. By nature I am sensitive and refined. A woman of untidy appearance disgusts me, a man who talks filthily without reason is utterly repellent to me. The ploughman with his loose jokes I loathed, the girls I despised even more than they despised me. Their dislike was more affected than real; my dislike was real though less ostentatious. It gave me no pleasure to tell a dirty slut that she was dirty, but a dirty woman annoyed me in those days. I could not imagine a man falling in love with one of those women, with their short, inelegant petticoats and hobnailed shoes caked with the dried muck of the farmyard. I could not imagine love in the midst of such filth, such squalid poverty. But I did not then understand the meaning of love; to me it was something which would exist when Norah Ryan became a lady, and when I had a grand house wherein to pay her homage. I am afraid that my knowledge of life was very small.

The talk of the two girls gave me the first real insight into love and all that it cloaks with the false covering of poetical illusion. Every poetical ideal, every charm and beauty which I had associated with love was dispelled by the talk of those two women. For a while I did not believe the things of which they spoke. My mind revolted. The ploughman and the two girls continued their disgusting anecdotes. I did my best not to listen. Knowing that I hated their talk the servants would persist in talking, and every particle of information collected by them was in course of time given to me.

My outlook on life became cynical and sour. I was a sort of outcast among men, liking few and liked by none. When the end of the season came I was pleased to get clear of Braxey Farm ; the more familiar I became with the people the more I disliked them. The farmer paid me nine pounds, and explained that he retained the other thirty shillings because he had to learn me how to milk.

. " Your feyther was a great liar," he added.

Out of my wages I sent seven pounds home to Glenmornan and kept the remainder for my own use, as I did not know when I could get a next job. My mother sent me a letter that another brother was born to me—the second since I left home—and asking me for some more money to help them along with the rent. But my disposition was changing ; my outlook on life was becoming bitter, and I hated to be slave to farmers, landlords, parents, and brothers and sisters. Every new arrival into the family was reported to me as something for which I should be grateful. " Send home some more money, you have another brother," ran the letters, and a sense of unfairness crept over me. The younger members of the family were taking the very life-blood out of my veins, and on account of them I had to suffer kicks, snubs, cold and hunger. New brothers and sisters were no pleasure to me. I rebelled against the imposition and did not answer the letter.

CHAPTER XVII

ON THE DEAD END

" He tramped through the colourless winter land or swined in the
    scorching heat,
The dry skin hacked on his sapless hands or blistering on his feet ;
He wallowed in mire, unseen, unknown where your houses of
    pleasure rise,
And hapless hungry and chilled to the bone he builded the
    edifice."

—From *A Song of the Dead End*.

IN this true story, as in real life, men and women crop
up for a moment, do something or say something,
then go away and probably never reappear again.
In my story there is no train of events or sequence
of incidents leading up to a desired end. When I started
writing of my life I knew not how I would end my story ;
and even yet, seeing that one thing follows another so
closely, I hardly know when to lay down my pen and say
that the tale is told. Sometimes I say, " I'll write my
life up to this day and no further," but suddenly it comes
to me that to-morrow may furnish a more fitting climax,
and so on my story runs. In fiction you settle upon the
final chapter before you begin the first, and every event
is described and placed in the fabric of the story to suit
an end already in view. A story of real life, like real life
itself, has no beginning, no end. Something happens
before and after ; the first chapter succeeds another and
another follows the last. The threads of a made-up story
are like the ribs of an open umbrella, far apart at one
end and joined together at the other. You close the

umbrella and it becomes straight; you draw the threads of the story together at the end and the plot is made clear. Emanating as it does from the mind of a man or woman, the plot is worked up so that it arouses interest and compels attention. Such an incident is unnecessary; then dispense with it. Such a character is undesirable; then away with him. Such a conversation is unfitting; then substitute one more suitable. But I, writing a true story, cannot substitute imaginary talk for real, nor false characters for true, if I am faithful to myself and the task imposed upon me when I took to writing the story of my life. No doubt I shall have some readers weak enough to be shocked by my disclosures; men and women, who like ascetic hermits, fight temptation by running from it, and avoid sin by shutting their eyes to it. But these need not be taken into account, their weakness is not worthy of attention. I merely tell the truth, speak of things as I have seen them, of people as I have known them, and of incidents as one who has taken part in them. Truth needs no apologies, frankness does not deserve reproof. I write of the ills which society inflicts on individuals like myself, and when possible I lay every wound open to the eyes of the world. I believe that there is an Influence for Good working through the ages, and it is only by laying our wounds open that we can hope to benefit by the Influence. Who doctors the wounds which we hide from everybody's eyes?

It was beautiful weather and the last day of May, 1906, when I left Braxey Farm and took to the road again. I obtained work, before night fell, on an estate in the vicinity. The factor, a pompous man with a large stomach, gave me the job; and I got lodgings with a labourer who worked on the estate. My pay was eighteen shillings a week, and I stopped a fortnight. At the end of that period I got sacked. This was how it happened.

Two men, a fat man and a fatter, came to the spot where I was working on the estate grounds. The fat man was the factor.

"Are you working here?" asked the fat man.

"Yes," I answered.

"'Yes, sir,' you mean," said the fatter man.

"I mean 'yes,'" I said. The man looked overbearing, and he annoyed me.

"I'm the master of this place," said the fatter man. "You must address me as 'sir' when speaking to me."

A fat man looks awfully ridiculous with his big stomach, his short breath, and short legs. An ugly man may look dignified; a gargoyle may even possess the dignity of unrivalled ugliness, but a fat man with a red face who poses as a dignified being is very funny to see. I never raise my hat to any man, and I was not going to say "sir" to the blown bubble in front of me.

"You had better say 'sir,'" said the factor. "This gentleman is your master."

The word "master" is repellent to me.

"Sir be damned!" I snapped out.

"Pay him off this evening," was all that gentleman said; and that evening I was on the road again.

Afterwards I kept mucking about on farms and other places, working a day here and a week there, earning a guinea clear at one job and spending it while looking for the next. Sometimes I tramped for days at a time, sleeping in haysheds, barns and ditches, and "bumming my grub," as we tramps say, from houses by the roadside. Often in the darkness of the night I lit my little fire of dried sticks under shelter of a rock or tree, and boiled my billy of tea in the red flames. Then I would fall asleep while looking at the pictures in the embers, and my dreams would take me back again to Glenmornan and the road that led from Greenanore to my home on the steep hillside of Donegal.

I

Often and often I went home to my own people in my nightly dreams. When morning came I would set out again on my journey, leaving nothing to tell of my passing but the ashes of my midnight fire. I had nothing to cheer me, no hopes, no joys, no amusements. It was hard to obtain constant employment; a farmer kept me a fortnight, a drainer a week, a roadmender a day, and afterwards it was the road, the eternal, soul-killing road again. When I had money I spent it easily; spending was my nearest approach to pleasure. When I had aught in my purse I lived in suspense, thinking of the time when all would be spent, but when the coin was gone I had the contentment of a man who knows that he can fall no lower. Always, however, I sought for work; I wanted something to do. My desire to labour became a craze, an obsession, and nothing else mattered if I got plenty of work to do.

"You are an idle, useless-lookin' lump o' a man," the women in roadside cottages said to me. "Why don't you work?" Looking for work meant laziness and idleness to them. For me they felt all the contempt which people with fixed abodes feel for vagabonds. They did not hate me; of that I was not worthy. They were very human, which is the worst that can be said of them, and they despised me. Work was scarce; I looked light and young, and a boy is not much good to a farmer. Yet for my age I was very strong, and many a man much older than myself I could work blind, if only I got the chance. But no one seemed to want me. "Run away, little impudence, and hide behind your big sister's petticoats!" were the words that I was greeted with when I asked for a job.

For a whole month I earned my living by gathering discarded metal from the corporation middens near Glasgow and selling the scrap to proprietors of the city rag-stores. Starvation has hold of the forelock of a man

who works at that job. Sometimes I made tenpence a
day. By night I slept on the midden, or, to be more exact,
in the midden. I dug a little hole in the warm refuse
sent out from the corporation stables, and curled myself
up there and went to sleep, somewhat after the manner
of Job of old. Once a tipster employed me to sell his tips
outside the enclosure of Ayr racecourse. I gave up that
job quickly, for I could only earn sixpence a day. During
the end of the summer I made a few shillings by carrying
luggage for passengers aboard the steamer at G——
Pier, but in the end the porters on the quay chased me
away. I was depriving decent men of their livelihood,
they said.

About this time I met Tom MacGuire, a countryman of
my own, an anarchist, a man with great courage, strength,
and love of justice. Tom said that all property was theft,
all religion was fraud, and a life lacking adventure was a
life for a pig. He had just come out of jail after serving
six months' hard because he shot the crow * in a Greenock
public-house. I met him on the roadside, where he was
sitting reading an English translation of some of Schopen-
hauer's works. We sat down together and talked of one
thing and another, and soon were the best of friends. I
told Tom the story of the man who wanted me to say
" Yes, sir," when speaking to him.

" I have a job on that man's place to-night," said Tom.
" Will you come and give me a hand ? "

" What is the job ? " I asked.

Tom lowered the left eyelid slightly as I looked at him.
That was his only answer. I guessed instinctively that
Tom's job was a good one, and so I promised to accompany
him.

---

* Ordering and drinking whisky, and having no intention of
paying for the drink, is known to navvies as "shooting the
crow."

We worked together on that estate not only that night, but for some weeks afterwards. Operations started at midnight and finished at four o'clock in the morning. We stopped in Paisley, and we went into the town in the morning, each on a different route, and sold the proceeds of our night's labour. At the end of a fortnight, or, to be exact, fifteen days' work on the estate, Tom was accosted by two policemen as he was going into Paisley. His belly looked bigger than any alderman's, and no wonder ! When searched he had three pheasants under his waistcoat. Because of that he got six months, and the magistrate spoke hard things against Tom's character. For all that, my mate was a sound, good fellow. In a compact made beforehand it was understood that if one was gripped by the law he would not give his comrade away, and Tom was good to his word when put to the test. From that time forward I forsook poaching. I loved it for its risks alone, but I was not an adept at the art, and I could never make a living at the game. I felt sorry for poor Tom and I have never seen him since.

Once, eighteen months after I had left Braxey Farm, I wrote home to my own people. I was longing to hear from somebody who cared for me. In reply an angry letter came from my mother. " Why was I not sending home some money ? " she asked. Another child had come into the family and there were many mouths to fill. I would never have a day's luck in all my life if I forgot my father and mother. I was working with a drainer at the time and I had thirty shillings in my possession. This I sent home, but not with a willing heart, for I did not know when I would be idle again. Three days later my mother wrote asking me to send some more money, for they were badly needing it. I did not answer the letter, for I got sacked that evening, and I went out on the road again with five shillings in my pocket and new thoughts in my head, thoughts that had never come there before.

Why had my parents brought me into the world? I asked myself. Did they look to the future? At home I heard them say when a child was born to such and such a person that it was the will of God, just as if man and woman had nothing to do with the affair. I wished that I had never been born. My parents had sinned against me in bringing me into the world in which I had to fight for crumbs with the dogs of the gutter. And now they wanted money when I was hardly able to keep myself alive on what I earned. Bringing me into the world and then living on my labour—such an absurd and unjust state of things! I was angry, very angry, with myself and with everyone else, with the world and the people on it.

The evening was wet; the rain came down heavily, and I got drenched to the skin. While wandering in the town of Kilmacolm, my eye caught the light of a fire through the window-blind of an inn parlour. It would be very warm inside there. My flesh was shivery and my feet were cold, like lumps of ice, in my battered and worn boots. I went in, sat down, and when the bar-tender approached me, I called for a half-glass of whisky. I did not intend to drink it, having never drunk intoxicating liquor before, but I had to order something and was quite content to pay twopence for the heat of the fire. It was so very comfortable there that I almost fell asleep three or four times. Suddenly I began to feel thirsty; it seemed as if I was drying up inside, and the glass of whisky, sparkling brightly as the firelight caught it, looked very tempting. I raised it to my mouth, just to wet my lips, and the whisky tasted good. Almost without realising what I was doing I swallowed the contents of the glass.

At that moment a man entered, a man named Fergus Boyle, who belonged to the same arm of the Glen as myself, and he was then employed on a farm in the neighbourhood.

I was pleased to see him. I had not seen a Glenmornan man since I had left Micky's Jim's squad, but Fergus brought no news from home ; he had been in Scotland for over five years without a break. Without asking me, he called for " two schooners * of beer, with a stick † in iviry wan of them."

" Don't pull the hare's foot, ‡ for I don't drink, Fergus," I said. I did not want to take any more liquor. I could hardly realise that I had just been drinking a moment before, the act being so unpremeditated. I came into the inn parlour solely to warm myself, and thinking still of that more than anything else I could hardly grasp what had resulted. I had a great dislike in my heart for drunken men, and I did not want to become one. Fergus sniffed at the glass beside me and winked knowingly. Evidences were against my assertion, and if I did not drink with Fergus he would say that I did not like his company. He was the first Glenmornan man whom I had seen for years, and I could not offend him. When the bar-tender brought the drinks I drained the schooner at one gulp, partly to please Fergus and partly because I was very dry. I stood treat then myself, as decency required, and my remembrance of subsequent events is very vague. In a misty sort of way I saw Fergus putting up his fists, as a Glenmornan man should when insulted, and knocking somebody down. There was a scuffle afterwards and I was somehow mixed up in it and laying out round me for all I was worth.

Dawn was breaking when I found myself lying on the

* Schooner. A large glass used for lager-beer and ale, which contains fourteen fluid ounces.

† A stick. A half-glass of whisky mixed with beer—a navvyism for *petite verre*.

‡ Pulling the hare's foot. A farmyard phrase. The hare in the cornfield takes refuge in the standing corn when the servants are reaping. To the farmer himself belongs the privilege of catching the animal. If he is unable to corner the hare he stands drinks to all the harvesters, and the drink is usually a sure one.

toll-road, racked by a headache and suffering from extreme thirst. It was still raining and my clothes were covered with mud ; one boot was gone and one sleeve of my coat was hanging by a mere thread. I found the sum of seven-pence in my pockets—the rest of the money had dis-appeared. I looked round for Fergus, but could not see him. About a hundred paces along the road I came on his cap and I saw the trace of his body in the wet muck. Probably he had slept there for a part of the night and crept away when the rain brought him to his senses. I looked high and low for my lost boot, but could not find it. I crept over the wall surrounding a cottage near the road and discovered a pair of boots in an outhouse. I put them on when I came back to the road and threw my own old one away. The pain in my head was almost intolerable, and my mind went back to the stories told by hard drinkers of the cure known as the " hair of the dog that bit you." So it was that I went into Kilmacolm again, not knowing how I came out, and waited until the pubs opened, when I drank a bottle of beer and a half-glass of whisky. My headache cleared away and I had threepence left and felt happy. By getting drunk the night before I made myself impervious to the rain and blind to the discomforts of the cold and the slush of the roadway. Drunkenness had no more terrors for me, and as a matter of course I often got drunk when a cold night rested over the houseless road, and when my body shuddered at the thought of spending hour after hour in the open. Drink kept me company, and there was no terror that we could not face together, drink and I.

I never have seen Fergus since, but often I think of the part which he played in my life. If he had not come into the inn at the moment when I was sitting by the fire I would probably never have drunk another glass of spirits in my life. I do not see anything wrong in taking liquor as long as a man makes it his slave. Drink was a slave to me. I used it for the betterment of my soul, and for the comfort of the body. In conformity with the laws of society an individual like me must sleep under a wet hedgerow now and again. There is nothing in the world more dismal. The water drops off the tree like water from the walls of a dungeon, splashes on your face, maybe dropping into the eyes when you open them. The hands are frozen, the legs are cold, heavy and dead ; you hum little songs to yourself over and over again, ever the same song, for you have not the will to start a fresh one, and the cold creeps all over the body, coming closer and closer, like a thief to your heart. Sometimes it catches men who are too cold to move even from the spectre of death. The nights spent in the cold are horrible, are soul-killing. Only drink can draw a man from his misery ; only by getting drunk may a man sleep well on the cold ground. So I have found, and so it was that I got drunk when I slept out on a winter's night. Maybe I would be dead in the morning, I sometimes thought, but no one would regret that, not even myself. Drink is a servant wonderfully efficient. Only when sober could I see myself as I really was, an outcast, a man rejected by society, and despised and forgotten. Often I would sit alone in a quiet place and think my life was hardly worth living. But somehow I kept on living a life that was to me as smoke is to the eyes, bitter and cruel. As time wore on I became primeval, animalised and brutish. Everything which I could lay hands on and which would serve my purposes was mine. The milk left by milkmen at the doors of houses in early morning was mine. How often in the grey dawn of a winter morning did I steal through a front gate silently as a cat and empty the milk-can hanging over some doorstep, then slip so silently away again that no one either heard my coming or going. It was most exciting, and excitement is one of the necessaries of life. Excitement appeals to me, I hanker after it as a hungry man hankers after food. I like to see people getting excited over something.

One evening in early spring, nearly two years after I had left Braxey Farm, I was passing a large house near G——, or was it P——? I now forget which of these towns was nearest the house. I had at that time a strange partiality for a curious form of amusement. I liked to steal up to large houses in the darkness and watch the occupants at dinner.

A large party was at dinner in the house on this spring evening, and I crept into the shrubbery and looked through the window into the lighted room. With the slushy earth under my body I lay and watched the people inside eating, drinking, and making merry. At the further end of the table a big fat woman in evening dress sat facing me, and she looked irrepressibly merry. Her low-cut frock exposed a great spread of bulging flesh stretching across from shoulder to shoulder. It was a most disgusting sight, and should have been hidden.

The damp of the earth came through my clothing and I rose to my feet, intending to go away. Before me lay the darkness, the night, and the cold. I am, as I said, very impulsive, and long for excitement. Some rash act would certainly enliven the dull dark hours. In rising, my hand encountered a large pebble, and suddenly an idea entered my mind. What would the old lady do if the pebble suddenly crashed through the window? If such a thing occurred it would be most amusing to witness her actions. I stepped out of the shrubbery in order to have a clear swing of the arm, and threw the stone through the window. There was a tinkling fall of broken glass, and everyone in the room turned to the window—everyone in the room except the old lady. She rose to her feet, and in another moment the door of the house opened and she stood in the doorway, her large form outlined against the light in the hall. So quickly had she come out that I had barely time to steal into the shrubbery. From there I crept backwards towards the road, but before I had completed half the journey I heard to my horror the fat lady calling for a dog. Then I heard a short, sharp yelp, and I turned and ran for all I was worth. Before I reached the gate a fairly-sized black animal was at my heels, squealing as I had heard dogs in Ireland squeal when pursuing a rabbit. I turned round suddenly, fearing to get bitten in the legs, and the animal, unable to restrain his mad rush, careered past. He tried to turn round, but my boot shot out and the blow took him on the head. This was an action that he did not relish, and he hurried back to the house, whimpering all the way. In a moment I was on the road, and I ran for a long distance, feeling that I had had enough excitement for one night. Needless to say I never threw a stone through a window again. I had been out of work for quite a long while and hunger was again pinching me. I remember well the day following my encounter with the fat lady and her dog, for on that day I sold my shirt in a rag-store in Glasgow and got the sum of sixpence for the same.

It was now two years and a half since I had seen Micky's Jim or any members of his squad, but often during that time I thought of Norah Ryan and the part she played in my life. Almost daily since leaving the squad I had thoughts of her in my mind. For a while I was angry with myself for allowing such thoughts to master me, but in the end I became resigned to them. Norah's fair face would persist in rising before my vision, and when other dreams, other illusions, were shattered, the memory of Norah Ryan still exercised a spell over me. In the end I resigned myself to the remembrances of her, and in the course of time remembrance gave rise to longings and I wanted to see her again. Now, instead of being almost entirely mental, the longing, different from the youthful longing, was both of the mind and body. I wanted to kiss her, take her on my knees and fondle her. But these desires were always damped by the thought of the other man, so much so that I recoiled from the very thought even of meeting Norah again.

Since meeting Gourock Ellen and hearing the loose talk of the women in Braxey Farm most women were repulsive in my sight. For all that, Norah Ryan was ever the same in my eyes. To me she was a wonder, a mystery, a dream. But when I desired to go and see her a certain pride held me back. She allowed another man to kiss her. I never kissed her, partly because kissing was practically unknown in Glenmornan, and partly because I thought Norah far above the mere caresses of my lips. To kiss her would be a violation and a wrong. Why had she allowed Morrison to kiss her? I often asked myself. She must have loved him, and, loving him, she would have no thought for me. Perhaps she would be annoyed if I went to see her, and it is wrong to annoy those whom we love. True love to a man should mean the doing of that which is most desirable in the eyes of her whom he loves. The man who disputes this has never loved; if he thinks that he has, he is mistaken. He has been merely governed by that most bestial passion, lust.

The year had already taken the best part of autumn to itself, and I was going along to Greenock by the Glasgow road when I came to a farmhouse. There I met with Micky's Jim and a squad of potato-diggers. It gave me pleasure to meet Jim again, and, the pleasure being mutual, he took me into the byre and gave me food and drink. There were many Glenmornan people in the squad, but there were none of those who were in it in my time, and of these latter people you may be certain I lost no time in asking. Gourock Ellen and Annie had not come back that season, and nobody knew where they had gone and what had become of them.

"It does not matter, anyhow," said Jim, who, curiously enough, had nothing but contempt for women of that class.

Norah Ryan, first in my thoughts, was the last for whom I made enquiries.

"She left us a week ago, and went away to Glasgow," said Jim.

"Indeed she did, poor girl," said one of the Glenmornan women.

"And her such a fine soncy lass too! Wasn't it a great pity that it happened?" said another.

"What happened?" I asked, bewildered. "Is she not well?"

"It's worse than that," said a woman.

"Much worse!" cackled another, shaking her head.

"The farmer's son kept gaddin' about with her all last year," broke in Jim, and I noticed the eyes of everybody in the byre turned on me. "But he has left her to herself now," he concluded.

"I'm glad to hear it," I said.

"I think that ye had a notion of her yerself," said Jim, "and the farmer's son was a dirty beast, anyhow."

"Why has she left the squad?" I asked again. "Has she got married?"

"When she left here she was in the family-way, ye know," answered Micky's Jim. "Such a funny thing, and no one would have thought of it, the dirty slut. Ye would think that butter would not melt in her mouth."

"That's just so," chorused the women. "Wan would think that butter would not melt in the girl's mouth."

" She was a dirty wench," said Micky's Jim, as if giving a heavy decision.

I was stunned by the news and could hardly trust my ears. Also I got mad with Micky's Jim for his last words. It comes naturally to some people to call those women betrayed by great love and innocence the most opprobrious names. The fact of a woman having loved unwisely and far too well often offers everybody excuses to throw stones at her. And there are other men who, in the company of their own sex, always talk of women in the most filthy manner, and nobody takes offence. Often have I listened to tirades of abuse levelled against all women, and I have taken no hand in suppressing it, not being worthy enough to correct the faults of others. But when Micky's Jim said those words against Norah Ryan I reached out, for-getting the bread eaten with him and the hand raised on the 'Derry boat on my behalf years before, and gripping him under the armpits I lifted him up into the air and threw him head foremost on the floor. He got to his feet and rushed at me, while the other occupants of the byre watched us but never interfered.

" I didn't think it was in ye, Dermod, to strike a friend," he said, and drove his fist for my face. But I had learned a little of the art of self-defence here and there ; so it was that at the end of five minutes Jim, still willing in spirit but weak in flesh, was unable to rise to his feet, and I went out to the road again, having fought one fight in which victory gave me no pleasure.

I walked along heedlessly, but in some inexplicable manner my feet turned towards Glasgow. My brain was afire, my life was broken, and I almost wished that I had not asked about Norah when I met Jim. My last dream, my greatest illusion, was shattered now, and only at that moment did I realise the pleasure which the remembrances of early days in Norah's company had given me. I believed so much in my ideal love for Norah that I thought the one whom I idealised was proof against temptation and sin. My mind went back to the night when I saw her give the two-shilling piece, nearly all her fortune, to the man with the pain in his back—the same night when she and I both blushed at the frowardness of Gourock Ellen. Such goodness and such innocence! Instinctively I knew that her sin—not sin, but mistake—was due to her innocence. And some day Norah might become like Gourock Ellen. The thought terrified me, and almost drove me frantic. Only now did I know what Norah Ryan really meant to me. For her I lived, and for her alone. I loved her, then it was my duty to help her. Love is unworthy of the name unless it proves its worth when put to the test. I went to Glasgow and made enquiries for my sweetheart. For three whole weeks I searched, but my search was unsuccessful, and at last hunger drove me from the city.

Perhaps Jim knew of her abode? After our last encounter it was hard to go back and ask a favour of him. In the end I humbled myself and went and spoke to one of the women in the squad. She did not know where Norah was ; and sour against Heaven and Destiny I went out on the long road again.

CHAPTER XVIII

THE DRAINER

" Voiceless slave of the solitude, rude as the draining shovel is rude :
   Man by the ages of wrong subdued, marred, misshapen, mis-
     understood,
   Such is the Drainer."

—From *Songs of a Navvy*.

LATE in the September of the same year I got a job at digging sheep drains on a moor in Argyll-shire. I worked with a man named Sandy, and I never knew his second name. I believe he had almost forgotten it himself. He had a little hut in the centre of the moor, and I lived with him there. The hut was built of piles shoved into the ground, and the cracks between were filled with moss to keep out the cold. In the wet weather the water came through the floor and put out the fire, what time we required it most.

One night when taking supper a beetle dropped from the roof into my tea-can.

" The first leevin' thing I've seen here for mony a day, barrin' oursel's," Sandy remarked. " The verra worms keep awa' frae the place."

We started work at seven o'clock in the morning. Each of us dug a sod six inches deep and nine inches wide, and threw it as far as we could from the place where it was lifted. All day long we kept doing the same thing, just as Sandy had been doing it for thirty years. We hardly ever spoke to one another, there was nothing to speak about. The moor spread out on all sides, and little could be seen save the brown rank grass, the crawling bogbine, and the dirty sluggish water. We had to drink this water. The nearest tree was two miles distant, and the nearest public-house a good two hours' walk away. Sandy got drunk twice a week.

" Just tae put the taste o' the feelthy water oot o' my mooth," he explained in apologetic tones when he got sober. I do not know why he troubled to make excuses for his drunkenness. It mattered very little to me, although I was now teetotal myself. I was even glad when the man got drunk, for intoxicated he gave a touch of the ridiculous to the scene that was so killingly sombre when he was sober. In the end I became almost as soulless and stupid as the sods I turned up, and in the long run I debated whether I should take to drink or the road in order to enliven my life. I had some money in my pocket, and my thoughts turned to Norah Ryan. Perhaps if I went to Glasgow I would find her. I took it in my head to leave ; I told Sandy and asked him to come.

" There's nae use in me leavin' here noo," he said. " I've stopped too lang for that."

The farmer for whom we wrought got very angry when I asked him for my wages.

" There's nae pleasin' o' some folk," he grumbled. " They'll nae keep a guid job when they get one."

The last thing I saw as I turned out on the high-road was Sandy leaning over his draining spade like some God-forsaken spirit of the moorland. Poor man I he had not a friend in all the world, and he was very old.

I stopped in Glasgow for four weeks, but my search for Norah was fruitless. She seemed to have gone out of the world and no trace of her was to be found.

CHAPTER XIX

A DEAD MAN'S SHOES

" In the grim dead-end he lies,
  With passionless filmy eyes,
English Ned, with a hole in his head,
  Staring up at the skies.

" The engine driver swore, as often he swore before :
  ' I whistled him back from the flamin' track,
And I couldn't do no more ! '

" The ganger spoke through the 'phone : ' Platelayer seventy-one
  Got killed to-day on the six-foot way
By a goods on the city run.

" ' English Ned is his name, no one knows whence he came ;
  He didn't take mind of the road behind,
And none of us is to blame.' "

                              —From *Songs of the Dead End.*

THE law has it that no man must work as a plate-layer on the running lines until he is over twenty-one years of age. If my readers look up the books of the —— Railway Company, they'll find that I started work in the service of the company at the age of twenty-two. My readers must not believe this. I was only eighteen years of age when I started work on the railway, but I told a lie in order to obtain the post.

One day, five weeks following my return from the Argyllshire moors, and long after all my money had been expended on the fruitless search for Norah Ryan, I clambered up a railway embankment near Glasgow with the intention of seeking a job, and found that a man had just

K

been killed by a ballast engine. He had been cut in two ; the fingers of his left hand severed clean away were lying on the slag. The engine wheels were dripping with blood. The sight made me sick with a dull heavy nausea, and numberless little blue and black specks floated before my eyes. An almost unbearable dryness came into my throat ; my legs became heavy and leaden, and it seemed as if thousands of pins were pricking them. All the men were terror-stricken, and a look of fear was in every eye. They did not know whose turn would come next.

A few of them stepped reluctantly forward and carried the .thing which had been a fellow-man a few minutes before and placed it on the green slope. Others pulled the stray pieces of flesh from amidst the rods, bars, and wheels of the engine and washed the splotches of blood from the sleepers and rails. One old fellow lifted the severed fingers from the slag, counting each one loudly and carefully as if some weighty decision hung on the correct tally of the dead man's fingers. They were placed beside the rest of the body, and prompted by a morbid curiosity I approached it where it lay in all its ghastliness on the green slope with a dozen men or more circled around it. The face was unrecognisable as a human face. A thin red sliver of flesh lying on the ground looked like a tongue. Probably the man's teeth in contracting had cut the tongue in two. I had looked upon two dead people, Dan and Mary Sorley, but they might have been asleep, so quiet did they lie in their eternal repose. This was also death, but death combined with horror. Here and there scraps of clothing and buttons were scrambled up with the flesh, but all traces of clothing were almost entirely hidden from sight. The old man who had gathered up the fingers brought a bag forward and covered up the dead thing on the slope. The rest of the men drew back,

quietly and soberly, glad that the thing was hidden from
their eyes.

"A bad sight for the fellow's wife," said the old man
to me. "I've seen fifteen men die like him, you know."

"How did it happen?" I asked.

"We was liftin' them rails into the ballast train, and
every rail is over half a ton in weight," said the man, who,
realising that I was not a railway man, gave full details.
"One of the rails came back. The men were in too big
a hurry, that's what I say, and I've always said it, but
it's not their fault. It's the company as wants men to
work as if every man was a horse, and the men daren't
take their time. It's the sack if they do that. Well,
as I was a-sayin', the rail caught on the lip of the waggon,
and came back atop of Mick—Mick Deehan is his name—
as the train began just to move. The rail broke his back,
snapped it in two like a dry stick. We heard the spine
crack, and he just gave one squeal and fell right under
the engine. Ugh! it was ill to look at it, and, mind you,
I've seen fifteen deaths like it. Fifteen, just think of
that!"

Then I realised that I had been saved part of the worst
terror of the tragedy. It must have been awful to see a
man suddenly transformed into that which lay under the
bag beside me. A vision came to me of the poor fellow
getting suddenly caught in the terrible embrace of the
engine, watching the large wheel slowly revolving downwards towards his face, while his ears would hear, the last
sound ever to be heard by them, the soft, slippery movement of that monstrous wheel skidding in flesh and blood.
For a moment I was in the dead man's place, I could feel
the flange of the wheel cutting and sliding through me
as a plough slides through the furrow of a field. Again
my feelings almost overcame me, my brain was giddy
and my feet seemed insecurely planted on the ground.

By an effort I diverted my thoughts from the tragedy, and my eyes fell on a spider's web hung between two bare twigs just behind the dead man. It glistened in the sunshine, and a large spider, a little distance out from the rim, had its gaze fixed on some winged insect which had got entangled in the meshes of the web. When the old man who had seen fifteen deaths passed behind the corpse, the spider darted back to the shelter of the twig, and the winged insect struggled fiercely, trying to free itself from the meshes of death.

On a near bough a bird was singing, and its song was probably the first love-song of the spring. In the field on the other side of the line, and some distance away, a group of children were playing, children bare-legged, and dressed in garments of many colours. Behind them a row of lime-washed cottages stood, looking cheerful in the sunshine of the early spring. Two women stood at one door, gossiping, no doubt. A young man in passing raised his hat to the women, then stopped and talked with them for a while. From far down the line, which ran straight for miles, an extra gang of workers was approaching, their legs moving under their apparently motionless bodies, and breaking the lines of light which ran along the polished upper bedes of the rails. The men near me were talking, but in my ears their voices sounded like the droning of bees that flit amid the high branches of leafy trees. The coming gang drew nearer, stepping slowly from sleeper to sleeper, thus saving the soles of their boots from the contact of the wearing slag. The man in front, a strong, lusty fellow, was bellowing out in a very unmusical voice an Irish love song. Suddenly I noticed that all the men near me were gazing tensely at the approaching squad, the members of which were yet unaware of the tragedy, for the rake of ballast waggons hid the bloodstained slag and scene of the accident from their eyes. The singer came round behind the rear waggon, still bellowing out his song.

> " I'll leave me home again and I'll bid good-bye to-morrow,
> I'll pass the little graveyard and the tomb anear the wall,
> I have lived so long for love that I cannot live for sorrow
> By the grave that holds me cooleen in a glen of Donegal."

Every eye was turned on him, but no man spoke. Apparently taking no heed of the splotches of blood, now darkly red, and almost the colour of the slag on which they lay, he approached the bag which covered the body.

" What the devil is this ? " he cried out, and gave the bag a kick, throwing it clear of the thing which it covered. The bird on the bough atop of the slope trilled louder ; the song of the man died out, and he turned to the ganger who stood near him, with a questioning look.

" It's Mick, is it ? " he asked, removing his cap.

" It's Micky," said the ganger.

The man by the corpse bent down again and covered it up slowly and quietly, then he sank down on the green slope and burst into tears.

" Micky and him's brothers, you know," said a man who stood beside me in a whisper. The tears came into my eyes, much though I tried to restrain them. The tragedy had now revealed itself in all its horrible intensity, and I almost wished to run away from the spot.

After a while the breakdown van came along ; the corpse was lifted in, the brother tottered weakly into the carriage attached to the van, and the engine puffed back to Glasgow. A few men turned the slag in the sleeper beds and hid the dark red clotted blood for ever. The man had a wife and several children, and to these the company paid blood money, and the affair was in a little while forgotten by most men, for it was no man's business. Does it not give us an easy conscience that this wrong and that wrong is no business of ours ?

When the train rumbled around the first curve on its return journey I went towards the ganger, for the work obsession still troubled me. Once out of work I long for a job, once having a job my mind dwells on the glories of the free-footed road again. But now I had an object in view, for if I obtained employment on the railway I could stop in Glasgow and continue my search for Norah Ryan during the spare hours. The ganger looked at me dubiously, and asked my age.

" Twenty-two years," I answered, for I was well aware that a man is never taken on as a platelayer until he has attained his majority.

There and then I was taken into the employ of the —— Railway Company, as Dermod Flynn, aged twenty-two years. Afterwards the ganger read me the rules which I had to observe while in the employment of the company. I did not take very much heed to his droning voice, my mind reverting continuously to the tragedy which I had just witnessed, and I do not think that the ganger took very much pleasure in the reading. While we were going through the rules a stranger scrambled up the railway slope and came towards us.

" I heard that a man was killed," he said in an eager voice. " Any chance of gettin' a start in his place ? "

" This man's in his shoes," said the ganger, pointing at me.

" Lucky dog ! " was all that the man said, as he turned away.

The ganger's name was Roche, " Horse Roche"—for his mates nicknamed him " Horse " on account of his enormous strength. He could drive a nine-inch iron spike through a wooden sleeper with one blow of his hammer. No other man on the railway could do the same thing at that time ; but before I passed my twenty-first birthday I could perform the same feat quite easily. Roche was a hard swearer, a heavy drinker, and a fearless fighter. He will not mind my saying these things about him now. He is dead over four years.

CHAPTER XX

BOOKS

" For me has Homer sung of wars,
   Æschylus wrote and Plato thought,
   Has Dante loved and Darwin wrought,
And Galileo watched the stars."

      —From *The Navvy's Scrap Book.*

UP till this period of my life I had no taste for literature. I had seldom even glanced at the daily papers, having no interest in the world in which I played so small a part. One day when the gang was waiting for a delayed ballast train, and when my thoughts were turning to Norah Ryan, I picked up a piece of paper, a leaf from an exercise book, and written on it in a girl's or woman's handwriting were these little verses :

" No, indeed ! for God above
   Is great to grant, as mighty to make,
And creates the love to reward the love,—
   I claim you still, for my own love's sake !
Delayed it may be for more lives yet,
   Through worlds I shall traverse, not a few—
Much is to learn and much to forget
   Ere the time be come for taking you.

" I have lived (I shall say) so much since then,
   Given up myself so many times,
Gained me the gains of various men,
   Ransacked the ages, spoiled the climes ;
Yet one thing, one, in my soul's full scope,
   Either I missed or itself missed me :
And I want and find you, Evelyn Hope
   What is the issue ? let us see ! "

While hardly understanding their import, the words went to my heart. They expressed thoughts of my own, thoughts lying so deeply that I was not able to explain or express them. The writer of the verse I did not know, but I thought that he, whoever he was, had looked deep into my soul and knew my feelings better than myself. All day long I repeated the words to myself over and over again, and from them I got much comfort and strength, that stood me in good stead in the long hours of searching on the streets of Glasgow for my luckless love. Under the glaring lamps that lit the larger streets, through the dark guttery alleys and sordid slums I prowled about nightly, looking at every young maiden's face and seeing in each the hard stare of indifference and the cold look of the stranger. Round the next corner perhaps she was waiting ; a figure approaching reminded me of her, and I hurried forward eagerly only to find that I was mistaken. Oh ! how many illusions kept me company in my search ! how many disappointments ! and how many hopes. For I wanted Norah ; for her I longed with a great longing, and a dim vague hope of meeting her buoyed up my soul.

> " And I want and find you, Evelyn Hope !
> What is the issue ? let us see ! "

Such comforting words, and the world of books might be full of them ! A new and unexplored world lay open before me, and for years I had not seen it, or seeing, never heeded. I had once more the hope that winged me along the leading road to Strabane when leaving for a new country. Alas ! the country that raised such anticipations was not what my hopes fashioned, but this newer world, just as enticing, was worthy of more trust and greater confidence. I began to read eagerly, ravenously. I read Victor Hugo in G—— Tunnel. One day a falling rail broke the top joint of the middle finger of my left hand. Being unable for some time to take part in the usual work of the squad I was placed on the look-out when my gang worked on the night-shift in the tunnel at G——. When the way was not clear ahead I had to signal the trains in the darkness, but as three trains seldom passed in the hour the work was light and easy. When not engaged I sat on the rail beside the naphtha lamp and read aloud to myself. I lived with Hugo's characters, I suffered with them and wept for them in their troubles. One night when reading *Les Miserables* I cried over the story of Jean Valjean and little Cosette. Horse Roche at that moment came through the darkness (in the tunnel it is night from dawn to dawn) and paused to ask me how I was getting along.

" Your eyes are running water, Flynn," he said. " You sit too close to the lamp smoke."

I remember many funny things which happened in those days. I read the chapter on *Natural Supernaturalism*, from *Sartor Resartus*, while seated on the footboard of a flying ballast train. Once, when Roche had left his work to take a drink in a near public-house, I read several pages from *Sesame and Lilies*, under shelter of a coal waggon, which had been shunted into an adjacent siding. I read Montaigne's *Essays* during my meal hours, while my mates gambled and swore around me.

I procured a ticket for the Carnegie Library, but bought some books, when I had cash to spare, from a second-hand bookseller on the south side of Glasgow. Every pay-day I spent a few shillings there, and went home to my lodgings with a bundle of books under my arm. The bookseller would not let me handle the books until I bought them, because my hands were so greasy and oily with the muck of my day's labour. I seldom read in my lodgings. I spent most of my evenings in the streets engaged on my unsuccessful search. I read in the spare moments snatched from my daily work. Soon my books were covered with iron-rust, sleeper-tar and waggon grease, where my dirty hands had touched them, and when I had a book in my possession for a month I could hardly decipher a word on the pages. There is some difficulty in reading thus.

I started to write verses of a kind, and one poem written by me was called *The Lady of the Line*. I personified the spirit that watched over the lives of railway men from behind the network of point-rods and hooded signals. The red danger lamp was her sign of power, and I wrote of her as queen of all the running lines in the world.

I read the poem to my mates. Most of them liked it very much and a few learned it by heart. When Horse Roche heard of it he said: " You'll end your days in the madhouse, or "—with cynical repetition—" in the House of Parliament."

On Sunday afternoons, when not at work, I went to hear the socialist speakers who preached the true Christian Gospel to the people at the street corners. The workers seldom stopped to listen ; they thought that the socialists spoke a lot of nonsense. The general impression was that socialists, like clergymen, were paid speakers ; that they endeavoured to save men's bodies from disease and poverty as curates save souls from sin for a certain number of shillings a day. From the first I looked upon socialist speakers as men who had an earnest desire for justice, and men who toiled bravely in the struggle for the regeneration of humanity. I always revolted against injustice, and hated all manner of oppression. My heart went out to the men, women, and children who toil in the dungeons and ditches of labour, grinding out their souls and bodies for meagre pittances. All around me were social injustices, affecting the very old and the very young as they affected the supple and strong. Social suffering begins at any age, and death is often its only remedy. That remedy is only for the individual; the general remedy is to be found in Socialism. Industry, that new Inquisition, has thousands on the rack of profit ; Progress, to millions, means slavery and starvation ; Progress and Profit mean sweated labour to railway men, and it meant death to many of them, as to Mick Deehan, whose place I had filled. I had suffered a lot myself: a brother of mine had died when he might have been saved by the rent which was paid to the landlord, and I had seen suffering all around me wherever I went ; suffering due to injustice and tyranny of the wealthy class. When I heard the words spoken by the socialists at the street corner a fire of enthusiasm seized me, and I knew that the world was moving and that the men and women of the country were waking from the torpor of poverty, full of faith for a new cause. I joined the socialist party.

For a while I kept in the background ; the discussions which took place in their hall in G—— Street made me conscious of my own lack of knowledge on almost any subject. The members of the party discussed Spencer, Darwin, Huxley, Karl Marx, Ricardo, and Smith, men of whom I had never even heard, and inwardly I chafed at my own absolute ignorance and want of the education necessary for promoting the cause which I advocated. · Hours upon hours did I spend wading through Marx's *Capital*, and Henry George's *Progress and Poverty*. The former, the more logical, appealed to me least.

I had only been two months in the socialist party when I organised a strike among the railway men, the thirty members of the Flying Squad on which I worked.

We were loading ash waggons at C—— engine shed, and shovelling ashes is one of the worst jobs on the railway. Some men whom I have met consider work behind prison walls a pleasure when compared with it. As these men spoke from experience I did not doubt their words. The ash-pit at C—— was a miniature volcano. The red-hot cinders and burning ashes were piled together in a deep pit, the mouth of which barely reached the level of the railway track. The Flying Squad under Horse Roche cleared out the pit once every month. The ashes were shovelled into waggons placed on the rails alongside for that purpose. The men stripped to the trousers and shirt in the early morning, and braces were loosened to give the shoulders the ease in movement required for the long day's swinging of the shovel. Three men were placed at each waggon and ten waggons were filled by the squad at each spell of work. Every three wrought as hard as they were able, so that their particular waggon might be filled before the others. The men who lagged behind went down in the black book of the ganger.

On the day of the strike the pit was a boiling hell. Chunks of coal half-burned and half-ablaze, lumps of molten slag, red-hot bricks and fiery ashes were muddled together in suffocating profusion. From the bottom of the pit a fierce impetus was required to land the contents of the shovel in the waggon overhead. Sometimes a brick would strike on the rim of the waggon and rebound back on the head of the man who threw it upwards. " Cripes ! we'll have to fill it ourselves now," his two mates would say as they bundled their bleeding fellow out of the reeking heat. A shower of fine ashes were continuously falling downwards and resting upon our necks and shoulders, and the ash-particles burned the flesh like thin red-hot wires. It was even worse when they went further down our backs, for then every move of the underclothing and every swing of the shoulders caused us intense agony. Under the run of the shirt the ashes scarred the flesh like sand-paper. All around a thick smoke rested and hid us from the world without, and within we suffered in a pit of blasting fire. I've seen men dropping at the job like rats in a furnace. These were usually carried out, and a bucket of water was emptied on their face. When they recovered they entered into the pit again.

Horse Roche stood on the coupling chains of the two middle waggons, timing the work with his watch and hastening it on with his curses. He was not a bad fellow at heart, but he could do nothing without flying into a fuming passion, which often was no deeper than his lips. Below him the smoke was so thick that he could hardly see his own labourers from the stand on the coupling chain. All he could see was the shovels of red ashes and shovels of black ashes rising up and over the haze that enveloped the pit beneath. But we could hear Roche where we wrought. Louder than the grinding of the ballast engine was the voice of the Horse cursing and swearing. His swearing was a gift, remarkable and irrepressible; it was natural to the man; it was the man.

"God's curse on you, Dan Devine, I don't see your shovel at work at all!" he roared. "Where the hell are you, Muck MaCrossan? Your waggon isn't nearly water-level yet, and that young whelp, Flynn, has his nearly full! If your chest was as broad as your belly, MacQueen, you'd be a danged sight better man on the ash-pile! It's not but that you are well enough used to the ashes, for I never yet saw a Heelin man who didn't spend the best part of his life before a fire or before grub! Come now, you men on the offside; you are slacking it like hell! If you haven't your waggon up over the lip, I'll sack every God-damned man of you on the next pay day! Has a brick fallen on Feeley's head? Well, shove the idiot out of the pit and get on with your work! His head is too big, anyhow, it's always in the road!"

This was the manner in which Horse Roche carried on, and most of the men were afraid of him. I felt frightened of the man, for I anticipated the gruelling which he would give me if I fell foul of him. But if we had come to blows he would not, I am certain, have much to boast about at the conclusion of the affair. However, I never quarrelled with Roche.

On the day of the strike, about three o'clock in the afternoon, when fully forespent at our work, the ballast engine brought in a rake of sixteen-ton waggons. Usually the waggons were small, just large enough to hold eight tons of ashes. The ones brought in now were very high, and it required the utmost strength of any one of us to throw a shovelful of ashes over the rim of the waggon. Not alone were the waggons higher, but the pile in the pit had decreased, and we had to work from a lower level. And those waggons could hold so much! They were like the grave, never satisfied, but ever wanting more, more. I suggested that we should stop work. Discontent was boiling hot, and the men scrambled out of the pit, telling Roche to go to hell, and get men to fill his waggons. Outside of the pit the men's anger cooled. They looked at one another for a while, feeling that they had done something that was sinful and wrong. To talk of stopping work in such a manner was blasphemy to most of them. Ronald MacQueen had a wife and a gathering of young children, and work was slack. Dan Devine was old, and had been in the service of the company for twenty years. If he left now he might not get another job. He rubbed the fine ashes out of his eyes, and looked at MacQueen. Both men had similar thoughts, and before the sweat was dry on their faces they turned back to the pit together. One by one the men followed them, until I was left alone on the outside. Horse Roche had never shifted his position on the coupling chains. "It'll not pain my feet much, if I stand till you come back!" he cried when we went out. He watched the men return with a look of cynical amusement.

"Come back, Flynn," he cried, when he saw me standing

alone. " You're a fool, and the rest of the men are cowards ; their spines are like the spines of earth worms."

I picked up my shovel angrily, and returned to my waggon. I was disgusted and disappointed and ashamed. I had lost in the fight, and I felt the futility of rising in opposition against the powers that crushed us down. That night I sent a letter to the railway company stating our grievance. No one except myself would sign it, but all the men said that my letter was a real good one. It must have been too good. A few days later a clerk was sent from the head of the house to inform me that I would get sacked if I wrote another letter of the same kind.

Then I realised that in the grip of the great industrial machine I was powerless ; I was a mere spoke in the wheel of the car of progress, and would be taken out if I did not perform my functions there. The human spoke is useful as long as it behaves like a wooden one in the socket into which it is wedged. So long will the Industrial Carriage keep moving forward under the guidance of heavy-stomached Indolence and inflated Pride. There is no scarcity of spokes, human and wooden. What does it matter if Devine and MacQueen were thrown away ? A million seeds are dropping in the forest, and all women are not divinely chaste. The young children are growing. Blessings be upon you, workmen, you have made spokes that will shove you from the sockets into which your feet are wedged, but God grant that the next spokes are not as wooden as yourselves !

Again the road was calling to me. My search in Glasgow had been quite unsuccessful, and the dull slavery of the six-foot way began to pall on me. The clerk who was sent by the company to teach me manners was a most annoying little fellow, and full of the importance of his mission. I told him quietly to go to the devil, an advice which he did not relish, but which he forbore to censure. That evening I left the employ of the —— Railway Company.

Just two hours before I lifted my lying time, the Horse was testing packed sleepers with his pick some distance away from the gang, when a rabbit ran across the railway. Horse dropped his pick, aimed a lump of slag at the animal and broke its leg. It limped off; we saw the Horse follow, and about a hundred paces from the point where he had first observed it Roche caught the rabbit, and proceeded to kill it outright by battering its head against the flange of the rail. At that moment a train passed us, travelling on the down line. Roche was on the up line, but as the train passed him we saw a glint of something bright flashing between the engine and the man, and at the same moment Roche fell to his face on the four-foot way. We hurried towards him, and found our ganger vainly striving to rise with both arms caught in his entrails. The pick which he had left lying on the line got caught in the engine wheels and was carried forward, and violently hurled out when the engine came level with the ganger. It ripped his belly open, and he died about three minutes after we came to his assistance. The rabbit, although badly wounded, escaped to its hole. That night I was on the road again.

CHAPTER XXI

A FISTIC ARGUMENT

" You're hungry and want me to give you food ? I'll see you in hell first !"—From *Words to the Hungry.*

I LEFT my job on Tuesday, and tramped about for the rest of the week foot-free and reckless. The nights were fine, and sleeping out of doors was a pleasure. On Saturday night I found myself in Burn's model lodging-house, Greenock. I paid for the night's bedding, and got the use of a frying-pan to cook a chop which I had bought earlier in the day. Although it was now midsummer a large number of men were seated around the hot-plate on the ground floor, where some weighty matter was under discussion. A man with two black eyes was carrying on a whole-hearted argument with a ragged tramp in one corner of the room. I proceeded to fry my trifle of meat, and was busily engaged on my job when I became aware of a disturbance near the door. A drunken man had come in, and his oaths were many, but it was impossible to tell what he was swearing at. All at once I turned round, for I heard a phrase that I knew full well.

" There's a good time comin', though we may never live to see it," said the drunken man. The speaker was Moleskin Joe, and face to face he recognised me immediately.

" Dermod Flynn, by God !" he cried. " Dermod—Flynn—by—God ! How did you get on with your milkin,' sonny ? You're the only man I ever cheated out of five bob, and there's another man cheatin' you out of your bit of steak this very minute."

I turned round rapidly to my frying-pan, and saw a man bending over it. This fellow, who was of middle age, and unkempt appearance, had broken an egg over my chop, and was busily engaged in cooking both. I had never seen the man before.

" You're at the wrong frying-pan," I roared, knowing his trick.

" You're a damned liar," he answered.

" No, but you are the damned liar," I shouted in reply.

" Good ! " laughed Moleskin, sitting down on a bench, and biting a plug of tobacco. " Good, Flynn ! Put them up to Carroty Dan ; he's worth keepin' your eye on."

" If he keeps his eye on me, he'll soon get it blackened," replied the man who was nick-named Carroty, on account of his red hair. " This is my frying-pan."

" It is not," I replied.

" Had you an egg on this chop when you turned round ? " asked Carroty.

" I had not."

" Well, there's an egg on this pan, cully, so it can't be yours."

I knew that it would be useless to argue with the man. I drew out with all my strength, and landed one on the jowl of Carroty Dan, and he went to the ground like a stuck pig.

" Good, Flynn ! " shouted Moleskin, spitting on the planking beneath his feet. " You'll be a fighter some day."

I turned to the chop and took no notice of my fallen enemy until I was also lying stretched amidst the sawdust on the floor, with a sound like the falling of many waters ringing in my head. Carroty had hit me under my ear while my attention was devoted to the chop. I scrambled to my feet but went to the ground again, having received a well-directed blow on my jaw. My mouth was bleeding now, but my mind was clear. My man stood waiting until I rose, but I lay prone upon the ground considering how I might get at him easily. A dozen men had gathered round and were waiting the result of the quarrel, but Moleskin had dropped asleep on the bench. I rose to my knees and reaching forward I caught Carroty by the legs. With a strength of which, until then, I never thought myself capable, I lifted my man clean off his feet, and threw him head foremost over my shoulders to the ground behind. Knowing how to fall, he dropped limply to the ground, receiving little hurt, and almost as soon as I regained my balance, he was in front of me squaring out with fists in approved fashion. I took up a posture of instinctive defence and waited. My enemy struck out; I stooped to avoid the blow. He hit me, but not before I landed a welt on the soft of his belly. My punch was good, and he went down, making strange noises in his throat, and rubbing his guts with both hands. His last hit had closed my left eye, but all fight was out of Carroty; he would not face up again. The men returned to their discussion, Moleskin slid from his bench and lay on the floor, and I went on with my cooking. When Carroty recovered I gave him back his egg, and he ate it as if nothing had happened to disturb him. He asked for a bit of the chop, and I was so pleased with the thrashing I had given him that I divided half the meat with the man.

Later in the evening somebody tramped on Moleskin Joe and awoke him.

" Who the hell thinks I'm a doormat ? " he growled on getting to his feet, and glowered round the room. No one answered. He went out with Carroty, and the two of them got as drunk as they could hold. I was in bed when they returned, and Carroty, full of a drunken man's courage, challenged me again to "put them up to him." I pretended that I was asleep, and took no notice of his antics, until he dragged me out of the bed. Stark naked and mad with rage, I thrashed him until he shrieked for mercy. I pressed him under me, and when he could neither move hand nor foot, I told him where I was going to hit him, and kept him sometimes over two minutes waiting for the blow. He was more than pleased when I gave him his freedom, and he never evinced any further desire to fight me.

"It's easy for anyone to thrash poor Carroty," said Joe, when I had finished the battle.

On Sunday we got drunk together in a speak-easy * near the model, and it was with difficulty that we restrained Carroty from challenging everybody whom he met to fistic encounter. By nightfall Moleskin counted his money, and found that he had fourpence remaining.

"I'm off to Kinlochleven in the morning," he said. "There's good graft and good pay for a man in Kinlochleven now. I'm sick of prokin' in the gutters here. Damn it all! who's goin' with me?"

"I'm with you," gibbered Carroty, running his fingers through the "blazing torch"—the term used by Joe when speaking of the red hair of his mate.

"I'll go too," I said impulsively. "I've only twopence left for the journey, though."

"Never mind that," said Moleskin absently. "There's a good time comin'."

Kinlochleven is situated in the wilderness of the Scottish Highlands, and I had often heard of the great job going on

* A shebeen. "You must speak easy in a shebeen when the police are around."

there, and in which thousands of navvies were employed. It was said that the pay was good and the work easy. That night I slept little, and when I slept my dreams were of the journey before me at dawn, and the new adventures which might be met with on the way.

CHAPTER XXII

THE OPEN ROAD

"The road runs north, the road runs south, and there foot-easy,
    slow,
The tramp, God speed him ! wanders forth, and nature's gentry
    go.
Gentlemen knights of the gravelled way, who neither toil nor
    spin,
Men who reck not whether or nay the landlord's rents come in,
Men who are close to the natal sod, who know not sin nor shame,
And Way of the World or Way of the Road, the end is much the
    same."

                    —From *A Song of the Road.*

IN the morning I was afoot before any of my mates,
full of impatience, and looking forward eagerly to
the start.

" Wake up, Moleskin ! " I cried, as I bent over my mate,
where he lay snoring loudly in the bed ; " it is time to be
away."

" It's not time yet, for I'm still sleepy," said Moleskin
drowsily. " Slow and easy goes far in a day," he added,
and fell asleep again. I turned my attention to Carroty.

" Get up, Carroty ! " I shouted. " It's time that we were
out on our journey."

" What journey ? " grumbled Carroty, propping himself
up on his elbow in the bed.

" To Kinlochleven," I reminded him.

" I never heard of it."

" You said that you would go this morning," I informed
him. " You said so last night when you were drunk."

" Well, if I said so, it must be so," said the red-haired

one, and slipped out of the blankets. Moleskin rose also, and as a proof of the bond between us, we cooked our food in common on the hot-plate, and at ten minutes to ten by the town clock we set out on the long road leading to Kinlochleven. Our worldly wealth amounted to elevenpence, and the distance to which we had set our faces was every inch, as the road turned, of one hundred miles, or a six days' tramp according to the computation of my two mates. The pace of the road is not a sharp one. " Slow and easy goes far in a day," is a saying amongst us, and it sums up the whole philosophy of the long journey. Besides our few pence, each man possessed a pipe, a knife, and a box for holding matches. The latter, being made of tin, was very useful for keeping the matches dry when the rain soaked the clothing. In addition, each man carried, tied to his belt, a tin can which would always come in handy for making tea, cooking eggs, or drinking water from a wayside well.

When we got clear of the town Moleskin opened his shirt front and allowed the wind to play coolly against his hairy chest.

" Man alive ! " he exclaimed, " this wind runs over a fellow's chest like the hands of a soncy wench ! " Then he spoke of our journey. Carroty was silent ; he was a morbid fellow who had little to say, except when drunk, and as for myself I was busy with my thoughts, and eager to tramp on at a quicker pace.

" We'll separate here, and each must go alone and pick up what he can lay his hands on," said Moleskin. " As I'm an old dog on the road, far more knowing than a torch-headed boozer or young mongrel, I'll go ahead and lead the way. Whenever I manage to bum a bit of tucker from a house, I'll put a white cross on the gatepost ; and both of you can try your luck after me at the same place. If you hear a hen making a noise in a bunch of brambles, just look about there and see if you can pick up an egg or

two   It would be sort of natural for you, Carroty, to talk
about your wife and young brats, when speaking to the
woman of a house.   You look miserable enough to have been
married more than once.   You're good lookin', Flynn ; just
put on your blarney to the young wenches and maybe they'll
be good for the price of a drink for three.   We'll sit for a
bite at the Ferry Inn, and that is a good six miles of country
from our feet.''

Without another word Joe slouched off, and Carroty
and I sat down and waited until he turned the corner of the
road, a mile further along.   The moment he was out of
sight, Carroty rose and trudged after him, his head bent
well over his breast and his hands deep in the pockets of
his coat.   This slowness of movement disgusted me.   I was
afire to reach Kinlochleven, but my mates were in no great
hurry.   They placed their faith in getting there to-morrow,
if to-morrow came.   Each man was calmly content, when
working out the problem of the day's existence, to allow
the next day to do for itself.

Carroty had barely turned the corner when I got up and
followed.   Over my head the sun burned and scalded with
its scorching blaze.   The grey road and its fine gravel,
crunching under the heels of my boots, affected the ears,
and put the teeth on edge.   Far in front, whenever I raised
my head, I could see the road winding in and out, now
losing itself from my view, and again, further on, reappear-
ing, desolate, grey, and lonely as ever.   Although memories
of the road are in a sense always pleasing to me, the road
itself invariably depressed me ; the monotony of the same
everlasting stretch of dull gravelled earth gnawed at my
soul.   Most of us, men of the road, long for comfort, for
love, for the smile of a woman, and the kiss of a child, but
these things are denied to us.   The women shun us as
lepers are shunned, the brainless girl who works with a
hoe in a turnip field will have nothing to do with a tramp

navvy. The children hide behind their mothers' petticoats when they see us coming, frightened to death of the awful navvy man who carries away naughty children, and never lets them back to their mothers again.

He is a lonely man who wanders on the roads of a strange land, shunned and despised by all men, and foul in the eyes of all women. Rising cold in the morning from the shadow of the hedge where the bed of a night was found, he turns out on his journey and begs for a crumb. High noon sees nor wife nor mother prepare his mid-day meal, and there is no welcome for him at an open door when the evening comes. Christ had a mother who followed him all along the road to Calvary, but the poor tramp is seldom followed even by a mother's prayers along the road where he carries the cross of brotherly hate to the Valley of the Shadow of Death.

Suddenly I saw a white cross on a gate in front of a little cottage. A girl stood by the door, and I asked for a slice of bread. From the inside of the house a woman cried out : " Don't give that fellow anything to eat. We're sick of the likes of him."

The maiden remonstrated. " Poor thing ! he must eat just like ourselves," she said.

Once I heard one of the servant girls on Braxey Farm use the same words when feeding a pig. I did not wait for my slice of bread. I walked on ; the girl called after me, but I never turned round to answer. And the little dignity that yet remained made me feel very miserable, for I felt that I was a man classed among swine, and that is a very bitter truth to learn at eighteen.

Houses were rare in the country, but alas ! rarer were the crosses of white. I had just been about two hours upon the journey, when as I was rounding a bend of the road I came upon Carroty sitting on a bank with his arms around a woman who sat beside him. I had been walking on the grass to ease my feet, and he failed to hear my approach. When he saw me, he looked half ashamed, and his companion gazed at me with a look half cringing and half defiant. She put me in mind of Gourock Ellen. Her face might have been handsome at one time, but it was blotched and repugnant now. Vice had forestalled old age and left its traces on the woman's features. Her eyes were hard as steel and looked as if they had never been dimmed by tears. I wondered what Carroty could see in such a person, and it was poor enough comfort to know that there was at least one woman who looked with favour upon a tramp navvy.

"Tell Moleskin that I'm not comin' any further," Carroty shouted after me as I passed him by.

"All right," I answered over my shoulder. Afterwards I passed two white crosses, and at each I was refused even a crust of bread. "Moleskin has got some, anyhow, and that is a comfort," I said to myself. Now I began to feel hungry, and kept an eye in advance for the Ferry Inn. Passing by a field which I could not see on account of the intervening hedgerow, I heard a voice crying "Flynn! Flynn!" in a deep whisper. I stopped and could hear some cows crop-cropping the grass in the field beyond. "Flynn!" cried the voice again. I looked through the hedgerow and there I saw Moleskin, the rascal, sitting on his hunkers under a cow and milking the animal into his little tin can. When he had his own can full I put mine through the branches and got it filled to the brim. Then my mate dragged himself through the branches and asked me where I had left Carroty. I told him about the woman.

"The damned whelp! I might have known," said Joe, but I did not know whether he referred to the woman or the man. We carried our milk cans for a little distance, then turning off the road we sat down in the corner of a field under a rugged tree and began our meagre meal. Joe had only one slice of bread. This he divided into equal shares, and when engaged in that work I asked him the meaning of the two white crosses by the roadside, the two crosses, which as far as I could see, had no beneficial results.

"They were all right," said Joe. "I got food at the three places."

"What happened to the other two slices?" I asked.

"I gave it to a woman who was hungrier than myself," said Joe simply.

We sat in a nice cosy place. Beside us rumbled a little stream; it glanced like anything as it ran over the stones and fine sands in its bed. From where we sat we could see it break in small ripples against the wild iris and green rushes on the bank. From above, the gold of the sunlight filtered through the waving leaves and played at hide and seek all over our muck-red moleskin trousers. Far down an osier bed covered the stream and hid it from our sight. From there a few birds flew swiftly and perched on the tree above our heads and began to examine us closely. Finding that we meant to do them no harm, and observing that Moleskin threw away little scraps which might be eatable, one bold little beggar came down, and with legs wide apart stood a short distance away and surveyed us narrowly. Soon it began to pick up the crumbs, and by-and-bye we had a score of strangers at our meal.

Later we lay on our backs and smoked. 'Twas good to watch the blue of the sky outside the line of leaves that shaded us from the sun. The feeling of rest and ease was sublime. The birds consumed every crumb which had been thrown to them; then they flew away and left us. When our pipes were finished we washed our feet in the passing stream, and this gave us great relief. Moleskin pared a corn; I turned my socks inside out and hit down a nail which had come through the sole of my bluchers, using a stone for a hammer.

" Now we'll get along, Moleskin," I said, for I was in a hurry.

" Along be damned ! " cried my mate. " I'm goin' to have my dog-sleep." *

" You have eaten," I said, " and you do not need your dog-sleep to-day."

Joe refused to answer, and turning over on his side he closed his eyes. At the end of ten minutes (his dog-sleep usually lasted for that length of time), he rose to his feet, and walked towards the Clyde, the foreshore of which spread out from the lower corner of the field. A little distance out a yacht heaved on the waves, and a small boat lay on the shingle, within six feet of the water. The tide was full. Joe caught hold of the boat and proceeded to pull it towards the water, meanwhile roaring at me to give him a hand. This was a new adventure. I pulled with all my might, and in barely a minute's space of time the boat was afloat and we were inside of it. Joe rowed for all he was worth, and soon we were past the yacht and out in the deep sea. A man on the yacht called to us, but Joe put down one oar and made a gesture with his hand. The man became irate and vowed that he would send the police after us. My mate took no further heed of the man.

" Can you row ? " he asked me.

" I've never had an oar in my hand in my life," I said.

" How much money have you ? " he asked as he bent to his oars again. " I gave all mine to that woman who was hungry."

" I have only a penny left," I said.

" We have to cross the Clyde somehow," said Joe, " and a penny would not pay two men's fares on a ferry-boat. It is too far to walk to Glasgow, so this is the only thing to do. I saw the blokes leavin' this boat when we were at

* A sleep on an empty stomach in the full sun.

our grubbin'-up, so there was nothin' to be done but to take a dog-sleep until they were out of the way."

My respect for Joe's cleverness rose immediately. He was a mate of whom anyone might have been proud.

When once on the other side, we shoved the boat adrift ; and went on the road again, outside the town of Dumbarton. Joe took the lead along the Lough Lomond road, and promised to wait for me when dusk was near at hand. The afternoon was very successful ; I soon had my pockets crammed with bread, and I got three pipefuls of tobacco from three several men when I asked for a chew from their plugs. An old lady gave me twopence and later I learned that she had given Moleskin a penny.

Far outside of Dumbarton in a wild country, I overtook my mate again. It was now nearly nightfall, and the sun was hardly a hand's breadth above the horizon. Moleskin was singing to himself as I came up on him. I overheard one verse and this was the kind of it. It was a song which I had heard often before sung by navvies in the models.

> " Oh ! fare you well to the bricks and mortar !
> And fare you well to the hod and lime !
> For now I'm courtin' the ganger's daughter,
> And soon I'll lift my lyin' time."

He finished off at that, as I came near, and I noticed a heavy bulge under his left oxter between the coat and waistcoat. It was something new ; I asked him what it was, but he wouldn't tell me. The road ran through a rocky moor, but here and there clumps of hazel bounded our way. We could see at times soft-eyed curious Highland steers gazing out at us from amongst the bushes, as if they were surprised to see human beings in that deserted neighbourhood. When we stood and looked at them they snorted in contempt and crashed away from our sight through the copsewood.

" I think that we'll doss here for the night," said Mole-skin when we had walked about a mile further. He crawled over a wayside dyke and threw down the bundle which he had up to that time concealed under his coat. It was a dead hen.

" The corpse of a hen," said Joe with a laugh. " Now we've got to drum up," he went on, " and get some supper before the dew falls. It is a hard job to light a fire when the night is on."

From experience I knew this to be the case ; so together we broke rotten hazel twigs, collected some dry brambles from the undergrowth and built them in a heap. Joe placed some crisp moss under the pile ; I applied a match and in a moment we had a brightly blazing fire. I emptied my pockets, proud to display the results of the afternoon's work, which, when totalled, consisted of four slices of bread, twopence, and about one half-ounce of tobacco. Joe produced some more bread, his penny, and three little packets which contained tea, sugar, and salt. These, he told me, he had procured from a young girl in a plough-man's cottage.

" But the hen, Moleskin—where did you get that ? " I asked, when I had gathered in some extra wood for the fire.

" On the king's highway, Flynn," he added with a touch of pardonable pride. " Coaxed it near me with crumbs until I nabbed it. It made an awful fuss when I was wringing its neck, but no one turned up, more by good luck than anything else. I never caught any hen that made such a noise in all my life before."

" You are used to it then ! " I exclaimed.

" Of course I am," was the answer. " When you are on the road as long as I've been on it, you'll be as big a belly-thief * as myself."

* One who steals to satisfy his hunger.

It was fine to look around as the sun went down. Far west the sky was a dark red, the colour of old wine. A pale moon had stolen up the eastern sky, and it hung by its horn from the blue above us. Looking up at it, my thoughts turned to home, and I wondered what my own people would say if they saw me out here on the ghostly moor along with old Moleskin.

I searched around for water, and found a little well with the moon at the bottom. As I bent closer the moon disappeared, and I could see the white sand beneath. I thought that the well was very holy, it looked so peaceful and calm out there alone in the wild place. I said to myself, " Has anybody ever seen it before ? What purpose does it serve here ? " I filled the billies, and when turning away I noticed that a pair of eyes were gazing at me from the depths of the near thicket where a heavy darkness had settled. I felt a little bit frightened, and hurried towards the fire, and once there I looked back. A large roan steer came into the clearing and drank at the well. Another followed, and another. Their spreading horns glistened in the moonshine, and Joe and I watched them from where we sat.

" Will I take some more water here ? " I asked my mate, as he cleaned out the hen, using the contents of the second billy in the operation.

" Wait a minute till all the bullocks have drunk enough," he replied. " It's a pity to drive them away."

The fowl was cooked whole on the ashes, and we ate it with great relish. When the meal was finished, Moleskin flung away the bones.

" The skeleton of the feast," he remarked sadly.

Next day was dry, and we got plenty of food, food enough and to spare, and we made much progress on the journey north. Joe had an argument with a ploughman. This was the way of it.

Coming round a bend of the road we met a man with the wet clay of the newly turned earth heavy on his shoes. He was knock-kneed in the manner of ploughmen who place their feet against the slant of the furrows which they follow day by day. He was a decent man, and he told Moleskin as much when my mate asked him for a chew of tobacco.

" I dinna gang aboot lookin' for work and prayin' to God that I dinna get it, like you men," said the plougher. " I'm a decent man, and I work hard and hae no reason to gang about beggin'."

I was turning my wits upside down for a sarcastic answer, when Joe broke in.

" You're too damned decent ! " he answered. " If you weren't, you'd give a man a plug of tobacco when he asks for it in a friendly way, you God-forsaken, thran-faced bell-wether, you ! "

" If you did your work well and take a job when you get one, you'd have tobacco of your own," said the ploughman. " Forbye you would have a hoose and a wife and a dinner ready for you when you went hame in the evenin'. As it is, you're daunderin' aboot like a lost flea, too lazy to leeve and too afeard to dee."

" By Christ ! I wouldn't be in your shoes, anyway," Joe broke in quietly and soberly, a sign that he was aware of having encountered an enemy worthy of his steel. " A man might as well expect an old sow to go up a tree backwards and whistle like a thrush, as expect decency from a nipple-noddled ninny-hammer like you. If you were a man like me, you would not be tied to a woman's apron strings all your life ; you would be fit to take your turn and pay for it. Look at me ! I'm not at the beck and call of any woman that takes a calf fancy for me."

" Who would take a fancy to you ? "

" You marry a wench and set up a beggarly house," said

M

Joe, without taking any heed of the interruption. "You work fourteen or fifteen hours a day for every day of the year. If you find the company of another woman pleasant you have your old crow to jaw at you from the chimney corner. You'll bring up a breed of children that will leave you when you need them most. Your wife will get old, her teeth will fall out, and her hair will get thin, until she becomes as bald as the sole of your foot. She'll get uglier until you loathe the sight of her, and find one day that you cannot kiss her for the love of God. But all the time you'll have to stay with her, growl at her, and nothin' before both of you but the grave or the workhouse. If you are as clever a cadger as me why do you suffer all this?"

"Because I'm a decent man," said the plougher.

Joe straightened up as if seriously insulted. "Well, I'm damned!" he muttered and continued on his journey. "It's the first time ever I got the worst of an argument, Flynn," he said after we had gone out of the sight of the ploughman, and he kept repeating this phrase for the rest of the day. For myself, I thought that Joe got the best of the argument, and I pointed out the merits of his sarcastic remarks and proved to him that if his opponent had not been a brainless man, he would be aware of defeat after the first exchange of sallies.

"But that about the decent man was one up for him," Joe interrupted.

"It was the only remark which the man was able to make," I said. "The pig has its grunt, the bull its bellow, the cock its crow, and the plougher his boasted decency. To each his crow, grunt, boast, or bellow, and to all their ignorance. It is impossible to argue against ignorance, Moleskin. It is proof against sarcasm and satire and is blind to its own failings and the merits of clever men like you."

Joe brightened perceptibly, and he walked along with elated stride.

" You're very clever, Flynn," he said. " And you think
I won ? "

" You certainly did. The last shot thrown at you
struck the man who threw it full in the face. He admitted
that he suffered because of his decency."

Joe was now quite pleased with himself, and the rest of
the day passed without any further adventure.

On the day following it rained and rained. We tasted
the dye of our caps as the water washed it down our faces
into our mouths. By noon we came to the crest of a hill
and looked into a wild sweep of valley below. The valley
—it was Glencoe—from its centre had a reach of miles
on either side, and standing on its rim we were mere midges
perched on the copestones of an amphitheatre set apart
for the play of giants. Far away, amongst grey boulders
that burrowed into steep inclines, we could see a pigmy
cottage sending a wreath of blue spectral smoke into the
air. No other sign of human life could be seen. The
cottage was subdued by its surroundings, the movement of
the ascending smoke was a sacrilege against the spell of
the desolate places.

" It looks lonely," I said to my mate.

" As hell ! " he added, taking up the words as they fell
from my tongue.

We took our meal of bread and water on the ledge and
saved up the crumbs for our supper. When night came
we turned into a field that lay near the cottage, which we
had seen from a distance earlier in the day.

" It's a god's charity to have a shut gate between us and
the world," said Moleskin, as he fastened the bars of the
fence. Some bullocks were resting under a hazel clump.
These we chased away, and sat down on the spot which
their bellies had warmed, and endeavoured to light our
fire. From under grey rocks, and from the crevices in the
stone dyke, we picked out light, dry twigs, and in the

course of an hour we had a blazing flame, around which we dried our wet clothes. The clouds had cleared away and the moon came out silently from behind the shadow of the hills. The night was calm as the face of a sleeping girl.

We lay down together when we had eaten our crumbs, but for a long while I kept awake. A wind, soft as the breath of a child, ruffled the bushes beside us and died away in a long-drawn swoon. Far in the distance I could hear another, for it was the night of many winds, beating against the bald peaks that thrust their pointed spires into the mystery of the heavens. From time to time I could hear the falling earth as it was loosened from its century-long resting place and flung heavily into the womb of some fathomless abyss. God was still busy with the work of creation !

I was close to the earth, almost part of it, and the smell of the wet sod was heavy in my nostrils. It was the breath of the world, the world that was in the eternal throes of change all around me. Nature was restless and throbbing with movement ; streams were gliding forward filled with a longing for unknown waters ; winds were moving to and fro with the indecision of homeless way-farers ; leaves were dropping from the brown branches, falling down the curves of the wind silently and slowly to the great earth that whispered out the secret of ever-lasting change. The hazel clump twined its trellises of branches overhead, leaving spaces at random for the eternal glory of the stars to filter through and rest on our faces. Joe, bearded and wrinkled, slept and dreamt perhaps of some night's heavy drinking and desperate fighting, or maybe his dreams were of some weary shift which had been laboured out in the lonely places of the world.

Coming across the line of hills could be heard the gather-ing of the sea, and the chant of the deep waters that were for ever voicing their secrets to the throbbing shores.

The fire burned down but I could not go to sleep. I looked in the dying embers, and saw pictures in the flames and the redness ; pictures of men and women, and strange pictures of forlorn hopes and blasted expectations. I saw weary kinless outcasts wandering over deserted roads, shunned and accursed of all their kind. Also I saw women, old women, who dragged out a sordid existence, labouring like beasts of burden from the cradle to the grave. Also pictures of young women with the blood of early life in them, and the fulness of maiden promise in them, walking one by one in the streets of the midnight city—young women, fair and beautiful, who knew of an easier means of livelihood than that which is offered by learning the uses of sewing-needle or loom-spindle in fetid garret or steam-driven mill. In the flames and the redness I saw pictures of men and women who suffered ; for in that, and that only, there is very little change through all the ages. Thinking thus I fell asleep.

When I awoke, all the glory of the naked world was aflame with the early sun. The red mud of our moleskins blended in harmony with the tints of the great dawn. The bullocks were busy with their breakfasts and bore us no ill-will for the wrong which we had done them the night before. Two snails had crawled over Joe's coat, leaving a trail of slimy silver behind them, and a couple of beetles had found a resting-place in the seams of his velvet waistcoat. He rubbed his eyes when I called to him and sat up.

The snails curled up in mute protest on the ground, and the beetles hurried off and lost themselves amid the blades of grass. Joe made no effort to kill the insects. He lifted the snails off his coat and laid them down easily on the grass. " Run, you little devils ! " he said with a laugh, as he looked at the scurrying beetles. " You haven't got hold of me yet, mind."

I never saw Joe kill an insect. He did not like to do so,

he often told me. " If we think evil of insects, what will they think of us ? " he said to me once. As for myself, I have never killed an insect knowingly in all my life. My house for so long has been the wide world, that I can afford to look leniently on all other inmates, animal or human. Four walls coffin the human sympathies.

When I rose to my feet I felt stiff and sore, and there was nothing to eat for breakfast. My mate alluded to this when he said bitterly : " I wish to God that I was a bullock ! "

A crow was perched on a bush some distance away, its head a little to one side, and it kept eyeing us with a look of half quizzical contempt. When Joe saw it he jumped to his feet.

" A hooded crow ! " he exclaimed.

" I think that it is as well to start off," I said. " We must try and pick up something for breakfast."

My mate was still gazing at the tree, and he took no heed to my remark. " A hooded crow ! " he repeated, and lifting a stone flung it at the bird.

" What about it ? " I asked.

" Them birds, they eat dead men," Moleskin answered, as the crow flew away. " There was Muck Devaney— Red Muck we called him—and he worked at the Toward waterworks three winters ago. Red Muck had a temper like an Orangeman, and so had the ganger. The two of them had a row about some contract job, and Devaney lifted his lyin' time and jacked the graft altogether. There was a heavy snow on the ground when he left our shack in the evenin', and no sooner were his heels out of sight than a blizzard came on. You know Toward Mountain, Flynn ? Yes. Well, it is seven long miles from the top of the hill to the nearest town. Devaney never finished his journey. We found him when the thaw came on, and he was lyin' stiff as a bone in a heap of snow. And them hooded crows !

There was dozens of them pickin' the flesh from his naked shoulder-blades. They had eat the very guts clean out of Red Muck, so we had to bury him as naked as a new-born baby. By God! Flynn, they're one of the things that I am afraid of in this world, them same hooded crows. Just think of it! maybe that one that I just threw the stone at was one of them as gobbled up the flesh of Muck Devaney."

CHAPTER XXIII

THE COCK OF THE NORTH

Though up may be up and down be down,
   Time will make everything even,
And the man who starves at Greenock town
   Will fatten at Kinlochleven ;

So what does it matter if time be fleet,
   And life sends no one to love us ?
We've the dust of the roadway under our feet
   And a smother of stars above us.

                     —*A Wee Song.*

I THINK that the two verses given above were the best verses of a song which I wrote on a bit of tea-paper and read to Moleskin on the last day of our journey to Kinlochleven. Anyhow, they are the only two which I remember. Since I had read part of the poem " Evelyn Hope," I was possessed of a leaning towards lilting rhymes, and now and again I would sit down and scribble a few lines of a song on a piece of paper. Times were when I had a burning desire to read my effusions to Moleskin, but always I desisted, thinking that he would perhaps laugh at me, or call me fool. Perhaps I would sink in my mate's estimation. I began to like Joe more and more, and daily it became apparent that he had a genuine liking for me.

We were now six days on our journey. Charity was cold, while belly-thefts were few and far between. We were hungry, and the weather being very hot at high noon, Moleskin lay down and had his dog-sleep. I wrote a few other verses in addition to those which herald this chapter, and read them to my mate when he awoke. When I had finished I asked Joe how he liked my poem.

"It's a great song," answered Moleskin. "You're nearly as good a poet as Two-shift Mullholland."

"Two-shift Mullholland?" I repeated. "I've never heard of him. Do you know anything written by him?"

"Of course I do. Have you never heard of 'The Shootin' of the Crow'?"

"Never," I replied.

"You're more ignorant than I thought," said Joe, and without any further explanation he started and sang the following song.

"THE SHOOTIN' OF THE CROW.

"Come all you true-born navvies, attend unto my lay !
While walkin' down through Glasgow town, 'twas just the other
    day,
I met with Hell-fire Gahey, and he says to me : ' Hallo !
Maloney has got seven days for shootin' of the crow ;
    With his fol the diddle, fol the diddle daddy.

" ' It happened near beside the docks in Moran's pub, I'm told
Maloney had been on the booze, Maloney had a cold,
Maloney had no beer to drink, Maloney had no tin,
Maloney could not pay his way and so they ran him in,
    With his fol the diddle, fol the diddle daddy.'

" The judge he saw Maloney and he says, ' You're up again !
To sentence you to seven days it gives me greatest pain,
My sorrow at your woeful plight I try for to control ;
And may the Lord, Maloney, have mercy on your soul,
    And your fol the diddle, fol the diddle daddy.'

" Oh ! labour in the prison yard, 'tis very hard to bear,
And many a honest navvy man may sometimes enter there ;
So here's to brave Maloney, and may he never go
Again to work in prison for the shootin' of the crow,
    With his fol the diddle, fol the diddle daddy."

The reader of this story can well judge my utter literary simplicity at the time when I tell him that I was angry with Joe for the criticism he passed upon my poem. While blind to the defects of my own verses I was wide awake to those of Mullholland, and I waited, angrily eager, until Joe finished the song.

" It's rotten ! " I exclaimed. " You surely do not think that it is better than mine. What does 'fol the diddle' mean ? A judge would not say that to a prisoner. Neither would he say, ' May the Lord have mercy on your soul,' unless he was going to pass the sentence of death on the man."

" What you say is quite right," replied Joe. " But a song to be any good at all must have a lilt at the tail of it ; and as to the judge sayin', ' May the Lord have mercy on your soul,' maybe he didn't say it, but if you have ' control' at the end of one line, what must you have at the end of the next one, cully ? ' May the Lord have mercy on your soul' may be wrong. I'll not misdoubt that. But doesn't it fit in nicely ? "

Moleskin gave me a square look of triumph, and went on with his harangue.

" Barrin' these two things, the song is a true one. Maloney did get seven days' hard for shootin' the crow, and I mind it myself. On the night of his release I saw him in Moran's model by the wharf, and it was in that same model that Mullholland sat down and wrote the song that I have sung to you. It's a true song, so help me God! but yours ! —How do *you* know that we'll fatten at Kinlochleven ? More apt to go empty-gutted there, if you believe me ! Then you say ' up is up, and down is down.' Who says that they are not ? No one will give the lie to that, and what's the good of sayin' a thing that everyone knows about ? You've not even a lilt at the tail of your screed, so it's not a song, nor half a song ; it's not even a decent ' Come-all-you.' Honest to God, you're a fool, Flynn ! Wait till you hear Broken-Snout Clancy sing ' The Bold Navvy Man ! ' That'll be the song that will make your heart warm. But your song was no good at all,

Flynn.   If it had only a lilt to it itself, it might be middlin'."

I recited the verse about Evelyn Hope, and when I finished, Joe asked me what it was about.   I confessed that I did not exactly know, and for an hour afterwards we walked together in silence.

Late in the evening we came to the King's Arms, a lonely public-house half-way between the Bridge of Orchy and Kinlochleven.   We hung around the building until night fell, for Joe became interested in an outhouse where hens were roosting.   By an estimation of the stars it was nearly midnight when both of us took off our boots, and approached the henhouse.   The door was locked, but my mate inserted a pointed steel bar, which he always carried in his pocket, in the keyhole, and after he had worked for half a minute the door swung open and he crept in.

" Leave all to me," he said in a whisper.

The hens were restless, and made little hiccoughy noises in their throats, noises that were not nice to listen to.   I stood in the centre of the building while Joe groped cautiously around.   After a little while he passed me and I could see his big gaunt form in the doorway.

" Come away," he whispered.

About twenty yards from the inn he threw down that which he carried and we proceeded to put on our boots.

" It's a rooster," he said, pointing to the dead fowl ; " a young soft one too.   When our boots are on, we'll slide along for a mile or so and drum up.   It's not the thing to cook your fowl on the spot where you stole it.   I mind once when I lifted a young pig——"

Suddenly the young rooster fluttered to its feet and started to crow.

" Holy hell ! " cried Moleskin, and jumping to his feet he flung one of his boots at the fowl.   The aim was bad, and the bird zig-zagged off, crowing loudly. Both of us gave chase.

The bird was a very demon. Several times when we thought that we had laid hands on it, it doubled in its tracks like a cornered fox and eluded us. Once I tried to hit it with my foot, but the blow swung clear, and my hobnailed boot took Moleskin on the shin, causing him to swear deeply.

" Fall on it, Joe ; it's the only way ! " I cried softly.

" Fall be damned ! You might as well try to fall on a moonbeam."

A light appeared at the window of the public-house ; a sash was thrown open, and somebody shouted, " Who is there ? "

" Can you get hold of it ? " asked Joe, as he stood to clean the sweat from his unshaven face.

" I cannot," I answered. " It's a wonderful bird."

" Wonderful damned fraud ! " said my mate bitterly. " Why didn't it die decent ? "

" Who's there ? I say," shouted the man at the window. I made a desperate rush after the rooster, and grabbed it by the neck.

" It will not get away this time, anyhow," I said.

" Where is my other boot, Flynn ? " called out Joe.

" I do not know," I replied truthfully.

The door opened, and Moleskin's boot was not to be found. We sank into the shadow of the earth and waited, meanwhile groping around with our hands for the missing property. Across the level a man came towards us slowly and cautiously.

" We had better run for it," I said.

We rushed off like the wind, and the stranger panted in pursuit behind us. Joe with a single boot on, struck the ground heavily with one foot ; the other made no sound. He struck his toe on a rock and swore ; when he struck it a

second time he stopped like a shot and turned round.
The pursuer came to a halt also.

" If you come another step nearer, I'll batter your head
into jelly ! " roared Moleskin.   The man turned hurriedly,
and went back.   Feeling relieved we walked on for a long
distance, until we came to a stream.   Here I lit a fire,
plucked the rooster and cooked it, while Joe dressed his
toe, and cursed the fowl that caused him such a calamity.
I gave one of my boots to Joe and threw the other one away.
Joe was wounded, and being used in my early days to go
barefooted, I always hated the imprisonment of boots.
I determined to go barefooted into Kinlochleven.

" Do you hear it ? " Joe suddenly cried, jumping up and
grabbing my arm.

I listened, and the sound of exploding dynamite could be
heard in the far distance.

" The navvies on the night-shift, blastin' rocks in Kinlochleven ! " cried Joe, jumping to his feet and waving a
wing of the fowl over his head.   " Hurrah !   There's a
good time comin', though we may never live to see it.
Hurrah ! "

" Hurrah ! " I shouted, for I was glad that our travels
were near at an end.

Although it was a long cry till the dawn, we kicked our
fire in to the air and set out again on our journey, Joe
limping, and myself barefooted.   We finished our supper
as we walked, and each man was silent, busy with his own
thoughts.

For myself I wanted to make some money and send it
home to my own people in Glenmornan.   I reasoned with
myself that it was unjust for my parents to expect me to
work for their betterment.   Finding it hard enough to
earn my own livelihood, why should I irk myself about
them ?   I was, like Moleskin, an Ishmaelite, who without
raising my hand against every man, had every man's hand

against me. Men like Moleskin and myself are trodden underfoot, that others may enjoy the fruit of centuries of enlightenment. I cursed the day that first saw me, but, strangely inconsistent with this train of thought, I was eager to get on to Kinlochleven and make money to send to my own people in Glenmornan.

CHAPTER XXIV

" Oh, God ! that this was ended ; that this our toil was past !
Our cattle die untended ; our lea-lands wither fast ;
Our bread is lacking leaven ; our life is lacking friends,
And short's our prayer to Heaven for all that Heaven sends."
—From *God's Poor.*

THE cold tang of the dawn was already in the air
and the smell of the earth was keen in our
nostrils, when Moleskin and I breasted the
steep shoulder of a hill together, and saw the outer line
of derricks standing gaunt and motionless against the bald
cliffs of Kinlochleven. From the crest of the rise we could
see the lilac gray vesture of the twilight unfold itself from
off the naked peaks that stood out boldly in the ghostly air
like carved gargoyles of some mammoth sculpture. A sense
of strange remoteness troubled the mind, and in the half-
light the far distances seemed vague and unearthly, and we
felt like two atoms frozen into a sea of silence amidst the
splendour of complete isolation. A long way off a line
of hills stood up, high as the winds, and over their storm-
scarred ribs we saw or fancied we saw the milky white
torrents falling. We could not hear the sound of falling
waters ; the white frothy torrents were the ghosts of
streams.

The mood or spell was one of a moment. A derrick near
at hand clawed out with a lean arm, and lifted a bucket of
red muck into the air, then turned noisily on its pivot, and
was relieved of its burden. The sun burst out suddenly

like an opening rose, and the garments of the day were thrown across the world. One rude cabin sent up a gray spiral of smoke into the air, then another and another. We sat on a rock, lit our pipes, and gazed on the Mecca of our hopes.

A sleepy hollow lay below ; and within it a muddle of shacks, roofed with tarred canvas, and built of driven piles, were huddled together in bewildering confusion. These were surrounded by puddles, heaps of disused wood, tins, bottles, and all manner of discarded rubbish. Some of the shacks had windows, most of them had none ; some had doors facing north, some south ; everything was in a most haphazard condition, and it looked as if the buildings had dropped out of the sky by accident, and were just allowed to remain where they had fallen. The time was now five o'clock in the morning ; the night-shift men were still at work and the pounding of hammers and grating noises of drills could be heard distinctly. The day-shift men, already out of bed, were busily engaged preparing breakfast, and we could see them hopping half-naked around the cabins, carrying pans and smoking tins in their hands, and roaring at one another as if all were in a bad temper.

" I'm goin' to nose around and look for a pair of under-standin's," said Joe, as he rose to his feet and sauntered away. " You wait here until I come back."

In fifteen minutes' time he returned, carrying a pair of well-worn boots, which he gave to me. I put them on, and then together we went towards the nearest cabin.

Although it was high mid-summer the slush around the dwelling rose over our boots, and dropped between the leather and our stockings. We entered the building, which was a large roomy single compartment that served the purpose of bedroom, eating-room, dressing-room, and gambling saloon. Some of the inmates had sat up all night playing banker, and they were still squatting around a rough plank where silver and copper coins clanked noisily in the intervals between the game. The room, forty feet square, and ten foot high, contained fifty bed-places, which were ranged around the walls, and which rose one over the other in three tiers reaching from the ground to the ceiling. A spring oozed through the earthen floor, which was nothing but a puddle of sticky clay and water.

A dozen or more frying-pans, crammed with musty, sizzling slices of bacon, were jumbled together on the red hot-plate in the centre of the room, and here and there amid the pile of pans, little black sooty cans of brewing tea bubbled merrily. The odour of the rank tea was even stronger than that of the roasting meat.

The men were very ragged, and each of them was covered with a fine coating of good healthy clay. The muck was caked brown on the bare arms, and a man, by contracting his muscles firmly, could break the dirt clear off his skin in hard, dry scales. No person of all those on whom I looked had shaved for many months, and the hair stood out strongly from their cheeks and jowls. I myself was the only hairless faced individual there. I had not begun to shave then, and even now I only shave once a fortnight. A few of the men were still in bed, and many were just turning out of their bunks. On rising each man stood stark naked on the floor, prior to dressing for the day. None were ashamed of their nakedness : the false modesty of civilisation is unknown to the outside places. To most people the sight of the naked human body is repulsive, and they think that for gracefulness of form and symmetry of outline man's body is much inferior to that of the animals of the field. I suppose all people, women especially, are conscious of this, for nothing else can explain the desire to improve nature's handiwork which is inherent in all human beings.

N

Joe and I approached the gamblers and surveyed the game, looking over the shoulders of one of the players.

" Much luck ? " inquired my mate.

" Not much," answered the man beside him, looking up wearily, although in his eyes the passion of the game still burned brightly.

" At it all night ? "

" All night," replied the player, wearily picking up the cards which had been dealt out and throwing them away with an air of disgust.

" I'm broke," he cried, and rising from his seat on the ground, he began to prepare his meal. The other gamblers played on, and took no notice of their friend's withdrawal.

" It's nearly time that you gamblers stopped," someone shouted from amidst the steam of the frying meat.

" Hold your damned tongue," roared one player, who held the bank and who was overtaking the losses of the night.

" Will someone cook my grub ? " asked another.

" Play up and never mind your mealy grub, you gutsy whelp ! " snarled a third, who was losing heavily and who had forgotten everything but the outcome of the game. Thus they played until the whistle sounded, calling all out to work ; and then each man snatched up a crust of bread, or a couple of slices of cold ham, and went out to work in the barrow-squads or muck-gangs where thousands laboured day by day.

Meanwhile my mate and I had not been idle. I asked several questions about the work while Joe looked for food as if nothing else in the world mattered. Having urged a young fellow to share his breakfast with me, he then nosed about on his own behalf, and a few minutes later when I glanced around me I saw my pal sitting on the corner of a ground bunk, munching a chunk of stale bread and gulping down mighty mouthfuls of black tea from the sooty can in which it had been brewed. On seeing me watching him he lowered his left eyelid slightly, and went solemnly on with his repast.

"We'll go out and chase up a job now," said Moleskin, emptying his can of its contents with a final sough. "It will be easy to get a start. Red Billy Davis, old dog that he is, wants three hammermen, and we'll go to him and get snared while it is yet early in the day."

"But how do you know that there are three men wanted?" I asked. "I heard nothing about it, although I asked several persons if there was any chance of a job."

"You've a lot to learn, cully," answered Moleskin. "The open ear is better than the open mouth. I was listenin' while you were lookin' around, and by the talk of the men I found out a thing or two. Come along."

We went out, full of belly and full of hope, and sought for Red Billy Davis and his squad of hammermen. I had great faith in Moleskin, and now being fully conscious of his superior knowledge I was ready to follow him anywhere. After a long search, we encountered a man who sat on the idle arm of a crane, whittling shavings off a splinter of wood with his clasp-knife. The man was heavily bearded and extremely dirty. When he saw us approaching he rose and looked at my mate.

"Moleskin, by God!" he exclaimed, closing the knife and putting it in his pocket. "Are you lookin' for a job?"

"Can you snare an old hare this mornin'?" asked Joe.

"H'm!" said the man.

"Pay?" asked Joe laconically.

"A tanner an hour, overtime seven and a half," said the man with the whiskers.

"The hammer?" asked Joe.

"Hammer and jumper," answered the man. "You can take off your coat now."

" This mate of mine is lookin' for work, too," said Joe, pointing at me.

" He's light of shoulder and lean as a rake," replied the bearded man, with undisguised contempt in his voice.

My temper was up in an instant. I took a step forward with the intention of pulling the old red-haired buck off his seat, when my mate put in a word on my behalf.

" He knocked out Carroty Dan in Burn's model," said Joe, by way of recommendation, and my anger gave way to pride there and then.

" If that is so he can take off his coat too," said the old fellow, pulling out his clasp-knife and restarting on the rod. " Hammers and jumpers are down in the cuttin', the dynamite is in the cabin at the far end on the right. Slide."

" Come back, lean-shanks," he called to me as I turned to go. " What is your name ? " he asked, when I turned round.

" Dermod Flynn," I replied.

" You have to pay me four shillin's when you lift your first pay," said Davis.

" That be damned ! " interrupted Moleskin.

" Four shillin's," repeated Red Billy, laying down his clasp-knife and taking out a note-book and making an entry. " That's the price I charge for a pair of boots like them."

Moleskin looked at my boots, which it appears he had stolen from Red Billy in the morning. Then he edged nearer to the ganger.

" Put the cost against me," he said. " I'll give you two and a tanner for the understandin's."

" Two and a tanner it is," said Red Billy, and shut the book.

" You must let me pay half," I said to Joe later.

"Not at all," he replied. "I have the best of the bargain."

He put his hand in his pocket and drew out something: It was the clasp-knife that Red Billy placed on the ground when making the entry in his note-book.

CHAPTER XXV

THE MAN WHO THRASHED CARROTY DAN

" He could fight like a red, roaring bull."

—Moleskin Joe.

SIXPENCE an hour meant thirty shillings a week, and a man was allowed to work overtime until he fell at his shift. For Sunday work ninepence an hour was given, so the navvies told me, and now I looked forward to the time when I would have money enough and to spare. In anticipation I computed my weekly earnings as amounting to two pounds ten, and I dreamt of a day in the near future when I could again go south, find Norah Ryan, and take her home as my wife to Glenmornan. I never thought of making my home in a strange land. Oh! what dreams came to me that morning as I took my place among the forty ragged members of Red Billy's gang! Life opened freshly; my morbid fancies were dispelled, and I blessed the day that saw my birth. I looked forward to the future and said that it was time for me to begin saving money. When a man is in misery he recoils from the thoughts of the future, but when he is happy he looks forward in eager delight to the time to come.

The principal labour of Red Billy's gang was rock-blasting. This work is very dangerous and requires skilful handling of the hammer. In the art of the hammer I was quite an adept, for did I not work under Horse Roche on the —— Railway before setting out for

Kinlochleven? Still, for all that, I have known men who could not use a hammer rightly if they worked with one until the crack of doom.

I was new to the work of the jumper gang, but I soon learned how operations were performed. One man—the " holder "—sat on the rock which was to be bored, his legs straight out in front of him and well apart. Between his knees he held the tempered steel drill with its sharp nose thrust into the rock. The drill or ": jumper " is about five feet long, and the blunt upper end is rounded to receive the full force of the descending hammer. Five men worked each drill, one holding it to the rock while the other four struck it with their hammers in rotation. The work requires nerve and skill, for the smallest error in a striker's judgment would be fatal to the holder. The hammer is swung clear from the hip and travels eighteen feet or more before it comes in contact with the inch-square upper end of the jumper. The whole course of the blow is calculated instinctively before the hammer rises to the swing. This work is classed as unskilled labour.

When it is considered that men often work the whole ten-hour shift with the eternal hammer in their hands it is really a wonder that more accidents do not take place, especially since the labour is often performed after a night's heavy drinking or gambling. A holder is seldom wounded; when he is struck he dies. Only once have I seen a man thus get killed. The descending hammer flew clear of the jumper and caught the poor fellow over the temple, knocking him stiff dead.

Red Billy's gang was divided into squads, each consisting of five persons. We completed a squad not filled up before our arrival, and proceeded to work with our two hammers. Stripped to our trousers and shirt, and puffing happily at our pipes, we were soon into the lie of the job, and swung our heavy hammers over our heads to the virile music of meeting steel. Most of the men knew Joe. He had worked somewhere and at some time with most on the place, and all had a warm word of welcome for Moleskin. " By God, it's Moleskin ! Have you a chew of 'baccy to spare ? " was the usual form of greeting. There was no handshake. It is unknown among the navvies, just as kissing is unknown in Glenmornan. For a few hours nobody took any notice of me, but at last my mate introduced me to several of those who had gathered around, when we took advantage of Red Billy's absence to fill our pipes and set them alight.

" Do you know that kid there, that mate of mine ? " he asked, pointing at me with his pipe-shank. I felt confused, for every eye was fixed on me, and lifting my hammer I turned to my work, trying thus to hide my self-consciousness.

" A blackleg without the spunk of a sparrow ! " said one man, a tough-looking fellow with the thumb of one hand missing, who, not satisfied with taking off his coat to work, had taken off his shirt as well. " What the hell are you workin' for when the ganger is out of sight ? "

I felt nettled and dropped my hammer.

" I did not know that it was wrong to work when the ganger was out of sight," I said to the man who had spoken. " But if you want to shove it on to me you are in the wrong shop ! "

" That's the way to speak, Flynn," said Moleskin approvingly. Then he turned to the rest of the men.

" That kid, that mate of mine, rose stripped naked from his bed and thrashed Carroty Dan in Burn's model lodging-house," he said. " Now it takes a good man to thrash Carroty."

" _I_ knocked Carroty out," said the man who accused me of working when the ganger was out of sight, and he looked covertly in my direction.

"There's a chance for you, Flynn!" cried Moleskin, in a delighted voice. "You'll never get the like of it again. Just pitch into Hell-fire Gahey and show him how you handle your pair of fives."

Gahey looked at me openly and eagerly, evincing all tokens of pleasure and willingness to come to fistic conclusions with me there and then. As for myself, I felt in just the right mood for a bit of a tussle, but at that moment Red Billy appeared from behind the crane handle and shouted across angrily:

"Come along, you God-damned, forsaken, lousy, beggarly, forespent wastrels, and get some work done!" he cried.

"Can a man not get time to light his pipe?" remonstrated Moleskin.

"Time in hell!" shouted Billy. "You're not paid for strikin' matches here."

We started work again; the fight was off for the moment, and I felt sorry. It is disappointing to rise to a pitch of excitement over nothing; and a fight keeps a man alert and alive.

Having bored the rock through to the depth of four or five feet, we placed dynamite in the hole, attached a fuse, lit it, and hurried off to a place of safety until the rock was blown to atoms. Then we returned to our labour at the jumper and hammer.

Dinner-time came around; the men shared their grub with my mate and me, Hell-fire Gahey giving me a considerable share of his food. Red Billy, who took his grub along with us, cut his bread into thin slices with a dirty tobacco-stained knife, and remarked that he always liked tobacco juice for kitchen. Red Billy chewed the cud after eating, a most curious, but, as I have learned since, not an unprecedented thing. He was very proud of this peculiarity, and said that the gift—he called it a gift—

was the outcome of a desire when young and hungry to chew over again the food which he had already eaten.

No one spoke of my proposed fight with Gahey, and I wondered at this silence. I asked Moleskin if Hell-fire was afraid of me.

"Not at all," said Joe. "But he won't put his dinner-hour to loss by thrashin' a light rung of a cully like you. That's the kind of him."

I laughed as if enjoying Joe's remark, but in my mind I resolved to go for Gahey as soon as I got the chance, and hammer him, if able, until he shrieked for mercy. It was most annoying to know that a man would not put his time to loss in fighting me.

We finished work at six o'clock in the evening, and Moleskin and I obtained two shillings of sub.* apiece. Then we set off for the store, a large rambling building in which all kinds of provisions were stored, and bought food. Having procured one loaf, one pound of steak, one can of condensed milk and a pennyworth of tea and sugar, we went to our future quarters in Red Billy's shack.

Our ganger built a large shack at Kinlochleven when work was started there, and furnished it with a hot-plate, beds, bedding, and a door. He forgot all about windows, or at least considered them unnecessary for the dwelling-place of navvy men. Once a learned man objected to the lack of fresh air in Billy's shack. "If you go outside the door you'll get plenty of air, and if you stay out it will be fresher here," was Billy's answer. To do Billy justice, it is necessary to say that he slept in the shack himself. Three shillings a week secured the part use of a bedplace for each man, and the hot-plate was used in common by the inmates of the shack. At the end of the week the three shillings were deducted from the men's pay. Moleskin and I had no difficulty in securing a bed, which we

* Wages paid on the day on which it is earned.

had to share with Gahey, my rival. Usually three men lay in each bunk, and sometimes it happened that four unwashed dirty humans were huddled together under the one evil-smelling, flea-covered blanket.

Red Billy's shack was built of tarred wooden piles, shoved endwise into the earth, and held together by iron cross-bars and wooden couplings. Standing some distance apart from the others, it was neither better nor worse than any of the rest. I mean that it could be no worse ; and there was not a better shack in all the place. As it happened to stand on a mountain spring a few planks were thrown across the floor to prevent the water from rising over the shoe-mouths of the inmates. In warm weather the water did not come over the flooring ; in the rainy season the flooring was always under the water. A man once said that the Highlands were the rain-trough of the whole world.

The beds were arranged one over another in three rows which ran round the entire hut, which was twelve feet high and about thirty feet square. The sanitary authorities took good care to see that every cow in the byre at Braxey farm had so many cubic feet of breathing space, but there was no one to bother about the navvies' byres in Kinlochleven ; it was not worth anybody's while to bother about our manner of living.

Moleskin and I had no frying-pan, but Gahey offered us the use of his, until such time as we raised the price of one. We accepted the offer and forthwith proceeded to cook a good square supper. It had barely taken us five minutes to secure our provisions, but by the time we started operations on the hot-plate the gamblers were busy at work, playing banker on a discarded box in the centre of the building. Gahey, who was one of the players, seemed to have forgotten all about the projected fight between himself and me.

" Is Gahey not going to fight ? " I asked Moleskin in a whisper.

" My God! don't you see that he's playin' banker? " said Joe, and I had to be content with that answer, which was also an explanation of the man's lack of remembrance. Fighting must be awfully common and boring to the man when he forgets one so easily, I thought. To me a fight was something which I looked forward to for days, and which I thought of for weeks afterwards. Now I felt a trifle afraid of Gahey. I was of little account in his eyes, and I concluded, for I jump quickly to conclusions, that I would not make much of a show if I stood up against such a man, a man who looked upon a fight as something hardly worthy of notice. I decided to let the matter drop and trouble about it no further. I think that if Gahey had asked me to fight at that moment I should have refused. The truth was that I became frightened of the man.

" Can I have a hand while I'm cookin' my grub ? " Joe asked the dealer, a man of many oaths whose name was Maloney, a personage already enshrined in the song written by Mullholland on the *Shootin' of the Crow.*

" The more the merrier ! " was the answer, given in a tone of hearty assent. On hearing these words Moleskin left the pan under my care, put down a coin on the table, and with one eye on the steak, and another on the game, he waited for the turn-up of the banker's card. During the whole meal my mate devoted the intervals between bites to the placing of money on the card table. Sometimes he won, sometimes he lost, and when the game concluded with a free fight my mate had lost every penny of his sub., and thirteen pence which he had borrowed from me. It was hard to determine how the quarrel started, but at the commencement nearly every one of the players was involved in the fight, which gradually resolved itself into an affair between two of the gamblers, Blasting Mick and Ben the Moocher.

Red Billy Davis came in at that moment, and between two planks, wallowing in the filth, he found the combatants tearing at one another for all they were worth.

" Go out and fight, and be damned to yous ! " roared Red Billy, catching the two men as they scrambled to their feet. " You want to break ev'rything in the place, you do ! Curses be on you ! go out into the world and fight ! " he cried, taking them by their necks and shoving them through the door.

Nothing daunted, however, both continued the quarrel outside in the darkness. No one evinced any desire to go out and see the result of the fight, but I was on the tip-toe of suspense waiting for the finish of the encounter. I could hear the combatants panting and slipping outside, but thinking that the inmates of the shack would consider me a greenhorn if I went to look at the fight I remained inside. I resolved to follow Moleskin's guidance for at least a little while longer ; I lacked the confidence to work on my own initiative.

" Clean broke ! " said Moleskin, alluding to his own predicament, as he sat down by the fire, and asked the man next to him for a chew of tobacco. " Money is made round to go round, anyway," he went on ; " and there is some as say that it is made flat to build upon, but that's damned rot. Doesn't ev'ryone here agree with that ? "

" Ev'ryone," was the hearty response.

" Why the devil do all of you agree ? " Joe looked savagely exasperated. " Has no man here an opinion of his own ? You, Tom Slavin, used to save your pay when you did graft at Toward Waterworks, and what did *you* do with your money ? " .

Tom Slavin was a youngish fellow, and Joe's enquiry caused him to look redder than the hot-plate.

" He bought penny ribbons and brass bracelets for Ganger Farley's daughter," put in Red Billy, who had quickly regained his good humour ; " but in the end the jade went and married a carpenter from Glasgow."

Red Billy chuckled in his beard. He was twice a widower, grass and clay, and he was a very cynical old man. I did not take much heed to the conversation ; I was listening to the scuffle outside.

" What did I always say about women ! " said Moleskin, launching into the subject of the fair sex. " Once get into the hands of a woman and she'll drive you to hell and leave you with the devil when she gets you there. How many fools can a woman put through her hands ? Eh ! How much water can run through a sieve ? No matter how many lovers a woman has, she has always room for one more. It's a well-filled barn that doesn't give room for the threshin' of one extra sheaf. Comin' back to that sliver of a Slavin's wenchin', who is the worst off now, the carpenter or Tom ? I'll go bail that one is jealous of the other ; that one's damned because he did and the other's damned because he didn't."

" There's a sort of woman, Gourock Ellen they call her," interrupted Red Billy with a chuckle, " and she nearly led you to hell in Glasgow three years ago, Mister Moleskin."

" And what about the old heifer you made love to in Clydebank, Moleskin ? " asked James Clancy, a man with a broken nose and great fame as a singer, who had not spoken before.

" Oh ! that Glasgow woman," said Moleskin, taking no heed of the second question. " I didn't think very much of her."

" What was wrong with her ? " asked Billy.

" She was a woman ; isn't that enough ? "

" It was a different story on the night when you and

Ginger Simpson fought about her in the Saltmarket," cut in some individual who was sitting in the bed sewing patches on his trousers.

"I've fought my man and knocked him out many a time, when there wasn't a wench within ten miles of me," cried Moleskin. "Doesn't ev'ryone here believe that ? "

"But that woman in Clydebank ! " persisted Clancy.

"Have you seen Ginger Simpson of late ? " said Moleskin, making an effort to change the subject, for he observed that he was cornered. It was evident that some of the inmates of the shack had learned facts relating to his career, which Moleskin would have preferred to remain unknown.

"Last winter I met him in Greenock," said Sandy Macdonald, a man with a wasting disease, who lay in a corner bunk at the end of the shack. "He told me all about the fight in the Saltmarket, and that Gourock Ellen——"

"But the Clydebank woman——"

"Listen ! " said Joe, interrupting Clancy's remark. "They're at it outside yet. It must be a hell of a fight between the two of them."

He referred to Blasting Mick and Ben the Moocher, who were still busily engaged in thrashing one another outside, and in the silence that followed Joe's remark I could hear distinctly the thud of many blows given and taken by the two combatants in the darkness.

"Let them fight ; that's nothin' to us," said Red Billy, taking a bite from the end of his plug. "But for my own part I would like to know where Gourock Ellen is now."

Joe made no answer ; he was visibly annoyed, and I saw his fists closing tightly.

"Do you mind the Clydebank woman, Moleskin ? " asked Clancy, making a final effort in his enquiries. "She was fond of her pint, and had a horrid squint "

"I'll squint you, by God ! " roared Moleskin, reaching

out and gripping Clancy by the scruff of the neck. " If I hear you talkin' about Clydebank again, I'll thicken your ear for you, seein' that I cannot break your nose ! And you, you red-bearded sprat, you ! " this to Red Billy Davis ; " if you mention Gourock Ellen again, I'll leave your eyes in such a state that you'll not be fit to see one of your own gang for six months to come."

Just at that moment the two fighters came in, and attracted the whole attention of the party inside by their appearance. They.looked worn and dishevelled, their clothes were torn to ribbons, their cheeks were covered with clay and blood, and their hair and beards looked like mops which had been used in sweeping the bottom of a midden. One good result of the two men's timely entrance was that the rest of the party forgot their own particular grievances.

" Quite pleased with yoursels now ? " asked Red Billy Davis, but the combatants did not answer. They sat down, took off their boots, scraped the clay from their wounds, and turned into bed.

" Moleskin, do you know Gourock Ellen ? " I asked my mate when later I found him sitting alone in a quiet corner.

Moleskin glared at me furiously. " By this and by that, Flynn ! if you talk to me about Gourock Ellen again I'll scalp you," he answered.

For a moment I felt a trifle angry, but having sense enough to see that Moleskin was sore cut with the outcome of the argument, and knowing that he was the only friend whom I had in all Kinlochleven I kept silent, stifling the words of anger that had risen to my tongue. By humouring one another's moods we have become inseparable friends.

One by one the men turned into bed. Maloney having collared all the day's sub. there was no more gambling that night. Joe sat for a while bare naked, getting a belly heat at the fire, as he himself expressed it, before he turned into bed.

" Where have you left your duds, Flynn ? " he asked, as he rose to his feet and extinguished the naphtha lamp which hung from the roof by a piece of wire. I was already under the blankets, glad of their warmth, meagre though it was, after so many long chilly nights on the road.

" They are under my pillow," I answered.

" And your bluchers ? "

" On the floor."

" Put them under your pillow too, or maybe you'll be without them in the mornin'."

Acting upon Joe's advice, I jumped out of bed, groped in the darkness, found my boots and placed them under my pillow. Presently, wedged in between the naked bodies of Moleskin Joe and Hell-fire Gahey, I endeavoured to test the strength of the latter's arms by pressing them with my fingers. The man was asleep, if snoring was to be taken as a sign, and presently I was running my hand over his body, testing the muscles of his arms, shoulders, and chest. He was covered with hair, more like a brute than a human ; long, curling, matted hair, that was rough as fine wire when the hand came in contact with it. The rubber-like pliability of the man's long arms impressed me, and assured me that he would be a quick hitter when he started fighting. Added to that he had a great fame as a fighting man in Kinloch-leven. He was a loud snorer too ; I have never met a man who could snore like Gahey, and snoring is one of the vices which I detest. Being very tired after the long homeless tramp from Greenock, I fell asleep by-and-bye ; but I did not sleep for long. The angry voice of Joe awakened me, and I heard him expostulate with Hell-fire on the unequal distribution of the blankets.

o

" You hell-forsaken Irish blanket-grabber, you ! " Joe was roaring ; " you've got all the clothes in the bed wrapped round your dirty hide."

" Ye're a hell-fire liar, and that's what ye are ! " snorted Gahey. " It's yerself that has got all the beddin'."

Joe replied with an oath and a vigorous tug at the blankets. In turn my other bedmate pulled them back, and for nearly five minutes both men engaged in a mad tug-of-war. Hell-fire got the best of it in the end, for he placed his back against the wall of the shack, planted his feet in my side, and pulled as hard as he was able until he regained complete possession of the disputed clothing. Just then Moleskin's hand passed over my head with a mighty swish in the direction of Gahey. I turned rapidly round and lay face downwards on the pillow in order to avoid the blows of the two men as they fought across my naked body. And they did fight ! The dull thud of fist on flesh, the grunts and pants of the men, the creaking of the joints as their arms were thrown outwards, the jerky spring of the wooden bunk-stanchions as they shook beneath the straining bodies, and the numberless blows which landed on me in the darkness makes the memory of the first night in Kinlochleven for ever green in my mind.

Rising suddenly to his feet Gahey stood over me in a crouching position with both his heels planted in the small of my back. The pain was almost unendurable, and I got angry. It was almost impossible to move, but by a supreme effort I managed to wriggle round and throw Gahey head-foremost into Moleskin's arms, whereupon the two fighters slithered out of bed, leaving the blankets to me, and continued their struggle on the floor.

Somewhere in the middle of the shack I could hear Red Billy swearing as he endeavoured to light a match on the upper surface of the hot-plate.

" My blessed blankets ! " he was lamenting. " You

damned scoundrels! you'll not leave one in the hut. Fighting in bed just the same as if you were lyin' in a pigsty. What the devil was I thinkin' of when I took on that pig of a Moleskin Joe?"

Billy ceased thinking just then, for a wild swing of Moleskin's heavy fist missed Gahey and caught the ganger under the ear. The whiskered one dropped with a groan amid the floor-planks and lay, kicking, shouting meanwhile that Moleskin had murdered him. Someone lit a match, and my bedmates ceased fighting and seemed little the worse for their adventure. Billy's face looked ghastly, and a red streak ran from his nose into the puddle in which he lay. He had now stopped speaking and was fearfully quiet. I jumped out of bed, shaking in every limb, for I thought that the old ganger was killed.

" A tin of water thrown in his face will bring him round," I said, but feared at the same time that it would not.

" Or a bucketful," someone suggested.

" Stab a pin under the quick of his nail."

" Burn a feather under his nose."

" Give him a dig in the back."

" Or a prod in the ribs."

The match had gone out, no one could find another, and the voices of advice came from the darkness in all the corners of the room. Even old Sandy MacDonald, who could find no cure for his own complaint, the wasting disease, was offering endless advice on the means of curing Red Billy Davis.

A match was again found ; the lamp was lit, and after much rough doctoring on the part of his gang, the ganger recovered and swore himself to sleep. Joe and Gahey came back together and stood by the bed.

" It's myself that has the hard knuckles, Moleskin," said Gahey. " And they're never loth to come in contact with flesh that's not belongin' to the man who owns them."

"There's a plot of ground here, and it's called the 'Ring,'" said Moleskin. "About seven o'clock the morrow evenin', I'll be out that way for a stroll. Many a man has broke a hard knuckle against my jaw, and if you just meet me in the Ring——"

"I'll take a bit of a dander round there, Joe," said Hell-fire, and filled with ineffable content both men slipped into their bed, and fell asleep. As for myself, the dawn was coming through a chink in the shack when my eyes closed in slumber.

CHAPTER XXVI

" When rugged rungs stand up to fight, stark naked to the buff,
Each taken blow but gives them zest, they cannot have enough,
For they are out to see red blood, to curse and club and clout,
And few men know and no one cares what brings the fuss about."

—From *Hard Knuckles*.

ABOUT fifty yards distant from Red Billy's hut a circle of shacks enclosed a level piece of ground, and this was used as a dumping place for empty sardine cans, waste tins, scrap iron, and broken bottles. This was also the favourite spot where all manner of quarrels were settled with the fists. It had been christened the Ring, and in those days many a heavy jowl was broken there and many a man was carried out of the enclosure seeing all kinds of dancing lights in front of his eyes. It was to this spot that Moleskin and Gahey came to settle their dispute on the evening of the second day, and I came with them, Joe having appointed me as his second, whose main duty would consist in looking on and giving a word of approval to my principal now and again. When we arrived two fights were already in progress, and my mates had to wait until one of these was brought to a satisfactory conclusion. Some men who had come out through sympathy with the combatants were seated on the ground in one corner, and had transferred their interest from the quarrels to a game of banker or brag. Moleskin and Gahey evinced not the slightest interest in the two fights that were taking place ; but grumbled a little because they had to wait their turn so long. For myself, I could hardly understand my mate's indifference to other people's quarrels. At that time, as a true Irishman, I could have spent all day long looking at fights. These men looked upon a fight as they looked upon a shift. " Hurry up and get it done, and when it is done trouble no more about it." Another man's shift or another man's fight was not their business.

I could not take my eyes away from the struggles which were going on already. A big Irishman, slow of foot, strong and heavy-going, was engaged in an encounter with a little Pole, who handled his fists scientifically, and who had battered his opponent's face to an ugly purple by the time we arrived. However, in the end the Irishman won. He lifted his opponent bodily, and threw him, naked shoulders and all, into the middle of a heap of broken bottles and scraggy tins. The Pole would fight no more. His mates pulled the edged scraps of tin out of his flesh, while his victor challenged all Poles (there were a fair sprinkling of them at Kinlochleven) who were yet on the safe side of hell to deadly battle.

The second fight was more vindictive. A Glasgow craneman had fallen foul of an English muck-filler, and the struggle had already lasted for the best part of an hour. Both men were stripped to the buff, and red splotches of blood and dirt covered their steaming bodies. The craneman thought that he had finished matters conclusively when he gave his opponent the knee in the stomach, and knocked him stiff to the ground. Just as he was on the point of leaving the ring the Englishman suddenly recovered, rose to his knees and, grabbing his adversary by the legs, inserted his teeth in the thick of the victor's right calf. Nothing daunted, however, the craneman bent down and tightened his thumbs under his enemy's ear, and pressed strongly until the latter let go his hold.

" Our turn now," said Moleskin affably, as he stripped to the waist and fastened his gallowses around his waist. " It'll give me much pleasure to blacken your eyes, Gahey."

Joe was a fine figure when stripped. His flesh was pure white below the brown of his neck, and the long muscles of his arms stood out in clearly defined ridges. When he stretched his arms his well-developed biceps rose and fell in graceful unison with every movement of his perfectly-shaped chest. When on the roads, dressed in every curious garment which he could beg, borrow, or thieve, Joe looked singularly unprepossessing ; but here, naturally garbed, and standing amidst the nakedness of nature, he looked like some magnificent piece of sculpture, gifted with life and fresh from the hands of the genius who fashioned it.

Gahey was of different build altogether. The profusion of hair that covered his body resolved itself into a mane almost in the hollow of the breast bone. His flesh was shrivelled and dried ; his limbs looked like raw pig-iron, which had in some strange manner been transformed into the semblance of a human being.

" Hell-fire and Moleskin Joe," I heard the gamblers say as they threw down their cards and scraped the money from the ground. " This will be a good set-to. Moleskin can handle his mits, and by this and that, Hell-fire is no slow one ! "

Joe stepped into the ring, hitched up his trousers and waited. Gahey followed, stood for a moment, then swung out for his enemy's head, only to find his blow intercepted by an upward sweep of the arm of Moleskin, who followed up his movement of defence by a right feint for the body of Gahey, and a straight left that went home from the shoulder. Gahey replied with a heavy smash to the ribs, and Joe looked at him with a smile.

" See and don't hurt your knuckles on my ribs, Gahey," he said.

"I was only feelin' if yer heart was beatin' just a trifle faster than the usual," replied Gahey.

Both men smiled, but the smile was a mask, behind which, clear-headed and cool-eyed, each of them looked for an opening and an opportunity to drive home a blow. To each belonged the wisdom bred of many weary, aching fights and desperate gruellings. Gahey was by far the quicker man ; his long brown arms shot out like whiplashes, and his footwork was very clever. He was a man, untrained in the art, but a natural fighter. His missing thumb seemed to place him at no disadvantage. Joe was slower but by far the stronger man. He never lost his head, and his blows had the impact of a knotted club. When he landed on the flesh of the body, every knuckle left its own particular mark ; when he landed on the face, there was a general disfigurement.

Gahey broke through the mask of his smile, and struck out with his right. In his eyes the purpose betrayed itself, and his opponent, forewarned, caught the blow on his arm. Hell-fire darted in with the left and took Joe on the stomach. The impact was sharp and sudden ; my mate winced a trifle slightly, but the next moment he forced a smile into his face.

"You're savin' your knuckles, matey," he said to Gahey. "There's no danger of you breakin' them on the soft of my belly."

"Well, I'll test them here," Gahey retorted, and came in with a resounding smack to Moleskin's jaw. Joe received the blow stolidly, and swung a right for Gahey, but, missing his man, he fell to the ground.

"See ! see ! " everyone around the ring shouted. "Who'd have thought that a light rung of a fellow like Gahey would have beat Moleskin Joe ? "

"Wait till he's beaten ! " I shouted back angrily. "I'll have something to say to some of you idiots."

"Good, Flynn!" said Moleskin, rising to his feet. "Just put in a word on my behalf with them lubberly coopers. I'll see to them myself in a minute or two, when I get this wee job off my hands."

So saying, my mate made for Gahey, who was afraid to come into contact with Joe when he was on the ground. The men fought to win, and the fight had no rules. All was fair, clinching, clutching, scraping, kicking, sarcasm, and repartee. Joe followed Gahey up, coming nearer every moment and eager to get into grips. When that would happen, Gahey was lost; but being wary, he avoided Moleskin's clutches, and kept hopping around, aiming in at intervals one of his lightning blows, and raising a red mark on Moleskin's white body whenever he struck. Joe kept walking after his man; nothing deterred him, he would keep at it until he achieved his purpose. The other man's hope lay in knocking Moleskin unconscious; but even that would ensure victory only for the moment. Joe once fought a man twenty-six times, and got knocked out every time. In the twenty-seventh fight, Joe knocked out his opponent. Joe did not know when he was beaten, and thus he was never defeated.

Now he kept walking stolidly round and round the ring after Gahey. Sometimes he struck out; nearly always he missed, and seldom was he quick enough to avoid the lightning blows of his enemy. Even yet he was smiling, although the smile had long gone from the face of Gahey, who was still angry and wanting to inflict punishment. He inflicted punishment, but it seemed to have no effect; apparently unperturbed, Joe took it all without wincing.

The crowd watched Gahey wistfully; now they knew instinctively that he was going to get beaten. Joe was implacable, resistless. He was walking towards an appointed goal steadily and surely; his pace was merciless, and it was slow, but in the end it would tell. For myself, I doubted if Joe could be successful. He was streaming with blood, one eyebrow was hanging, and the flesh of the breast was red and raw. Gahey was almost without a scratch ; if he finished the fight at that moment, he would leave the ring nearly as fresh as when he came into it. Joe still smiled, but the smile looked ghastly, when seen through the blood. Now and again he passed a joke.

The look of fear came into Gahey's eyes suddenly. It came to him when he realised that he would be beaten if he did not knock Joe out very soon. Then he endeavoured at every opportunity to strike fully and heavily, trying to land on the point, but this Joe kept jealously guarded. Gahey began to lose confidence in himself ; once or twice he blundered and almost fell into Joe's arms, but saved himself by an effort.

" I'll get you yet, my Irish blanket-grabber ! " Joe said each time.

" Get him now and put an end to the fight," I cried to Moleskin. " It's not worth your while to spend so much time over a little job."

Joe took my advice and rushed. Gahey struck out, but Joe imprisoned the striking arm, and drawing it towards him, he gripped hold of Gahey's body. Then, without any perceptible effort, he lifted Gahey over his head and held him there at arm's length for a few minutes. Afterwards he took him down as far as his chest.

" For God's sake don't throw me into the tins, Moleskin," cried Gahey.

" I don't want to dirty the tins," answered Joe. " Now I want to ask you a question. Who was right about the blankets last night ? "

Gahey gave no answer. Joe threw him on the ground, went on top of him, and began knuckling his knees along Gahey's ribs.

" Who was right about the blankets last night ? " asked
Moleskin again.

" You were," said Gahey sulkily. Joe smiled and rose
to his feet.

" That's a wee job finished," he said to me. " You
could knock Gahey out, yourself, Flynn."

" Could ye, bedamned ! " roared Gahey, dancing around
me and making strange passes with his fist.

" Go on, Flynn, give it to him same as you did with
Carroty in Greenock ! " shouted Joe as he struggled with
the shirt which he was pulling over his head. Gahey's lip
was swollen, his left ear had been thickened, but otherwise he had not received a scratch in the fight with
Moleskin, and he was now undoubtedly eager to try conclusions with me. As I have said, I was never averse to
a stand-up fight, and though the exhibition which Hell-
fire made against Joe filled me with profound respect for
the man, I looked at him squarely between the eyes for a
moment, and then with a few seasonable oaths I stripped
to the waist, my blood rushing through my veins at the
thought of the coming battle.

I am not much to look at physically, but am strong-
boned, though lacking muscle and flesh. I can stand any
amount of rough treatment ; and in after days men, who
knew something about the art of boxing, averred that I was
gifted with a good punch. Though very strong, my bearing
is deceptive ; new mates are always disinclined to believe
that my strength is out of keeping with my appearance,
until by practical demonstration they are taught otherwise.
While slender of arm my chest measurement is very good,
being over forty-three inches, and height five feet eleven.
In movement inclined to be slow, yet when engaged in a
sight I have an uncommonly quick eye for detail, and can
preserve a good sound striking judgment even when getting
the worst of the encounter, and never yet have I given in

to my man until he knocked me unconscious to the ground.

Gahey stood in the centre of the enclosure, and waited for me with an air of serene composure, and carried the self-confident look of a man who is going to win.

Despite the ease with which Moleskin had settled Gahey a few minutes previously, I felt a bit nervous when I took my way into the open and glanced at the circle of dirty, animated faces that glared at me from all corners of the ring. Gahey did not seem a bit afraid, and he laughed in my face when I raised my hands gingerly in assuming an attitude of defence. I did not feel angry with the man. I was going to fight in a cold-blooded manner without reason or excuse. In every previous fight I had something to annoy me before starting; I saw red before a blow was given or taken. But now I had no grievance against the man and he had none against me. We wanted to fight one another—that was all.

Gahey, though apparently confident of victory, was taking no chances. He swung his right for my head in the first onslaught, and I went slap to the ground like a falling log.

" Oh, Flynn ! " cried Joe in an agonised voice ; and I thought that his words were whispered in my ear where I lay. Up to my feet I jumped, and with head lowered down a nd wedged between my shoulder joints, I lunged forward at Gahey, only to recoil from an upward sweep of his fist, which sent all sorts of dancing lights into my eyes. My mouth filled with blood and a red madness of anger came over me. I was conscious no more of pain, or of the reason for the fight. All that I now wanted was to overcome the man who stood in front of me. I heard my opponent laugh, but I could not see him ; he struck out at me again and I stumbled once more to the ground.

"Flynn! Dermod Flynn!" shouted Joe, and there was a world of reproach in his voice.

Again I stood up, and the blindness had gone from my eyes. My abdomen heaved frankly, and I gulped down mighty mouthfuls of air. Gahey stood before me laughing easily. My whole mind was centred on the next move of the contest; but in some subconscious way I took in every detail of the surroundings. The gamblers stood about in clusters, and one of them carried the pack of cards in his hand, the front of it facing me, and I could see the seven of clubs on top of the pack. Joe was looking tensely at me, his lips wide apart and his tobacco-stained teeth showing between. Behind him, and a little distance off, the rest of the crowd, shouldered together, stood watching; and behind and above the circle of dirty faces the ring of cabins spread outwards under the shadow of the hair-poised derricks and firmly-set hills.

A vicious jab from Gahey slipped along the arm with which I parried it. I hit with my left, and the soft of my enemy's throat jellied inwards under the stroke. I followed up with two blows to the chest and one to the face. A stream of blood squirted from Gahey's jowl as my fist took it; and this filled me with new hopes of victory. Joe had drawn very little blood from the man, but then, though faster than my mate on my feet, I was not gifted with his staying power.

Behind me Moleskin clapped his hands excitedly, and urged me afresh with hearty words of cheer.

"Burst him up!" he yelled.

"Sure," I answered. My anger had subsided, and a feeling of confidence had taken its place.

"Will ye, be God!" cried Gahey, and he rushed at me like a mad wind, landing his brown hard fists repeatedly on my face and chest, and receiving no chastisement in return.

" I'll burst yer ear ! " he cried, and did so, smashing the lobe with one of his lightning blows. The blood from the wound fell on my shoulders for the rest of the fight. Another blow, a light one on the stomach, sickened me slightly, and my confidence began to ooze away from me. It went completely when I endeavoured to trip my opponent, and got tripped myself instead. My head took the ground, and I felt a little groggy when I regained my feet ; but in rising I got in a sharp jab to Gahey's nose and drew blood again.

The battle sobered down a little. Both of us circled around, looking for an opening. Suddenly I drove forward with my right, passed Gahey's guard, and with a well-directed blow on the chest, I lifted him neatly off his feet, and left him sitting on the ground. Rising, he rushed at me furiously, caught me by the legs, raised, and tried to throw me over his shoulders.

Then the fight turned in my favour. I had once on my wanderings met a man who had been a wrestler, and he taught me certain tricks of his art. I had a good opening before me now for one of them. Gahey had hold of me by the knees, and both his arms were twined tightly around my joints. I stooped over him, gripped him around the waist, and threw myself backwards flat to the ground. As I reached the earth I let Gahey go, and flying clean across my head, he slid along the rough ground on his naked back. When he regained his feet I was up and ready for him, and I knocked him down again with a good blow delivered on the fleshy part, where the lower ribs fork inward to the breast, bone. That settled him for good. The crowd cheered enthusiastically and went back to their cards. One or two stopped with Gahey, and it took him half an hour to recover. When he was well again Moleskin and I escorted him back to the shack.

We washed our wounds together and talked of every-

thing but the fights which had just taken place. The
result of the quarrels seemed to have had no effect on the
men, but my heart was jumping out of my mouth with
pleasure. I had beaten one of the great fighters of Kinlochleven ; I, a boy of nineteen, who had never shaved yet,
had knocked Gahey to the ground with a good hard punch,
and Gahey was a man twice my age and one who was
victor in a thousand battles. Excitement seized hold of
me, my step became alert, and I walked into the shack
with the devil-may-care swagger of a fighting man. The
gamblers were sitting at the table and the bright glitter
of silver caught my eye. Big Jim Maloney was banker.

"Come here, ye fightin' men," he cried ; "and take a
hand at another game."

The excitement was on me. In my pocket I had three
shillings sub., and I put it down on the board, the whole
amount, as befitted a fighting man. I won once, twice,
three times. I called for drinks for the school. I put
Maloney out of the bank, I backed any money, and all the
time I won. The word passed round that Flynn was playing
a big game ; he would back any money. More and more
men came in from the other shacks and remained. I
could hear the clink of bottles all round me. The men were
drinking, smoking, and swearing, and those who could not
get near the table betted on the result of the game.

My luck continued. The pile of silver beside me grew
and grew, and stray pieces of gold found their way into the
pile as well. Every turn-up was an ace or court-card.
My luck was unheard of : and all around me Kinlochleven
stood agape, and played blindly, as if fascinated. Gain
was nothing to me, the game meant all. I called for
further drinks ; I drank myself, although I was already
drunk with excitement. I had forgotten all about the
good resolutions made on the doorstep of Kinlochleven
but what did it matter ? Let my environment mould me,

let Nature follow out its own course, she knows what is best. I was now living large; the game held me captive, and the pile of glistening silver grew in size.

A man beside made some objection to my turn-up. He was one of the fiercest men in the shack, and he was known as a fighter of merit. I looked him between the eyes for a minute and he flinched before my gaze.

" I'll thrash you till you roar for mercy ! " I called at him and he became silent.

The drink went to my head and the cards turned up began to play strange antics before my eyes. The knaves and queens ran together, they waltzed over the place, and the lesser cards would persist in eluding my hand when it went out to grip them. I was terribly drunk, the whisky and the excitement were overpowering me.

" I'm going to stop, mateys," I said, and I caught a hand-ful of gold and silver and put it into my pocket, then staggered to my feet. A cry of indignation and contempt arose. " I was not going to allow any of them to overtake their luck; I was not a man ; I was a mere rogue." I was well aware of the fact that a winner is always honour bound to be the last to leave the table.

" I'm going to play no more," I said bluntly.

The crowd burst into a torrent of abuse. My legs were faltering under me, and I wanted to get into bed. I would go to bed, but how ? The players might not allow it ; they wanted their money. Then I would give it to them. I put my hand in my pocket, pulled out the cash, and flung it amongst the crowd of players. There was a hurried scramble all round me, and the men groped in the muck and dirt for the stray coins. I got into bed with my clothes on and fell asleep. In a vague sort of way I heard the gamblers talk about my wonderful luck, and some of them quarrelled about the money lifted from the floor. When morning came I was still lying, fully-dressed, over the blankets on the centre of the bed, while Joe and Gahey were under the blankets on each side of me.

I still had two half-sovereigns in my pocket along with a certain amount of smaller cash, and these coins reminded me of my game. But I did not treasure them so much as the long scar stretching across my cheek, and the disfigured eye, which were tokens of the fight in which I thrashed Hell-fire Gahey. All that day I lived the fight over and over again, and the victory caused me to place great confidence in myself. From that day forward I affected a certain indifference towards other fights, thus pretending that I considered myself to be above such petty scrapes.

By instinct I am a fighter. I never shirk a fight, and the most violent contest is a tonic to my soul. Sometimes when in a thoughtful mood I said to myself that fighting was the pastime of a brute or a savage. I said that because it is fashionable for the majority of people, spineless and timid as they are, to say the same. But fighting is not the pastime of a brute ; it is the stern reality of a brute's life. Only by fighting will the fittest survive. But to man, a physical contest is a pastime and a joy. I love to see a fight with the bare fists, the combatants stripped naked to the buff, the long arms stretching out, the hard knuckles showing white under the brown skin of the fists, the muscles sliding and slipping like live eels under the flesh, the steady and quick glance of the eye, the soft thud of fist on flesh, the sharp snap of a blow on the jaw, and the final scene where one man drops to the ground while the other, bathed in blood and sweat, smiles in acknowledgment of the congratulations on the victory obtained.

Gambling was another manner of fighting, and brim full of excitement. In it no man knew his strength until he paid for it, and there was excitement in waiting for the turn-up. Night after night I sat down to the cards, sometimes out in the open and sometimes by the deal plank on the floor of Red Billy's shack. Gambling was rife and unchecked. All night long the navvies played banker and brag; and those who worked on the night-shift took up the game that the day labourers left off. One Sunday evening alone I saw two hundred and fifty banker schools gathered in a sheltered hollow of the hills. That Sunday I remembered very well, for I happened to win seven pounds at a single sitting, which lasted from seven o'clock on a Saturday evening until half-past six on the Monday morning. I finished the game, went out to my work, and did ten hours' shift, although I was half asleep on the drill handle for the best part of the time.

One day a man, a new arrival, came to me and proposed a certain plan whereby he and I could make a fortune at the gambling school. It was a kind of swindle, and I do not believe in robbing workers, being neither a thief nor a capitalist. I lifted the man up in my arms and took him into the shack, where I disclosed his little plan to the inmates. A shack some distance off was owned by a Belfast man named Ramsay, and several Orangemen dwelt in this shack. Moleskin proposed that we should strip the swindler to the pelt, paint him green, and send him to Ramsay's shack. Despite the man's entreaties, we painted him a glorious green, and when the night came on we took him under cover of the darkness to Ramsay's shack, and tied him to the door. In the morning we found him, painted orange, outside of ours, and almost dead with cold. We gave him his clothes and a few kicks, and chased him from the place.

I intended, when I came to Kinlochleven, to earn money and send it home to my own people, and the intention was nursed in good earnest until I lifted my first day's pay. Then Moleskin requested the loan of my spare cash, and I could not refuse him, a pal who shared his very last crumb of bread with me time and again. On the second evening the gamble followed the fight as a matter of course; and on the third evening and every evening after I played—because I was a gambler by nature. My luck was not the best; I lost most of my wages at the card-table, and the rest went on drink. I know not whether drink and gambling are evils. I only know that they cheered many hours of my life, and caused me to forget the miseries of being. If drunkenness was a vice, I humoured it as a man might humour sickness or any other evil. But drink might have killed me, one will say. And sickness might have killed me, I answer. When a man is dead he knows neither hunger nor cold; he suffers neither from the cold of the night nor the craving of the belly. The philosophy is crude, but comforting, and it was mine. To gamble and drink was part of my nature, and for nature I offer no excuses. She knows what is best.

I could not save money, I hated to carry it about; it burned a hole in my pocket and slipped out. I was no slave to it; I detested it. How different now were my thoughts from those which buoyed up my spirit on first entering Kinlochleven! those illusions, like previous others, had been dispelled before the hard wind of reality. I looked on life nakedly, and henceforth I determined to shape my own future in such a way that neither I, nor wife, nor child, should repent of it. Although passion ran riot in my blood, as it does in the blood of youth, I resolved never to marry and bring children into the world to beg and starve and steal as I myself had done. I saw life as it was, saw it clearly, standing out stark from its covering of illusions. I looked on love cynically, unblinded by the fumes off the midden-heap of lust, and my life lacked the phantom happiness of men who see things as they are not.

The great proportion of the navvies live very pure lives, and women play little or no part in their existence.

The women of the street seldom come near a model, even when the navvies come in from some completed job with money enough and to spare. The purity of their lives is remarkable when it is considered that they seldom marry. "We cannot bring children into the world to suffer like ourselves," most of them say. That is one reason why they remain single. Therefore the navvy is seldom the son of a navvy ; it is the impoverished and the passionate who breed men like us, and throw us adrift upon the world to wear out our miserable lives.

CHAPTER XXVII

DE PROFUNDIS

" I've got kitchen for my grub out of the mustard-pot of sorrow."
—MOLESKIN JOE.

AT that time there were thousands of navvies working at Kinlochleven waterworks   We spoke of waterworks, but only the contractors knew what the work was intended for.   We did not know, and we did not care.   We never asked questions concerning the ultimate issue of our labours, and we were not supposed to ask questions.   If a man throws red muck over a wall to-day and throws it back again to-morrow, what the devil is it to him if he keeps throwing that same muck over the wall for the rest of his life, knowing not why nor wherefore, provided he gets paid sixpence an hour for his labour ? There were so many tons of earth to be lifted and thrown somewhere else ; we lifted them and threw them somewhere else : so many cubic yards of iron-hard rocks to be blasted and carried away ; we blasted and carried them away, but never asked questions and never knew what results we were labouring to bring about.   We turned the Highlands into a cinder-heap, and were as wise at the beginning as at the end of the task.   Only when we completed the job, and returned to the town, did we learn from the newspapers that we had been employed on the construction of the biggest aluminium factory in the kingdom.   All that we knew was that we had gutted whole mountains and hills in the operations.

We toiled on the face of the mountain, and our provisions came up on wires that stretched from the summit to the depths of the valley below. Hampers of bread, casks of beer, barrels of tinned meat and all manner of parcels followed one another up through the air day and night in endless procession, and looked for all the world like great gawky birds which still managed to fly, though deprived of their wings.

The postman came up amongst us from somewhere every day, bringing letters from Ireland, and he was always accompanied by two policemen armed with batons and revolvers. The greenhorns from Ireland wrote home and received letters now and again, but the rest of us had no friends, or if we had we never wrote to them.

Over an area of two square miles thousands of men laboured, some on the day-shift, some on the night-shift, some engaged on blasting operations, some wheeling muck, and others building dams and hewing rock facings. A sort of rude order prevailed, but apart from the two policemen who accompanied the letter-carrier on his daily rounds no other minion of the law ever came near the place. This allowed the physically strong man to exert considerable influence, and fistic arguments were constantly in progress.

Sometimes a stray clergyman, ornamented with a stainless white collar, had the impudence to visit us and tell us what we should do. These visitors were most amusing, and we enjoyed their exhortations exceedingly. Once I told one of them that if he was more in keeping with the Workman whom he represented, some of the navvies stupider than myself might endure his presence, but that no one took any heed of the apprentice who dressed better than his Divine Master. We usually chased these faddists away, and as they seldom had courage equal to their impudence, they never came near us again.

There was a graveyard in the place, and a few went there

from the last shift with the red muck still on their trousers, and their long unshaven beards still on their faces. Maybe they died under a fallen rock or broken derrick jib. Once dead they were buried, and there was an end of them.

Most of the men lifted their sub. every second day, and the amount left over after procuring food was spent in the whisky store or gambling-school. Drunkenness enjoyed open freedom in Kinlochleven. I saw a man stark naked, lying dead drunk for hours on a filthy muck-pile. No one was shocked, no one was amused, and somebody stole the man's clothes. When he became sober he walked around the place clad in a blanket until he procured a pair of trousers from some considerate companion.

I never stole from a mate in Kinlochleven, for it gave me no pleasure to thieve from those who were as poor as myself; but several of my mates had no compunction in relieving me of my necessaries. My three and sixpenny keyless watch was taken from my breast pocket one night when I was asleep, and my only belt disappeared mysteriously a week later. No man in the place save Moleskin Joe ever wore braces. I had only one shirt in my possession, but there were many people in the place who never had a shirt on their backs. Sometimes when the weather was good I washed my shirt, and I lost three, one after the other, when I hung them out to dry. I did not mind that very much, knowing well that it only passed to one of my mates, who maybe needed it more than I did. If I saw one of my missing shirts afterwards I took it from the man who wore it, and if he refused to give it to me, knocked him down and took it by force. Afterwards we bore one another no ill-will. Stealing is rife in shack, on road, and in model, but I have never known one of my kind to have given up a mate to the police. That is one dishonourable crime which no navvy will excuse.

As the days went on, I became more careless of myself,

and I seldom washed. I became like my mates, like Moleskin, who was so fit and healthy, and who never washed from one year's end to another. Often in his old tin-pot way he remarked that a man could often be better than his surroundings, but never cleaner. " A dirty man's the only man who washes," he often said. When we went to bed at night we hid our clothes under the pillows, and sometimes they were gone in the morning. In the bunk beneath ours slept an Irishman named Ward, and to prevent them passing into the hands of thieves he wore all his clothes when under the blankets. But nevertheless, his boots were unlaced and stolen one night when he was asleep and drunk.

One favourite amusement of ours was the looting of provisions as they came up on the wires to the stores on the mountains. Day and night the hampers of bread and casks of beer were passing over our heads suspended in mid-air on the glistening metal strings. Sometimes the weighty barrels and cases dragged the wires downwards until their burdens rested on the shoulder of some uprising knoll. By night we sallied forth and looted all the provisions on which we could lay our hands. We rifled barrels and cases, took possession of bread, bacon, tea, and sugar, and filled our stomachs cheaply for days afterwards. The tops of fallen casks we staved in, and using our hands as cups drank of the contents until we could hold no more. Sometimes men were sent out to watch the hillocks and see that no one looted the grub and drink. These men were paid double for their work. They deserved double pay, for of their own accord they tilted the barrels and cases from their rests and kept them under their charge until we arrived. Then they helped us to dispose of the contents. Usually the watcher lay dead drunk beside his post in the morning. Of course he got his double pay.

CHAPTER XXVIII

A LITTLE TRAGEDY

" The sweat was wet on his steaming loins and shoulders bent and
    scarred,
And he dropped to earth like a spavined mule that's struck in
    the knacker's yard.
Bury him deep in the red, red muck, and pile the clay on his
    breast,
For all that he needs for his years of toil are years of unbroken
    rest.''

—From the song that follows.

TALKING of thieving puts me in mind of the tragedy of English Bill. Bill was a noted thief. He would have robbed his mother's corpse, it was said. There were three sayings in Kinloch-leven, and they were as follows :

Moleskin Joe would gamble on his father's tombstone.
English Bill would rob his mother of her winding-sheet.
Flynn would fight his own shadow and get the best of it.

The three of us were mates, and we were engaged on a special job, blasting a rock facing, in the corner of a secluded cutting. There was very little room for movement, and we had to do the job all by ourselves. One evening we set seven charges of dynamite in the holes which we had drilled during the day, put the fuses alight, and hurried off to a place of safety, and there waited until the explosion was over. While the thunder of the riven earth was still in our ears the ganger blew his whistle, the signal to cease work and return to our shacks.

Next morning Bill reappeared wearing a strong heavily-soled pair of new bluchers which he had purchased on the evening previously.

" They're a good pair of understandings, Bill," I said, as I examined my mate's boots with a feeling of envy.

" A damned good pair ! " said Moleskin ruefully, looking at his own bare toes peeping through the ragged leather of his emaciated uppers.

Bill's face glowed with pride as he lifted his pick and proceeded to clean out the refuse from the rock face. Bill was always in a hurry to start work, and Joe often prophesied that the man would come to a bad end. On this morning Joe was in a bad temper, for he had drunk too well the night before.

" Stow it, you fool," he growled at Bill. " You're a damned hasher, and no ganger within miles of you ! "

Bill made no reply, but lifted his pick and drove it into the rock which we had blasted on the day before. As he struck the ground there was a deadly roar ; the pick whirled round, sprung upwards, twirled in the air like a wind-swept straw, and entered Bill's throat just a finger's breadth below the Adam's apple. One of the dynamite charges had failed to explode on the previous day, and Bill had struck it with the point of the pick, and with this tool which had earned him his livelihood for many years sticking in his throat he stood for a moment swaying unsteadily. He laughed awkwardly as if ashamed of what had happened, then dropped silently to the ground. The pick slipped out, a red foam bubbled on the man's lips for a second, and that was all.

The sight unnerved us for a moment, but we quickly recovered. We had looked on death many times, and our virgin terror was now almost lost.

" He's no good here now," said Moleskin sadly. " We'll look for a muck-barrow and wheel him down to the hut. Didn't I always say that he would come to a bad end, him with his hurry and flurry and his frothy get-about way ? "

" He saved us by his hurry, anyhow," I remarked.

We turned the man over and straightened his limbs, then hurried off for a muck-barrow. On coming back we discovered that some person had stolen the man's boots.

" They should have been taken by us before we left him," I said.

" You're damned right," assented Joe.

Several of the men gathered around, and together we wheeled poor Bill down to the hut along the rickety barrow road. His face was white under the coating of beard, and his poor naked feet looked very blue and cold. All the workmen took off their caps and stood bareheaded until we passed out of sight. No one knew whose turn would come next. When Bill was buried I wrote, at the request of Moleskin Joe, a song on the tragedy. I called the song "A Little Tragedy," and I read it to my mate as we sat together in a quiet corner of the hut.

" A LITTLE TRAGEDY.

" The sweat was wet on his steaming loins and shoulders bent and
    scarred,
And he dropped to earth like a spavined mule that's struck in the
    knacker's yard.
Bury him deep in the red, red muck, and pile the clay on his
    breast,
For all that he needs for his years of toil are years of unbroken
    rest.

"And who has mothered this kinless one ? Why should we want
    to know
As we hide his face from the eyes of men and his flesh from the
    hooded crow ?
Had he a sweetheart to wait for him, with a kiss for his toil-
    worn face ?
It doesn't matter, for here or there another can fill his place.

" Is there a prayer to be prayed for him ? Or is there a bell to toll ?
We'll do the best for the body that's dead, and God can deal
    with the soul.
We'll bury him decently out of sight, and he who can may pray,
For maybe our turn will come to-morrow though his has come
    to-day.

" And maybe Bill had hopes of his own and a sort of vague desire
 For a pure woman to share his home and sit beside his fire ;
 Joys like these he has maybe desired, but living and dying wild,
 He has never known of a maiden's love nor felt the kiss of a child.

" In life he was worth some shillings a day when there was work
     to do,
 In death he is worth a share of the clay which in life he laboured
     through ;
 Wipe the spume from his pallid lips, and quietly cross his hands,
 And leave him alone with the Mother Earth and the Master who
     understands."

My mate seemed very much impressed by the poem, and
remained silent for a long while after I had finished reading
it from the dirty scrap of tea-paper on which it was written.

" Have you ever cared a lot for some one girl, Flynn ? "
he asked suddenly.

" No," I answered, for I had never disclosed my little
love affair to any man.

" Have you ever cared a lot for one girl, Flynn ? "
repeated Joe.

" I have cared—once," I replied, and, obeying the impulse
of the moment, I told Joe the story.   He looked grave when
I had finished.

" They're all the same," he said ; " all the same.   I
cared for a wench myself one time and I intended to marry
her."

I looked at my mate's unshaven face, his dirty clothes,
and I laughed outright.

" I'm nothin' great in the beauty line," went on Moleskin as if divining my thoughts ; " but when I washed
myself years ago I was pretty passable.   She was a fine
girl, mine, and I thought that she was decent and above-
board.   It cost me money and time to find out what she
was, and in the end I found that she was the mother of
two kids, and the lawful wife of no man.   It was a great
slap in the face for me, Flynn."

" It must have been," was all that I could say.

" By God ! it was," Moleskin replied. " I tried to drink my regret away, but I never could manage it.   Have you ever wrote a love song ? "

" I've written one," I said.

" Will you say it to me ? " asked Joe.

I had written a love song long before, and knew it by heart, for it was a song which I liked very much.   I recited it to my mate, speaking in half-whispers so that the gamblers at the far end of the shack could not hear me.

" A LOVE SONG

" Greater by far than all that men know, or all that men see is this—
   The lingering clasp of a maiden's hand and the warmth of her
     virgin kiss,
   The tresses that cover the pure white brow in many a clustering
     curl,
   And the deep look of honest love in the grey eyes of a girl.

" Because of that I am stronger than death and life is barren no
    more,
   For otherwise wrongs that I hardly feel would sink to the heart's
     deep core,
   For otherwise hope were utterly lost in the endless paths of wrong—
   But only to look in her soft grey eyes—I am strong, I am strong !

Does she love as I love ? I do not know, but all that I know is
    this—
   'Tis enough to stay for an hour at her side and dream awhile of
     her kiss,
   'Tis enough to clasp the hands of her, and 'neath the shade of
     her hair
   To press my lips on her lily brow and leave my kisses there.

" In the dreary days on the vagrant ways whereon my feet have
    trod
   She came as a star to cheer my way, a guiding star from God,
   She came from the dreamy choirs of heaven, lovely and wondrous
     wise,
   And I follow the path that is lighted up by her eyes, her eyes."

" I don't like that song, because I don't know what it is about," said Moleskin when I had finished. " The one about English Bill is far and away better.   When you talk about a man that drops like a spavined mule in the knacker's yard, I know what you mean, but a girl that comes from the dreamy choirs of heaven, wherever they are, is not the kind of wench for a man like you and me, Flynn."

I felt a little disappointed, and made no reply to the criticism of my mate.

" Do you ever think how nice it would be to have a home of your own ? " asked Moleskin after a long silence, and a vigorous puffing at the pipe which he held between his teeth. " It would be fine to have a room to sit in and a nice fire to warm your shins at of an evenin'. I often think how roarin' it would be to sit in a parlour and drink tea with a wife, and have a little child to kiss me as you talk about in the song on the death of English Bill."

I did not like to hear my big-boned, reckless mate talk in such a way. Such talk was too delicate and sentimental for a man like him.

" You're a fool, Joe," I said.

" I suppose I am," he answered. " But just you wait till you come near the turn of life like me, and find a sort of stiffness grippin' on your bones, then you'll maybe have thoughts kind of like these. A young fellow, cully, mayn't care a damn if he is on the dead end, but by God ! it is a different story when you are as stiff as a frozen poker with one foot in the grave and another in hell, Flynn."

" It was a different story the day you met the plough-man, on our journey from Greenock," I said. " You must have changed your mind, Moleskin ? "

" I said things to that ploughman that I didn't exactly believe myself," said my mate. " I would do anything and say anything to get the best of an argument."

Many a strange conversation have I had with Moleskin Joe. One evening when I was seated by the hot-plate engaged in patching my corduroy trousers Joe came up to me with a question which suddenly occurred to him.

I was held to be a sort of learned man, and everybody in the place asked me my views upon this and that, and no one took any heed of my opinions. Most of them acknowledged that I was nearly as great a poet as Two-shift Mullholland, now decently married, and gone from the ranks of the navvies.

" Do you believe in God, Flynn ? " was Joe's question.

" I believe in a God of a sort," I answered. " I believe in the God who plays with a man, as a man plays with a dog, who allows suffering and misery and pain. The ' Holy-Willy ' look on a psalm-singing parson's dial is of no more account to Him than a blister on a beggar's foot."

" I only asked you the question, just as a start-off to tellin' you my own opinion," said Joe. " Sometimes I think one thing about God, and sometimes I think another thing. The song that you wrote about English Bill talks of God takin' care of the soul, and it just came into my head to ask your opinion and tell you my own. As for myself, when I see a man droppin' down like a haltered gin-horse at his work I don't hold much with what parsons say about the goodness of Providence. At other times, when I am tramping about in the lonely night, with the stars out above me and the world kind of holding its breath as if it was afraid of something, I do be thinking that there is a God after all. I'd rather that there is none ; for He is sure to have a heavy tally against me if He puts down all the things I've done. But where is heaven if there is such a place ? "

" I don't know," I replied.

" If you think of it, there is no end to anything," Moleskin went on. " If you could go up above the stars, there is surely a place above them, and another place in turn above that again. You cannot think of a place where there is nothing, and as far as I can see there is no end to anything. You can't think of the last day as they talk about, for that would mean the end of time. It's funny to think of a man sayin' that there'll be no time after such and such a time. How can time stop ? "

I tried to explain to Joe that time and space did not exist, that they were illusions used for practical purposes.

" No man can understand these things," said Joe, as I fumbled through my explanation of the non-existence of time and space. " I have often looked at the little brooks by the roadside and saw the water runnin', runnin', always lookin' the same, and the water different always. When I looked at the little brooks I often felt frightened, because I could not understand them. All these things are the same, and no man can understand them. Why does a brook keep runnin' ? Why do the stars come out at night ? Is there a God in Heaven ? Nobody knows, and a man may puzzle about these things till he's black in the face and grey in the head, but he'll never get any further."

" English Bill may know more about these things than we do," I said.

" How could a dead man know anything ? " asked Joe, and when I could not explain the riddle, he borrowed a shilling from me and lost it at the gaming-table.

That was Joe all over. One moment he was looking for God in Nature, and on the next instant he was looking for a shilling to stake on the gaming-table. Once in an argument with me he called the world " God's gamblin' table," and endeavoured to prove that God threw down men, reptiles, nations, and elements like dice to the earth, one full of hatred for the other and each filled with a desire for supremacy, and that God and His angels watched the great struggle down below, and betted on the result of its ultimate issue.

" Of course the angels will not back Kinlochleven very heavily," he concluded.

CHAPTER XXIX

I WRITE FOR THE PAPERS

" ' Awful Railway Disaster,'
The newspapers chronicle,
The men in the street are buying.
My ! don't the papers sell.
And the editors say in their usual way,
' The story is going well.' "

—From *Songs of the Dead End.*

DAY after day passed and the autumn was waning. The work went on, shift after shift, and most of the money that I earned was spent on the gambling table or in the whisky store. Now and again I wrote home, and sent a few pounds to my people, but I never sent them my address. I did not want to be upbraided for my negligence in sending them so little. The answers to my letters would always be the same: "Send more money; send more money. You'll never have a day's luck if you do not help your parents!" I did not want answers like that, so I never sent my address.

One night towards the end of October I had lost all my money at the gambling school, although Moleskin had twice given me a stake to retrieve my fallen fortunes. I left the shack, went out into the darkness, a fire in my head and emptiness in my heart. Around me the stark mountain peaks rose raggedly against the pale horns of the anæmic moon. Outside the whisky store a crowd of men stood, dark looks on their faces, and the wild blood of mischief behind. Inside each shack a dozen or more gamblers sat cross-legged in circles on the ground, playing banker or brag, and the clink of money could be heard as it passed from hand to hand. Above them the naphtha lamps hissed and spluttered and smelt, the dim, sickly light showed the unwashed and unshaven faces beneath, and the eager eyes that sparkled brightly, seeing nothing but the movements of the game. Down in the cuttings men were labouring on the night-shift, gutting out the bowels of the mountain places, and forcing their way through the fastness steadily, slowly and surely. I could hear the dynamite exploding and shattering to pieces the rock in which it was lodged. The panting of weary hammermen was loud in the darkness, and the rude songs which enlivened the long hours of the night floated up to me from the trough of the hills.

I took my way over the slope of the mountain, over the pigmies who wrought beneath, fighting the great fight which man has to wage eternally against nature. Down in the cuttings I could see my mates toiling amidst the broken earth, the sharp ledges of hewn rock, and the network of gang-planks and straining derricks that rose all around them. The red glare of a hundred evil-smelling torches flared dismally, and over the sweltering men the dark smoke faded away into the rays of the pallid moon. With the rising smoke was mingled the steam of the men's bent shoulders and steaming loins.

Above and over all, the mystery of the night and the desert places hovered inscrutable and implacable. All around the ancient mountains sat like brooding witches, dreaming on their own story of which they knew neither the beginning nor the end. Naked to the four winds of heaven and all the rains of the world, they had stood there for countless ages in all their sinister strength, undefied and unconquered, until man, with puny hands and little tools of labour, came to break the spirit of their ancient mightiness.

And we, the men who braved this task, were outcasts of the world. A blind fate, a vast merciless mechanism, cut and shaped the fabric of our existence. We were men flogged to the work which we had to do, and hounded from the work which we had accomplished. We were men despised when we were most useful, rejected when we were not needed, and forgotten when our troubles weighed upon us heavily. We were the men sent out to fight the spirit of the wastes, rob it of all its primeval horrors, and batter down the barriers of its world-old defences. Where we were working a new town would spring up some day ; it was already springing up, and then, if one of us walked there, " a man with no fixed address," he would be taken up and tried as a loiterer and vagrant.

Even as I thought of these things a shoulder of jagged rock fell into a cutting far below. There was the sound of a scream in the distance, and a song died away in the throat of some rude singer. Then out of the pit I saw men, red with the muck of the deep earth and redder still with the blood of a stricken mate, come forth, bearing between them a silent figure. Another of the pioneers of civilisation had given up his life for the sake of society.

I returned to the shack, and, full of the horror of the tragedy, I wrote an account of it on a scrap of tea-paper. I had no design, no purpose in writing, but I felt compelled to scribble down the thoughts which entered my mind. I wrote rapidly, but soon wearied of my work. I was proceeding to tear up the manuscript when my eye fell on a newspaper which had just come into the shack wrapped around a chunk of mouldy beef. A thought came to me there and then. I would send my account of the tragedy to the editor of that ;paper. It was the

Dawn, a London halfpenny daily. I had never heard of it before.

I had no envelope in my possession. I searched through the shack and found one, dirty, torn, and disreputable in appearance. Amongst all those men there was not another to be found. I did not rewrite my story. Scrawled with pencil on dirty paper, and enclosed in a dirtier envelope, I sent it off to Fleet Street and forgot all about it. But, strange to say, in four days' time I received an answer from the editor of the *Dawn*, asking me to send some more stories of the same kind, and saying that he was prepared to pay me two guineas for each contribution accepted.

The acceptance of my story gave me no great delight ; I often went into greater enthusiasm over a fight in the Kinlochleven ring. But outside a fight or a stiff game of cards, there are few things which cause me to become excited. My success as a writer discomfited me a little even. I at first felt that I was committing some sin against my mates. I was working on a shift which they did not understand ; and men look with suspicion on things beyond their comprehension. A man may make money at a fight, a gaming table or at a shift, but the man who made money with a dirty pencil and a piece of dirty paper was an individual who had no place in my mates' scheme of things.

For all that, the editor's letter created great stir amongst my mates. It passed round the shack and was so dirty on coming back that I couldn't read a word of it. Red Billy said that he could not understand it, and that I must have copied what I had written from some other paper. Moleskin Joe said that I was the smartest man he had ever met, by cripes ! I was. He took great pleasure in calling me " that mate of mine " ever afterwards. Old Sandy MacDonald, who had come from the Isle of Skye, and who was wasting slowly away, said that he knew a young lad like me who went from the Highlands to London and made his fortune by writing for the papers.

"He had no other wark but writin', and he made his fortune," Sandy asserted, and everyone except myself laughed at this. It was such a funny thing to hear old Sandy make his first joke, my mates thought. A man to earn his living by writing for the papers! Whoever heard of such a thing?

In all I wrote five articles for the *Dawn*, then found that I could write no more. I had told five truthful and exciting incidents of my navvying life, and I was not clever enough to tell lies about it. Ten guineas came to me from Fleet Street. Six of these I sent home to my own people, and for the remainder I purchased many an hour's joy in the whisky store and many a night's life-giving excitement at the gaming table.

I sent my address home with the letter, and when my mother replied she was so full of her grievances that she had no time to enquire if I had any of my own. Another child had been born, and the family in all now consisted of thirteen.

CHAPTER XXX

WINTER

" Do you mind the nights we laboured, boys, together,
  Spreadeagled at our travail on the joists,
  With the pulley-wheels a-turning and the naphtha lamps
    a-burning,
  And the mortar crawling upwards on the hoists,
  When our hammers clanked like blazes on the facing,
  When the trestles shook and staggered as we struck,
  When the derricks on their pivots strained and broke the
    crank-wheel rivets
  As the shattered jib sank heavy in the muck ? "

—From *Songs of the Dead End.*

THE winter was at hand. When the night drew near, a great weariness came over the face of the sun as it sank down behind the hills which had seen a million sunsets. The autumn had been mild and gentle, its breezes soft, its showers light and cool. But now, slowly and surely, the great change was taking place ; a strange stillness settled softly on the lonely places. Nature waited breathless on the threshold of some great event, holding her hundred winds suspended in a fragile leash. The heather bells hung motionless on their stems, the torrents dropped silently as smoke from the scarred edges of the desolate ravines, but in this silence there lay a menace ; in its supreme poise was the threat of coming danger. The crash of our hammers was an outrage, and the exploding dynamite a sacrilege against tired nature.

A great weariness settled over us ; our life lacked colour, we were afraid of the silence, the dulness of the surrounding mountains weighed heavily on our souls. The sound of labour was a comfort, the thunder of our hammers went up as a threat against the vague implacable portent of the wild.

Life to me had now become dull, expressionless, stupid. Only in drink was there contentment, only in a fight was there excitement. I hated the brown earth, the slushy muck and gritty rock, but in the end hatred died out and I was almost left without passion or longing. My life now had no happiness and no great sadness. My soul was proof against sorrow as it was against joy. Happiness and woe were of no account; life was a spread of brown muck, without any relieving splash of lighter or darker colours. For all that, I had no great desire (desire was almost dead even) to go down to the Lowlands and look for a newer job. So I stayed amidst the brown muck and existed.

When I had come up my thoughts for a long while were eternally straying to Norah Ryan, but in the end she became to me little more than a memory, a frail and delightful phantom of a fleeting dream.

The coming of winter was welcome. The first nipping frost was a call to battle, and, though half afraid, most of the men were willing to accept the challenge. A few, it is true, went off to Glasgow, men old and feeble who were afraid of the coming winter.

In the fight to come the chances were against us. Rugged cabins with unplanked floors, leaking roofs, flimsy walls, through the chinks of which the winds cut like knives, meagre blankets, mouldy food, well-worn clothes, and battered bluchers were all that we possessed to aid us in the struggle. On the other hand, the winter marshalled all her forces, the wind, the hail, frost, snow, and rain, and it was against these that we had to fight, and for the coming of the opposing legions we waited tensely and almost eagerly.

But the north played a wearing game, and strove to harry us out with suspense before thundering down upon us with her cold and her storm. The change took place slowly. In a day we could hardly feel it, in a week something intangible and subtle, something which could not be defined, had crept into our lives. We felt the change, but could not localise it. Our spirits sank under the uncertainty of the waiting days, but still the wild held her hand. The bells of the heather hung from their stems languidly and motionless, stripped of all their summer charm, but lacking little of the hue of summer. Even yet the foam-flecked waters dropped over the cliffs silently as figures that move in a dream. When we gathered together and ate our midday meal, we wrapped our coats around our shoulders, whereas before we had sat down without them. When night came on we drew nearer to the hot-plate, and when we turned naked into bed we found that the blankets were colder than usual. Only thus did the change affect us for a while. Then the cold snap came suddenly and wildly.

The plaintive sunset waned into a sickly haze one evening, and when the night slipped upwards to the mountain peaks never a star came out into the vastness of the high heavens. Next morning we had to thaw the door of our shack out of the muck into which it was frozen during the night. Outside the snow had fallen heavily on the ground, and the virgin granaries of winter had been emptied on the face of the world.

Unkempt, ragged, and dispirited, we slunk to our toil, the snow falling on our shoulders and forcing its way insistently through our worn and battered bluchers. The cuttings were full of slush to the brim, and we had to grope through them with our hands until we found the jumpers and hammers at the bottom. These we held under our coats until the heat of our bodies warmed them, then we went on with our toil.

At intervals during the day the winds of the mountain put their heads together and swept a whirlstorm of snow down upon us, wetting each man to the pelt. Our tools froze until the hands that gripped them were scarred as if by red-hot spits. We shook uncertain over our toil, our sodden clothes scalding and itching the skin with every movement of the swinging hammers. Near at hand the lean derrick jibs whirled on their pivots like spectres of some ghoulish carnival, and the muck-barrows crunched backwards and forwards, all their dirt and rust hidden in woolly mantles of snow. Hither and thither the little black figures of the workers moved across the waste of whiteness like shadows on a lime-washed wall. Their breath steamed out on the air and disappeared in space like the evanescent and fragile vapour of frying mushrooms.

" On a day like this a man could hardly keep warm on the red-hot hearth of hell ! " Moleskin remarked at one time, when the snow whirled around the cutting, causing us to gasp with every fiercely-taken breath.

" Ye'll have a heat on the same hearthstone some day," answered Red Billy, who held a broken lath in one mittened hand, while he whittled away with his eternal clasp-knife.

When night came on we crouched around the hot-plate and told stories of bygone winters, when men dropped frozen stiff in the trenches where they laboured. A few tried to gamble near the door, but the wind that cut through the chinks of the walls chased them to the fire. Moleskin told the story of his first meeting with me on the Paisley toll-road, and suddenly I realised that I was growing old. It was now some years since that meeting took place, and even then I was a man, unaided and alone, fighting the great struggle of existence. I capped Moleskin's story with the account of Mick Deehan's death on the six-foot way. Afterwards the men talked loudly of many adventures. Long lonely shifts were spoken of, nights and days when the sweat turned to ice on the eyelashes, when the cold nipped to the bone and chilled the workers at their labours. One man slipped off the snow-covered gang-plank and fell like a rock forty feet through space.

" Flattened out like a jelly-fish on the groun' he was," said Clancy, who told the story.

Red Billy, who worked on the railway line in his younger days, gave an account of Mick Cassidy's death. Mick was sent out to free the ice-locked facing points, and when they were closed by the signalman, Cassidy's hand got wedged between the blades and the rail.

" Held like a louse was Cassidy, until the train threw him clear," concluded Billy, adding reflectively that " he might have been saved if he had had somethin' in one hand to hack the other hand off with."

Joe told how one Ned Farley got his legs wedged between the planks of a mason's scaffold and hung there head downwards for three hours. When Farley got relieved he was a raving madman, and died two hours afterwards. We all agreed that death was the only way out in a case like that.

Gahey told of a night's doss at the bottom of a coal ship in a railway siding. He slept there with three other people, two men and a woman. As the woman was a bad one it did not matter very much to anyone where she slept. During the night a waggon of coal was suddenly shot down the ship. Gahey got clear, leaving his thumb with the three corpses which remained behind.

" It was a bad endin', even for a woman like that," someone said.

Outside the winds of the night scampered madly, whistling through every crevice of the shack and threatening to smash all its timbers to pieces. We bent closer over the hot-plate, and the many who could not draw near to the heat scrambled into bed and sought warmth under the meagre blankets. Suddenly the lamp went out, and a darkness crept into the corners of the dwelling, causing the figures of my mates to assume fantastic shapes in the gloom. The circle around the hot-plate drew closer, and long lean arms were stretched out towards the flames and the redness. Seldom may a man have the chance to look on hands like those of my mates. Fingers were missing from many, scraggy scars seaming along the wrists or across the palms of others told of accidents which had taken place on many precarious shifts. The faces near me were those of ghouls worn out in some unholy midnight revel. Sunken eyes glared balefully in the dim unearthly light of the fire, and as I looked at them a moment's terror settled on my soul. For a second I lived in an early age, and my mates were the cave-dwellers of an older world than mine. In the darkness, near the door, a pipe glowed brightly for a moment, then the light went suddenly out and the gloom settled again. The reaction came when Two-shift Mullholland's song, *The Bold Navvy Man*, was sung by Clancy of the Cross. We joined lustily in the chorus, and the roof shook with the thunder of our voices.

" THE BOLD NAVVY MAN.

" I've navvied here in Scotland, I've navvied in the south,
Without a drink to cheer me or a crust to cross me mouth,
I fed when I was workin' and starved when out on tramp,
And the stone has been me pillow and the moon above me lamp.
I have drunk me share and over when I was flush with tin,
For the drouth without was nothin' to the drouth that burned
    within !
And where'er I've filled me billy and where'er I've drained me can,
I've done it like a navvy, a bold navvy man.
         A bold navvy man,
         An old navvy man,
And I've done me graft and stuck it like a bold navvy man.

" I've met a lot of women and I liked them all a spell—
They drive some men to drinkin' and also some to hell,
But I have never met her yet, the woman cute who can
Learn a trick to Old Nick or the bold navvy man.
Oh ! the sly navvy man,
And the fly navvy man,
Sure a woman's always runnin' to the bold navvy man.

" I do not care for ladies grand who are of high degree,
A winsome wench and willin', she is just the one for me,
Drink and love are classed as sins, as mortal sins by some,
I'll drink and drink whene'er I can, the drouth is sure to come—
And I will love till lusty life runs out its mortal span,
The end of which is in the ditch for many a navvy man.
The bold navvy man,
The old navvy man,
Safe in a ditch with heels cocked up, so dies the navvy man.

" I've splashed a thousand models red and raised up fiery Cain
From Glasgow down to Dover Pier and back that road again ;
I've fought me man for hours on end, stark naked to the buff
And me and him, we never knew when we had got enough.
'Twas skin and hair all flyin' round and red blood up and out,
And me or him could hardly tell what brought the fight about.—
'Tis wenches, work and fight and fun and drink whene'er I can
That makes the life of stress and strife as suits the navvy man !

" Let her go, boys ; let her go now ! " roared Clancy,
rising to his feet, kicking a stray frying-pan and causing
it to clatter across the shack. " All together, boys ; damn
you, all together !

" Then hurrah ! ev'ry one
For the bold navvy man,
For fun and fight are damned all right for any navvy man ! "

Even old Sandy MacDonald joined in the chorus with
his weak and querulous voice. The winter was touching
him sharply, and he was worse off than any of us. Along
with the cold he had his wasting disease to battle against,
and God alone knew how he managed to work along with
his strong and lusty mates on the hammer squad at Kinlochleven. Sandy was not an old man, but what with the
dry cough that was in his throat and the shivers of cold

that came over him after a long sweaty shift, it was easily
seen that he had not many months to live in this world.
He looked like a parcel of bones covered with brown
withered parchment and set in the form of a man. How
life could remain fretting within such a frame as his was
a mystery which I could not solve. Almost beyond the
effects of heat or cold, the cold sweat came out of his
skin on the sweltering warm days, and when the winter
came along, the chilly weather hardly made him colder
than he was by nature. His cough never kept silent;
sometimes it was like the bark of a dog, at other times
it seemed as if it would carry the very entrails out of
the man. In the summer he spat blood with it, but usually
it was drier than the east wind.

At one period of his life Sandy had had a home and a wife
away down in Greenock; but in those days he was a strong
lusty fellow, fit to pull through a ten-hour shift without
turning a hair. One winter's morning he came out from
the sugar refinery, in which he worked, steaming hot from
the long night's labour, and then the cold settled on him.
Being a sober, steady-going man, he tried to work as long
as he could lift his arms, but in the end he had to give
up the job which meant life and home to him. One by
one his little bits of things went to the pawnshop; but all
the time he struggled along bravely, trying to keep the
roof-tree over his head and his door shut against the lean
spectre of hunger. Between the four bare walls of the
house Sandy's wife died one day; and this caused the
man to break up his home.

He came to Kinlochleven at the heel of the summer,
and because he mastered his cough for a moment when
asking for a job, Red Billy Davis started him on the
jumper squad. The old ganger, despite his swearing
habits and bluntness of discourse, was at heart a very
good-natured fellow. Sandy stopped with us for a long

while and it was pitiful to see him labouring there, his old bones creaking with every move of his emaciated body, and the cold sweat running off him all day. He ate very little ; the tame robin which flitted round our shack nearly picked as much from off the floor. He had a bunk to himself at the corner of the shack, and there he coughed out the long sleepless hours of the night, bereft of all hope, lacking sympathy from any soul sib to himself, and praying for the grave which would end all his troubles. For days at a stretch he lay supine in his bed, unable to move hand or foot, then, when a moment's relief came to him, he rose and started on his shift again, crawling out with his mates like a wounded animal.

Winter came along and Sandy got no better ; he could hardly grow worse and remain alive. Life burned in him like a dying candle in a ruined house, and he waited for the end of the great martyrdom patiently. Still, when he could, he kept working day in and day out, through cold and wet and storm. Heaven knows that it was not work which he needed, but care, rest, and sympathy. All of us expressed pity for the man, and helped him in little ways, trying to make life easier for him. Moleskin usually made gruel for him, while I read the *Oban Times* to the old fellow whenever that paper came into the shack. One evening as I read something concerning the Isle of Skye Sandy burst into tears, like a homesick child.

" Man ! I would like tae dee there awa' in the Isle of Skye," he said to me in a yearning voice.

" Die, you damned old fool, you ? " exclaimed Joe, who happened to come around with a pot of gruel just at that moment and overheard Sandy's remark. " You'll not die for years yet. I never saw you lookin' so well in all your life."

" It's all over with me, Moleskin," said poor Sandy. " It's a great wonder that I've stood it so long, but just now the thocht came to me that I'd like tae dee awa' back in my own place in the Isle of Skye. If I could just save as muckle siller as would take me there, I'd be content enough."

"Some people are content with hellish little!" said Joe angrily. "You've got to buck up, man, for there's a good time comin', though you'll never—I mean that ev'rything will come right in the end. We'll see that you get home all right, you fool, you!"

Joe was ashamed to find himself guilty of any kind impulse, and he endeavoured to hide his good intentions behind rough words. When he called Sandy an old fool Sandy's eyes sparkled, and he got into such good humour that he joined in the chorus of the *Bold Navvy Man* when Clancy, who is now known as Clancy of the Cross, gave bellow to Mullholland's *magnum opus*.

Early on the morning of the next day, which was pay-day, Moleskin was busy at work sounding the feelings of the party towards a great scheme which he had in mind; and while waiting at the pay-office when the day's work was completed, Joe made the following speech to Red Billy's gang, all of whom, with the exception of Sandy MacDonald, were present.

"Boys, Sandy MacDonald wants to go home and die in his own place," said Joe, weltering into his subject at once. "He'll kick the bucket soon, for he has the look of the grave in his eyes. He only wants as much tin as will take him home, and that is not much for any man to ask, is it? So what do you say, boys, to a collection for him, a shillin' a man, or whatever you can spare? Maybe some day, when you turn respectable, one of you can say to yourself, 'I once kept myself from gettin' drunk, by givin' some of my money to a man who needed it more than myself.' Now, just look at him comin' across there."

We looked in the direction of Joe's outstretched finger and saw Sandy coming towards us, his rags fluttering around him like the duds of a Michaelmas scarecrow.

"Isn't he a pitiful sight!" Moleskin went on. "He looks like the Angel of Death out on the prowl! It's a God's charity to help a man like Sandy and make him happy as we are ourselves. We are at home here; he is not. So it is up to us to help him out of the place. Boys, listen to me!" Moleskin's voice sank into an intense whisper. "If every damned man of you don't pay a shillin' into this collection I'll look for the man that doesn't, and I'll knuckle his ribs until he pays for booze for ev'ry man in Billy's shack, by God! I will."

Everyone paid up decently, and on behalf of the gang I was asked to present the sum of three pounds fifteen shillings to Sandy MacDonald. Sandy began to cry like a baby when he got the money into his hands, and every man in the job called out involuntarily: "Oh! you old fool, you!"

Pay-day was on Saturday. On Monday morning Sandy intended starting out on his journey home. All Saturday night he coughed out the long hours of the darkness, but in the morning he looked fit and well.

"You'll come through it, you fool!" said Moleskin. "I'll be dead myself afore you."

On the next night he went to bed early, and as we sat around the gaming table we did not hear the racking cough which had torn at the man's chest for months.

"He's getting better," we all said.

"Feeling all right, Sandy?" I asked, as I turned into bed.

"Mon! I'm feelin' fine now," he answered. "I'm goin' to sleep well to-night, and I'll be fit for the journey in the morn."

That night Sandy left us for good. When the morning

came we found the poor wasted fellow lying dead in his bunk, his eyes wide open, his hands closed tightly, and the long finger-nails cutting into the flesh of the palm. The money which we gave to the man was bound up in a little leathern purse tied round his neck with a piece of string.

The man was very light and it was an easy job to carry him in the little black box and place him in his home below the red earth of Kinlochleven. The question as to what should be done with the money arose later. I suggested that it should be used in buying a little cross for Sandy's grave.

" If the dead man wants a cross he can have one," said Moleskin Joe. And because of what he said and because it was more to our liking, we put the money up as a stake on the gaming table. Clancy won the pile, because his luck was good on the night of the game.

That is our reason for calling him Clancy of the Cross ever since.

The winter rioted on its way. Snow, rain, and wind whirled around us in the cutting, and wet us to the bone. It was a difficult feat to close our hands tightly over the hammers with which we took uncertain aim at the drill heads and jumper ends. The drill holder cowered on his seat and feared for the moment when an erring hammer might fly clear and finish his labours for ever. Hourly our tempers grew worse, each movement of the body caused annoyance and discomfort, and we quarrelled over the most trivial matters. Red Billy cursed every man in turn and all in general, until big Jim Maloney lost his temper completely and struck the ganger on the jaw with his fist, knocking him senseless into a snowdrift.

That night Maloney was handed his lying time and told to slide. He padded from Kinlochleven in the darkness, and I have never seen him since then. He must have died on the journey. No man could cross those mountains

R

in the darkness of mid-winter and in the teeth of a snow-storm.

Some time afterwards the copy of a Glasgow newspaper, either the *Evening Times* or *News* (I now forget which), came into our shack wrapped around some provisions, and in the paper I read a paragraph concerning the discovery of a dead body on the mountains of Argyllshire. While looking after sheep a shepherd came on the corpse of a man that lay rotting in a thawing snowdrift. Around the remains a large number of half-burnt matches were picked up, and it was supposed that the poor fellow had tried to keep himself warm by their feeble flames in the last dreadful hours. Nobody identified him, but the paper stated that he was presumably a navvy who lost his way on a journey to or from the big waterworks of Kinlochleven.

As for myself, I am quite certain that it was that of big Jim Maloney. No man could survive a blizzard on the houseless hills, and big Jim Maloney never appeared in model or shack afterwards.

CHAPTER XXXI

THE GREAT EXODUS

'We'll lift our time and go, lads,
  The long road lies before,
The places that we know, lads,
  Will know our like no more.
Foot forth! the last bob's paid out,
  Some see their last shift through,
But the men who are not played out
  Have other jobs to do."

—From *Tramp Navvies.*

'TWAS towards the close of a fine day on the following summer that we were at work in the dead end of a cutting, Moleskin and I, when I, who had been musing on the quickly passing years, turned to Moleskin and quoted a line from the Bible.

" Our years pass like a tale that is told," I said.

" Like a tale that is told damned bad," answered my mate, picking stray crumbs of tobacco from his waistcoat pocket and stuffing them into the heel of his pipe. " It's a strange world, Flynn. Here to-day, gone to-morrow; always waitin' for a good time comin' and knowin' that it will never come. We work with one mate this evenin', we beg for crumbs with another on the mornin' after. It's a bad life ours, and a poor one, when I come to think of it, Flynn."

" It is all·that," I assented heartily.

" Look at me ! " said Joe, clenching his fists and squaring his shoulders. " I must be close on forty years, maybe on the graveyard side of it, for all I know. I've horsed it since ever I can mind; I've worked like a mule for years, and what have I to show for it all to-day, matey? Not the price of an ounce of tobacco! A midsummer scarecrow wouldn't wear the duds that I've to wrap around my hide! A cockle-picker that has no property only when the tide is out is as rich as I am. Not the price of an ounce of tobacco! There is something wrong with men like us, surely, when we're treated like swine in a sty for all the years of our life. It's not so bad here, but it's in the big towns that a man can feel it most. No person cares for the likes of us, Flynn. I've worked nearly ev'rywhere; I've helped to build bridges, dams, houses, ay, and towns! When they were finished, what happened? Was it for us—the men who did the buildin'—to live in the homes that we built, or walk through the streets that we laid down? No earthly chance of that! It was always, 'Slide! we don't need you any more,' and then a man like me, as helped to build a thousand houses big as castles, was hellish glad to get the shelter of a ten-acre field and a shut gate between me and the winds of night. I've spent all my money, have I? It's bloomin' easy to spend all that fellows like us can earn. When I was in London I saw a lady spend as much on fur to decorate her carcase with as would keep me in beer and tobacco for all the rest of my life. And that same lady would decorate a dog in ribbons and fol-the-dols, and she wouldn't give me the smell of a crust when I asked her for a mouthful of bread. What could you expect from a woman who wears the furry hide of some animal round her neck, anyhow? We are not thought as much of as dogs, Flynn. By God! them rich buckos do eat an awful lot. Many a time I crept up to a window just to see them gorgin' themselves."

"I have often done the same kind of thing," I said.

"Most men do,". answered Joe. "You've heard of old Moses goin' up the hill to have a bit peep at the

Promist Land. He was just like me and you, Flynn, wantin' to have a peep at the things which he'd never lay his claws on."

" Those women who sit half-naked at the table have big appetites," I said.

" They're all gab and guts, like young crows," said Moleskin. " And they think more of their dogs than they do of men like me and you. I'm an Antichrist ! "

" A what ? "

" One of them sort of fellows as throws bombs at kings."

" You mean an Anarchist."

" Well, whatever they are, I'm one. What is the good of kings, of fine-feathered ladies, of churches, of anything in the country, to men like me and you ? One time, 'twas when I started trampin' about, I met an old man on the road and we mucked about, the two of us as mates, for months afterwards. One night in the winter time, as we were sleepin' under a hedge, the old fellow got sick, and he began to turn over and over on his beddin' of frost and his blankets of snow, which was not the best place to put a sick man, as you know yourself. As the night wore on, he got worse and worse. I tried to do the best I could for the old fellow, gave him my muffler and my coat, but the pains in his guts was so much that I couldn't hardly prevent him from rollin' along the ground on his stomach. He would do anythin' just to take his mind away from the pain that he was sufferin'. At last I got him to rise and walk, and we trudged along till we came to a house by the roadside. 'Twas nearly midnight and there was a light in one of the windows, so I thought that I would call at the door and ask for a bit of help. My mate, who bucked up somewhat when we were walkin', got suddenly worse again, and fell against the gatepost near beside the road, and stuck there as if glued on to the thing. I left him by himself and went up to the door and knocked.

A man drew the bolts and looked out at me. He had his collar on back to front, so I knew that he was a clergyman.

"' What do you want ? ' he asked.

"' My mate's dyin' on your gatepost,' I said.

"' Then you'd better take him away from here,' said the parson.

"' But he wants help,' I said. ' He can't go a step further, and if you could give me a drop of brandy——'

" I didn't get any further with my story. The fellow whistled for his dog, and a big black animal came boundin' through the passage and started snarlin' when it saw me standin' there in the doorway.

"' Now, you get away from here,' said the clergyman to me.

"' My mate's dyin','I said.

"' Seize him,' said the man to the dog."

" What a scoundrel that man must have been," I said, interrupting Moleskin in the midst of his story.

" He was only a human being, and that's about as bad as a man can be," said Joe. " Anyway, he put the dog on me and the animal bounded straight at the thick of my leg, but that animal didn't know that it was up against Moleskin Joe. I caught hold of the dog by the throat and twisted its throttle until it snapped like a dry stick. Then I lifted the dead thing up in my arms and threw it right into the face of the man who was standin' in the hallway.

"' Take that an' be thankful that the worst dog of the two of you is not dead,' I shouted. ' And when it comes to a time that sees you hangin' on the lower cross-bars of the gates of heaven, waitin' till you get in, may you be kept there till I give the word for you to pass through.'

" My mate was still hangin' on the gatepost when I came back, and he was as dead as a maggot. I could do nothin' for a dead man, so I went on my own, leavin' him hangin' there like a dead crow in a turnip field. Next mornin' a cop lifted me and I was charged with assaultin' a minister and killin' his dog. I got three months hard, and it was hard to tell whether for hittin' the man or killin' the dog. Anyway, the fellow got free, although he allowed a man to die at his own doorstep. I never liked clergy before, and I hate them ever since; but I know, as you know, that it's not for the likes of you and me that they work for."

"Time to stop lookin' at your work, boys!" interrupted Red Billy, as he approached us, carrying his watch and eternal clasp-knife in his hands. "Be damned to you, you could look at your work all day, you love it so much. But when you go to the pay-office to-night, you'll hear a word or two that will do you good, you will!"

On arriving at the pay-office, every man in turn was handed his lying time and told that his services were no longer required. Red Billy passed the money out through the window of the shack which served as money-box. Moleskin came after me, and he carefully counted the money handed to him.

"Half-a-crown wrong in your tally, old cock," he said to Red Billy. "Fork out the extra two-and-a-tanner, you unsanctified, chicken-chested cheat. I didn't think that it was in your carcase to cheat a man of his lyin' time."

"No cheatin'," said Billy.

"Well, what the hell——!"

"No cheatin'," interrupted Billy.

"I'm two-and-a-tanner short——"

"No cheatin'," piped Billy maliciously.

"I'll burst your nut, you parrot-faced, gawky son of a Pontius Pilate, if you don't fork out my full lyin' time!" roared Moleskin.

" I always charge two-and-six for a pair of boots and the same for a clasp-knife," said the ganger.

Billy had a long memory, and Joe was cornered and crestfallen. I, myself, had almost forgotten about the knife which Joe had lifted from Red Billy on the morning of our arrival in Kinlochleven, and Joe had almost lost memory of it as well.

" I had the best of that bargain," Red Billy went on sweetly. " The knife was on its last legs and I just intended to buy a new one. A half-crown was a good penny for a man like me to spend, so I thought that if Moleskin paid for it, kind of quiet like, it would be a very nice thing for me—a—very—nice—thing—for—me."

" I grant that you have the best of me this time," said Moleskin, and a smile passed over his face. " But my turn will come next, you know. I wouldn't like to do you any serious harm, Billy, but I must get my own back. I have only to look for that old woman of yours and send her after you. I can get her address easy enough, and I have plenty of time to look for it. You don't care much for your old wife, Billy, do you ? "

Billy made no answer. It was rumoured that his wife was a woman with a tongue and a temper, and that Billy feared her and spent part of his time in endeavouring to get out of her way. Joe was working upon this rumour now, and the ganger began to look uncomfortable.

" Of course, if I get my half-crown and another to boot, I'll not trouble to look for the woman," said Joe. " It won't be hard to find her. She'll have gone back to her own people, and it is well known that they belong to Paisley. Her brothers are all fightin' men, and ready to maul the man that didn't play fairly with their own blood relations. By God ! they'll give you a maulin', Billy, when I send them after you. They'll come up here, and further, until they find you out. You'll have to shank it when they come, run like hell, in fact, and lose your job and your lyin' time. If you give me seven-and-six I'll not give you away ! "

" I'll give you the half-crown," said Billy.

" I'm losin' my time talkin' to you," said Joe pleasantly, and he pulled out his watch. " Every minute I stop here I'm goin' to put my charge up a shillin'."

" I'll give you the five shillin's if you go away and keep clear of Paisley," growled the ganger. " Five shillin's ! you damned cheat ! Are you not content with that ? "

" One minute," said Joe solemnly. " Eight-and-six."

" My God ! " Billy cried. " You're goin' to rob me. I'll give you the seven-and-six."

We were heartily enjoying it. There were over one hundred men looking on, and Joe, now master of the strained situation, kept looking steadfastly at his watch, as if nothing else in the world mattered.

" Two minutes ; nine-and-six," he said at the end of the stated time.

" Here's your nine-and-six ! " roared Billy, passing some silver coins through the grating. " Here, take it and be damned to you ! "

Joe put the money in his pocket, cast a benevolent glance at Billy, and my mate and I went out from Kinlochleven. We did not go into the shack which we had occupied for over a year. There was nothing there belonging to us, all our property was on our backs or in our pockets, so we turned away straight from the pay-office and took to the road again.

The great procession filed down the hillside. Hundreds of men had been paid off on the same evening. The job was nearly completed, and only a few hands were required to finish the remainder of the labour. Some men decided to stay, but a great longing took possession of them at the last moment, and they followed those who were already on the road.

Civilisation again ! Away behind the hunchbacked mountains the sunset flamed in all its colours. Islands of jasper were enshrined in lakes of turquoise, rivers of blood flowed through far-spreading plains of dark cumulus that were enshrouded in the spell of eternal silence. Overhead the blue was of the deepest, save where one stray cloud blushed to find itself alone in the vastness of the high heavens.

We were an army of scarecrows, ragged, unkempt scare crows of civilisation. We came down from Kinlochleven in the evening with the glow of the setting sun full in our faces, and never have I looked on an array of men such as we were. Some were old, lame men who might not live until they obtained their next job, and who would surely drop at their post when they obtained it. These were the veterans of labour, crawling along limply in the rear, staggering over boulders and hillocks, men who were wasted in the long struggle and who were now bound for a new place—a place where a man might die. They had built their last town and were no longer wanted there or anywhere else. Strong lusty fellows like myself took the lead. We possessed hale and supple limbs, and a mile or two of a journey meant very little to any of us.

Now and again I looked behind at the followers. The great army spread out in the centre and tailed away towards the end. A man at the rear sat down and took a stone out of his boot. His comrades helped him to his feet when he had finished his task. He was a very old, decrepit, and weary man ; the look of death was in his eyes, but he wanted to walk on. Maybe he would sit down again at the foot of the mountain. Maybe he would sleep there, for further down the night breezes were warmer, much warmer, than the cold winds on the hillside. Probably the old fellow thought of these things as he tumbled down the face of the mountain ; and perhaps he knew that death was waiting for him at the bottom.

Some sang as they journeyed along. They sang about love, about drink, about women and gambling. Most of us joined in the singing. Maybe the man at the rear sang none, but we could not hear him if he did, he was so far behind.

The sun paled out and hid behind a hump of the mountain. Overhead a few stars twinkled mockingly. In the distance the streams could be heard falling over the cliffs. Still the mountain vomited out the human throng, and over all the darkness of the night settled slowly.

What did the men think of as they walked down from Kinlochleven ? It is hard to say, for the inmost thoughts of a most intimate friend are hidden from us, for they lack expression and cannot be put into words. As to myself, I found that my thoughts were running back to Norah Ryan and the evenings we spent on the shores of the Clyde. I was looking backward ; I had no thoughts, no plans, for the future.

I was now almost careless of life, indifferent towards fortune, and the dreams of youth had given place to a placid acceptance of stern realities. On the way up to the hills I had longed for things beyond my reach—wealth, comfort, and the love of fair women. But these longings had now given place to an almost unchanging calm, an indifference towards women, and an almost stoical outlook on the things that are. Nothing was to me pleasurable, nothing made me sad. During the last months in Kinlochleven I had very little desire for drink or cards, but true to custom I gave up neither. With no man except Moleskin did I exchange confidences, and even these were of the very slightest. To the rest of my mates I was always the same, except perhaps in the whisky saloon or in a fight. They thought me very strong in person and in character, but when I pried deeply into my own nature I found that I was full of vanity and weaknesses. The heat of a good fire after a hard day's work caused me to feel happier; hunger made me sour, a good meal made me cheerful. One day I was fit for any work; the next day I was lazy and heedless, and at times I so little resembled myself that I might be taken for a man of an entirely opposite character. Still, the river cannot be expected to take on the same form in shine as in shadow, in level as in steep, and in fall as in freshet. I am a creature of environment, an environment that is eternally changing. Not being a stone or clod, I change with it. I was a man of many humours, of many inconsistencies. The pain of a corn changed my outlook on life. Moleskin himself was sometimes disgusting in my sight; at other times I was only happy in his company. But all the time I was the same in the eyes of my mates, stolid, unsympathetic, and cold. In the end most of my moods went, and although I had mapped out no course of conduct, I settled into a temperate contentment, which, though far removed from gladness, had no connection with melancholy.

Since I came to Kinlochleven I had not looked on a woman, and the thoughts of womankind had almost entirely gone from my mind. With the rest of the men it was the same. The sexual instinct was almost dead in them. Women were merely dreams of long ago; they were so long out of sight that the desire for their company had almost expired in every man of us. Still, it was strange that I should think of Norah Ryan as I trudged down the hillside from Kinlochleven.

The men were still singing out their songs, and Joe hummed the chorus through the teeth that held his empty pipe as he walked along.

Suddenly the sound of singing died and Moleskin ceased

his bellowing chorus. A great silence fell on the party. The nailed shoes rasping on the hard earth, and the half-whispered curse of some falling man as he tripped over a hidden boulder, were the only sounds that could be heard in the darkness.

And down the face of the mountain the ragged army tramped slowly on.

CHAPTER XXXII

A NEW JOB

" The more you do, the more you get to do."
—Cold Clay Philosophy.

WHEN we arrived in Glasgow I parted company with Moleskin Joe. I told him that I was going to work on the railway if I got an opening, but my mate had no liking for a job where the pay could be only lifted once a fortnight ; he wanted his sub. every second day at least. He set out for the town of Carlisle. There was a chance of getting a real job there, he said.

" Mind you, if there's a chance goin' for another man, I'll let you know about it," he added. " I would like you to come and work along with me, matey, for me and you get on well together. Keep clear of women and always stand up to your man until he knocks you out—that's if you're gettin' the worst of the fight."

We parted without a handshake, as is the custom with us navvy men. He never wrote to me, for I had no address when he left, and he did not know the exact model to which he was going. Once out of each other's sight, the link that bound us together was broken, and being homeless men we could not correspond. Perhaps we would never meet again.

I got a job on the railway and obtained lodgings in a dismal and crooked street, which was a den of disfigured children and a hothouse of precocious passion, in the south side of Glasgow. The landlady was an Irishwoman, bearded like a man, and the mother of several children. When indoors, she spent most of her time feeding one child, while swearing like a carter at all the others. We slept in the one room, mother, children and myself, and all through the night the children yelled like cats in the moonshine. The house was alive with vermin. The landlady's husband was a sailor who went out on ships to foreign parts and always returned drunk from his voyages. When at home he remained drunk all the time, and when he left again he was as drunk as he could hold. I had no easy job to put up with him at first, and in the end we quarrelled and fought. He accused me of being too intimate with his wife when he was away from home. I told him that my taste was not so utterly bad, for indeed I had no inclination towards any woman, let alone the hairy and unkempt person who was my landlady. I struck out for him on the stair head. Three flights of stairs led from the door of the house down to the ground floor. I threw the sailor down the last flight bodily and headlong; he threw me down the middle flight. Following the last throw, he would not face up again, and I had won the fight. Afterwards the woman came to her husband's aid. She scratched my face with her fingers and tore at my hair, clawing like an angry cat. I did not like to strike her back, so I left her there with her drunken sailor and went out to the streets. Having no money I slept until morning beside a capstan on Glasgow quay. Next day I obtained lodgings in Moran's model, and I stopped there until I went off to London eleven months afterwards.

I did not find much pleasure in the company of my new railway mates. They were a spineless and ignorant crowd of men, who believed in clergycraft, psalm-singing, and hymn-hooting Not one of them had the pluck to raise his hands in a stand-up fight, or his voice in protest against the conditions under which he laboured. Most of them raised their caps to the overseers who controlled their starved bodies and to the clergy who controlled their starved souls. They had no rational doctrine, no comprehension of a just God. To them God took on the form of a monstrous and irritable ganger who might be pacified by prayers instead of by the usual dole of drink.

Martin Rudor was the name of my new ganger. He was very religious and belonged to the Railway Mission (whatever that is). He read tracts at his work, which he handed round when he finished perusing them. These contained little stories about the engine-driver who had taken the wrong turning, or the signalman who operated the facing points on the running line leading to hell. Martin took great pleasure in these stories, and he was an earnest supporter of the psalm-singing enthusiasts who raised a sound of devilry by night in the back streets of Glasgow. Martin said once that I was employed on the permanent way that led to perdition. I caught Martin by the scruff of the neck and rubbed his face on the slag. He never thought it proper to look out my faults afterwards. Martin ill-treated his wife, and she left him in the end. But he did not mind; he took one of his female co-religionists to his bosom and kept her in place of his legal wife. and seemed quite well pleased with the change. Meanwhile he sang hymns in the street whenever he got two friends to help and one to listen to him.

What a difference between these men and my devil-may-care comrades of Kinlochleven. I looked on Martin Rudor and his gang with inexpressible contempt, and their talk of religion was a source of almost unendurable torment. I also looked upon the missions with disgust. It is a paradox to pretend that the thing called Christianity was what the Carpenter of Galilee lived and died to establish. The Church allows a criminal commercial system to continue, and wastes its time trying to save the souls of the victims of that system. Christianity preaches contentment to the wage-slaves, and hob-nobs with the slave drivers ; therefore, the Church is a betrayer of the people. The Church soothes those who are robbed and never condemns the robber, who is usually a pillar of Christianity. To me the Church presents something unattainable, which, being out of harmony with my spiritual condition, jars rather than soothes. To me the industrial system is a great fraud, and the Church which does not condemn it is unfaithful and unjust to the working people. I detest missions, whether organised for the betterment of South Sea Islanders or unshaven navvies. A missionary canvasses the working classes for their souls just in the same manner as a town councillor canvasses them for their votes.

I have heard of workers' missions, railway missions, navvies' missions, and missions to poor heathens, but I have never yet heard of missions for the uplifting of M.P.'s, or for the betterment of stock exchange gamblers ; and these people need saving grace a great deal more than the poor untutored working men. But it is in the nature of things that piety should preach to poverty on its shortcomings, and forget that even wealth may have sins of its own. Clergymen dine nowadays with the gamblers who rob the working classes ; Christ used the lash on the gamblers in the Temple.

I heard no more of Norah Ryan. I longed to see her, and spent hours wandering through the streets, hoping that I would meet her once again. The old passion had come back to me ; the atmosphere of the town rekindled my desire, and, being a lonely man, in the midst of many men and women, my heart was filled with a great longing for my sweetheart. But the weary months went by and still there was no sign of Norah.

When writing home I made enquiries about her, but

s

my people said that she had entirely disappeared; no
Glenmornan man had seen Norah Ryan for many years.
My mother warned me to keep out of Norah's company
if ever I met her, for Norah was a bad woman. My mother
was a Glenmornan woman, and the Glenmornan women
have no fellow-feeling for those who sin.

Manual labour was now becoming irksome to me, and
eight shillings a week to myself at the end of six days'
heavy labour was poor consolation for the danger and worry
of the long hours of toil. I did not care for money, but I
was afraid of meeting with an accident, when I might get
maimed and not killed. It would be an awful thing if a
man like me got deprived of the use of an arm or leg, and
an accident might happen to me any day. In the end
I made up my mind that if I was to meet with an accident
I would take my own life, and henceforth I looked at the
future with stoical calm.

I have said before that I am very strong. There was no
man on the railway line who could equal me at lifting
rails or loading ballast waggons. I had great ambitions
to become a wrestler and go on the stage. No workman
on the permanent way could rival me in a test of
strength. Wrestling appealed to me, and I threw the
stoutest of my opponents in less than three minutes. I
started to train seriously, bought books on physical im-
provement, and spent twelve shillings and sixpence on a
pair of dumb-bells. During meal hours I persuaded my
mates to wrestle with me. Wet weather or dry, it did not
matter! We went at it shoulder and elbows in the muddy
fields and alongside the railway track. We threw one
another across point-rods and signal bars until we bled
and sweated at our work. I usually took on two men at
a time and never got beaten. For whole long months I
was a complete mass of bruises, my skin was torn from
my arms, my clothes were dragged to ribbons, and my

bones ached so much that I could hardly sleep at night owing to the pain. I attended contests in the music-halls, eager to learn tips from the professionals who had acquired fame in the sporting world

The shunter of our ballast train was a heavy-shouldered man, and he had a bad temper and an unhappy knack of lifting his fists to those who were afraid of him. He was a strong rung of a man, and he boasted about the number of fights in which he had taken part. He was also a lusty liar and an irrepressible swearer. Nearly everyone in the job was afraid of him, and to the tune of a wonderful vocabulary of unprintable words he bullied all Martin Rudor's men into abject submission. But that was an easy task. He felt certain that every man on the permanent way feared him, and maybe that was why he called me an Irish cur one evening. We were shovelling ashes from the ballast waggons on one line into the four-foot way of the other, and the shunter stood on the foot-board of the break-van two truck lengths away from me. I threw my shovel down, stepped across the waggons, and taking hold of the fellow by the neck and waist I pulled him over the rim of the vehicle and threw him headlong down the railway slope. I broke his coupling pole over my knee, and threw the pieces at his head. The breaking of the coupling pole impressed the man very much. Few can break one over their knees. When the shunter came to the top of the slope again, he was glad to apologise to me, and thus save himself further abuse.

That evening, when coming in from my work, I saw a printed announcement stating that a well-known Japanese wrestler was offering ten pounds to any man whom he could not overcome in less than five minutes in a ju-jitsu contest. He was appearing in a hall on the south side of the city, and he was well-known as an exponent of the athletic art.

I went to the hall that evening, hoping to earn the ten pounds. The shunter was four stone heavier than I was, yet I overcame him easily, and the victory caused me to place great reliance on myself.

I took a threepenny seat in the gallery, and waited breathless for the coming of the wrestler. Several artists appeared, were applauded or hissed, then went off the stage, but I took very little heed of their performances. All my thoughts were centred on the pose which I would assume when rising to accept the challenge.

Sitting next to me was a fat foreigner, probably a seller of fish-suppers or ice-cream. I wondered what he would think of me when he saw me rise to my feet and accept the challenge. What would the girl who sat on the other side of me think ? She kept eating oranges all the evening, and giggling loudly at every indecent joke made by the actors. She was somewhat the worse for liquor, and her language was far from choice. She was very pretty and knew it. A half-dressed woman sang a song, every stanza of which ended with a lewd chorus. The girl beside me joined in the song and clapped her hands boisterously when the artiste left the stage.

Th wrestler was the star turn of the evening, and his exhibition was numbered two on the programme. When the number went up my heart fluttered madly, and I felt a great difficulty in drawing my breath.

The curtain rose slowly. A man in evening dress, bearing a folded paper in his hand, came out to the front of the stage. One of the audience near me applauded with his hands.

" That's nae a wrestler, you fool ! " someone shouted. " You dinna ken what you're clappin' about."

" Silence ! "

The audience took up the word and all shouted silence, until the din was deafening.

" Ladies and gentlemen," began the figure on the stage, when the noise abated.

Everyone applauded again. Even the girl beside me blurted out " Hear ! hear ! " through a mouthful of orange juice. Those who pay threepence for their seats love to be called ladies and gentlemen.

" Ladies and gentlemen, I have great pleasure in introducin' U—— Y——, the well-known exponent of the art of ju-jitsu."

A little dark man with very bright eyes stepped briskly on the stage, and bowed to the audience, then folded his arms over his breast and gazed into vacancy with an air of boredom. He wore a heavy overcoat which lay open at the neck and exposed his chest muscles to the gaping throng.

" Everybody here has heard of U—— Y——, no doubt." The evening dress was speaking again. " He is well known in America, in England, and on the continent. At the present time he is the undefeated champion of his weight in all the world. He is now prepared to hand over the sum of ten pounds to any man in the audience who can stand against him for five minutes. Is there any gentleman in the audience prepared to accept the challenge ? "

" I could wrestle him mysel'," said the girl of the orange-scented breath in a whisper. Apart from that there was silence.

" Is any man in the audience prepared to accept the offer and earn the sum of ten pounds ? " repeated the man on the stage.

" I am."

Somehow I had risen to my feet, and my words came out spasmodically. Everyone in front turned round and stared at me. My seat-mate clapped her hands, and the audience followed her example.

There is no need to give an account of the contest.

Suffice to say that I did not collar the ten-pound note, and that I had not the ghost of a chance in the match. It only lasted for forty-seven seconds. The crowd hissed me off the stage, and I got hurriedly into the street when I regained my coat in the dressing-room. I went out into the night, sick at heart, a defeated man, with another of my illusions dashed to pieces. I took no interest in wrestling afterwards.

CHAPTER XXXIII

A SWEETHEART OF MINE

" She learned the pitiful story, that they must suffer who live,
While selling her soul in the gutters for all that the gutters give."
—From *Lost Souls.*

THERE was a cold air running along the street when I stepped into the open and took my way along the town to Moran's model where I lodged. I felt disappointed, vexed, and ashamed of my ludicrous exhibition on the stage. Forty-seven seconds! As I walked along I could hear the referee repeating the words over and over again. Forty-seven seconds! I was both angry and ashamed, angry at my own weakness, and ashamed of the presumption which urged me to attack a professional athlete. I walked quickly, trying to drive all memories of the night from my mind.

The hour of midnight rang out, and the streets were almost deserted. Here and there a few night-prowlers stole out from some gloomy alley and hurried along, bent, no doubt, upon some fell mission which could only be carried through under cover of the darkness. Once a belated drunken man swayed in front of me, and asked for a match to light his pipe. I had none to give him, and he cursed me as I passed on. I met a few women on the streets, young girls whose cheeks were very red, and whose eyes were very bright. This was the hour when these, our little sisters, carry on the trade which means life to their bodies

and death to their souls. It is so easy to recognise them !
Their eyes sparkle brightly in the lamplight ; they speak
light and trivial words to the men whom they meet, and
ever they hold their skirts lifted well over their ankles so
that those whom they meet may know of the goods which
they sell. The sisters of the street barter their chastity
for little pieces of silver, and from them money can purchase
the rightful heritage of love.

These, like navvies, are outcasts and waifs of society.
They are despised by those who hide imperfections under
the mask of decency, men and women who are so conscious of their own shortcomings that they make up for
them by censuring those of others.

White slavery is now the term used in denoting these
girls' particular kind of slavery. But, bad as it is, it is
chosen by many women in preference to the slavery of the
mill and the needle. As I write this, there are many noble
ladies, famed for having founded several societies for the
suppression of evils that never existed, who believe that
the solution of the white slave problem can only be arrived
at by flogging men who live on the immoral earnings of
women. This solution if extended might meet the case.
In all justice the lash should be laid on the backs of
the employers who pay starvation wages, and the
masters who fatten on sweated labour. The slavery of
the shop and the mill is responsible for the shame of the
street.

A girl came out from the shadow of a doorway, and
walked along the street in front of me, her head held down
against the cutting breeze. Sometimes she spoke words
to the men who passed her, but all went on unheeding.
Only to those who were well-dressed and prosperous-
looking did she speak.

I thought of my own sisters away home in Ireland, and
here, but for the grace of God, went one of them. At that

moment I felt sick of life and sorry for civilisation and all
its sin.

I detected something familiar in the figure of the woman
before me. Perhaps I had met the woman before. I
overtook her, and when passing looked at her closely.

"Under God, the day and the night, it's Dermod
Flynn that's in it!" she cried in a frightened voice.

I was looking at Norah Ryan. Just for a moment she
was far from my thoughts, and my mind was busy with
other things. I had almost lost all hopes of meeting her,
and thought that she was dead or gone to a strange country.

"Is this you, Norah?" I asked, coming to a standstill,
and putting out the hand of welcome to her.

She seemed taken aback, and placed her hand timorously
in mine. Her cheeks were very red and her brow was as
white as snow. She had hardly changed in features since
I had last seen her, years before. Now her hair was hidden
under a large hat ; long ago it hung down in brown waving
tresses over her shoulders. The half-timid look was still
in the grey eyes of her, and Norah Ryan was very much
the same girl who had been my sweetheart of old. Only,
now she had sinned and her shame of all shames was the
hardest to bear.

"Is it ye, yerself, that's in it, Dermod Flynn?" she asked,
as if not believing the evidence of her own eyes.

In her voice there was a great weariness, and at that
moment the sound of the waters falling over the high rocks
of Glenmornan were ringing in my ears. Also I thought of
an early delicate flower which I had once found killed by
the cold snows on the high uplands of Danaveen, ere yet
the second warmth of the spring had come to gladden the
bare hills of Donegal. In those days, being a little child, I
felt sorry for the flower that died so soon.

"I didn't expect to meet ye here," said Norah. "Have
ye been away back and home since I saw ye last?"

" I have never been at home since," I answered. " Have you ? "

" Me go home ! " she replied. " What would I be doin' goin' home now with the black mark of shame over me ? Do ye think that I'd darken me mother's door with the sin that's on me heavy, on me soul ? Sometimes I'm thinkin' long, but I never let on to anyone, and it's meself that would like to see the old place again. It's a good lot I'd give to see the grey boats of Dooey goin' out again beyont Trienna Bar in the grey duskus of the harvest evenin' ! Do ye mind the time ye were at school, Dermod, and the way ye hit the master with the pointer ? "

" I mind it well," I answered. " You said that he was dead when he dropped on the form."

" And do ye mind the day that ye went over beyont the mountains with yer bundle under yer arm ? I met ye on the road and ye said that ye were never comin' back."

" You did not care whether I returned or not," I said resentfully, unable to account for my mood of the moment. " You did not even stop to bid me good-bye."

" I was frightened of ye."

" Why were you frightened ? "

" I don't know."

" But you did not even turn and look after me," I said.

" That was because I knew that ye, yerself, was lookin' behind."

" Do you remember the night on the 'Derry boat ? " I asked.

" Quite well do I mind it, Dermod," she replied. " I often be thinkin' of them days, I do, indeed."

She was looking at me with wistful and pathetic eyes, and the street lamp beside us shone full on her face. There was a long interval of silence, and I did not know what to say next. Many a time had I thought of our next

meeting, and my head was usually teeming with the words
of welcome which I would say to her. But now I was
almost at a loss for one single word. The situation was
strained, and she showed signs of taking her departure.

" Where are you going at this hour of the night, Norah ? "
I asked impulsively.

" I'm goin' for a walk."

" Where are you working ? "

Well did I know her work, but I could not resist asking
her the question. The next moment I was sorry for my
words. Norah's face became white, she stammered a few
words about being a servant in a gentleman's house, then
suddenly burst into tears.

" Don't cry," I said in a lame sort of manner. " What's
wrong ? "

She kept her eyes fixed on the pavement, and did not
answer. I could see her bosom heaving, and hear the low
sobs that she tried vainly to suppress. We stood there for
nearly five minutes without a word. Then she held out
her hand.

" Slan agiv,* Dermod," she said. " I must be goin'.
It was good of ye to speak to me in that nice way of yers,
Dermod."

The hand which she placed in mine was limp and cold.
I struggled to find words to express my feelings at the
moment, but my tongue was tied, and my mind was teeming
with thoughts which I could not express. She drew her
hand softly from mine and walked back the way she had
come.

I stood there nonplussed, feeling conscious of some great
wrong in allowing that grey-eyed Irish girl to wander alone
through the naked streets of Glasgow. For years I had
recognised the evils of prostitution, but never had those
evils come home so sharply to me as they did at that

* Good-bye ; literally, " Health be with you."

moment. Despite my cynical views on love I had always a feeling deeper than friendship for Norah Ryan, and at times when I tried to analyse this feeling I found that it was not love; it was something more constant, less rash and less wavering. It was not subject to changes or stints, it was a hold-fast, the grip of which never lessened.

It was a love without any corporal end; its greatest desire did not turn to the illusive delights of the marriage bed. My love had none of the hunger of lust; it was not an appetite which might be satiated—it was something far holier and more enduring. To me Norah represented a poetical ideal; she was a saint, the angel of my dreams. Never for a moment did I think of winning her love merely for the purpose of condemning her to a hell of bearing me children. In all our poetry and music of love we delight merely in the soft glance of eyes, the warm touch of lips, the soft feel of a maiden's breast and the flutter of one heart beating against another. But all love of women leads to passion, and poetry or music cannot follow beyond a certain boundary. There poetry dies, music falters, and the mark of the beast is over man in the moments of his desire. But my love for Norah was different. To me she represented a youthful ideal which was too beautiful and pure to be degraded by anything in the world.

Norah had given her love to another. Who was I that I should blame her? In her love she was helpless, for love is not the result of effort. It cannot be stopped; its course cannot be stayed. As well ask the soft spring meadows to prevent the rising freshet from wetting the green grass, as ask a maiden to stem the torrent of the love which overwhelms her. Love is not acquired; it is not a servant. It comes and is master.

Norah's sufferings were due to her innocence. She was betrayed when yet a child, and a child is easily led astray.

But to me she was still pure, and I knew that there was no stain on the soul of her.

For a long while I stood looking after her and turning thoughts over in my mind. In the far distance I could see her stealing along the pavement like a frightened child who is afraid of the shadows. I turned and followed her, keeping well in the gloom of the houses which lined the pavement. She passed through many streets, stopping now and again to speak to the men whom she met on her journey. Never once did she look back. At the corner of Sauciehall Street, a well-dressed and half-intoxicated man stopped and spoke to her. For a few seconds they conversed ; then the man linked his arm in hers and the two of them walked off together.

I stood at the street corner, unable to move or act, and almost unable to think. A blind rage welled up in my heart against the social system that compelled women to seek a livelihood by pandering to the impurity of men. Norah had come to Scotland holy and pure, and eager to earn the rent of her mother's croft. She had earned many rents for the landlord who had caused me sufferings in Mid-Tyrone and who was responsible for the death of my brother Dan. To the same landlord Norah had given her soul and her purity. The young girls of Donegal come radiantly innocent from their own glens and mountains, but often, alas ! they fall into sin in a far country. It is unholy to expect all that is good and best from the young girls who lodge with the beasts of the byre and swine of the sty. I felt angry with the social system which was responsible for such a state of affairs, but my anger was thrown away ; it was a monstrous futility. The social system is not like a person ; one man's anger cannot remedy it, one man's fist cannot strike at its iniquities.

Norah had now disappeared, and with my brain afire I followed her round the turn of the street. What I intended to do was even a riddle to myself. When I overtook them the man who accompanied Norah would bear the impress of my knuckles for many days. Only of this was I certain. I turned into several streets and searched until three o'clock in the morning. But she had gone out of my sight once again. Then I went home to bed, but not to sleep.

Sick at heart and a prey to remorse, I prowled through the streets for many nights afterwards, looking for Norah. I did not meet her again, and only too late did I realise the opportunity which I had let slip when I met her at midnight in the city. But meeting her as I had met her on the streets, I found myself faced with a new problem, which for a moment overwhelmed and snapped the springs of action within me. In Glenmornan Norah would now be known as " that woman," and the Glenmornan pride makes a man much superior to women who make the great mistake of life. Thank goodness ! the Glenmornan pride was almost dead within my heart. I thought that I had killed it years before, but there, on the streets of Glasgow, I found that part of it was remaining when I met with Norah Ryan. It rose in rebellion when I spoke to the girl who had sinned, it checked the impulse of my heart for just a moment, and in that moment she whom I loved had passed out of my sight and perhaps out of my life.

Life on the railway, always monotonous, became now dreary and dragging. Day and night my thoughts were turning to her whom I loved, and my heart went out to the girl who was suffering in a lonely town because she loved too well. I was now almost a prey to despair, and in order to divert my mind somewhat from the thoughts that embittered my life I began to write for the papers again.

Ideas came to me while at work, and these I scribbled down on scraps of paper when the old psalm-singing ganger was not watching me. When I got back to Moran's in the evening I worked the ideas into prose or verse which I sent out to various papers. Many of my verses appeared in a Glasgow paper, and I got paid at the rate of three-and-sixpence a poem. Later on I wrote for London weeklies, and these paid me better for my work. Some editors wrote very nice letters to me, others sent my stuff back, explaining that lack of space prevented them from publishing it. I often wondered why they did not speak the truth. A navvy who generally speaks the truth finds it difficult to distinguish the line of demarcation which runs between falsehood and politeness. Most of my spare evenings I gave up to writing, but often I found myself out in the street where I had met Norah Ryan, and sometimes I wandered there until four o'clock in the morning, but never once set eyes on her.

A literary frenzy took possession of me for a while. I bought second-hand books on every subject, and studied all things from the infinitely great to the infinitesimally little. Microbes and mammoths, atoms and solar systems— I learned a little of all and everything of none. I wrote, not for the love of writing as much as to drown my own introspective humours, but in no external thing was I interested enough to forget my own thoughts.

I studied literary style, and but for that I might have by this time cultivated a style of my own ; I read so much that now I have hardly an original idea left. Only lately have I come to the conclusion that true art, the only true art, is that which appeals to the simple people. When writing this book I have been governed by this conclusion, and have endeavoured to tell of things which all people may understand.

Most of my articles and stories came back with the precision of boomerangs, weapons of which I have heard much talk, and which are said to come back to the hand of the man who throws them away ; some were published and never paid for, and some never came back at all.

Suddenly it occurred to me that editors might like to publish articles on subjects which were seldom written about. I wrote about the navvies' lives again ; the hopes and sorrows and aspirations of the men of the hovel, model, and road. Several papers took my articles, and for a while I drew in a decent penny for my literary work. Indeed, I had serious intentions of giving up manual labour and taking to the pen for good. Some of my stories again appeared in the *Dawn*, the London daily paper which had published my Kinlochleven stories, and on one fine morning I received a letter from the editor asking me to come and take a job on the staff of his paper. He offered me two pounds a week as salary, and added that I was certain to attain eminence in the position which was now open to me. I decided to go, not because I had any great desire for the job, but because I wanted to get rid of old Rudor and his gang, and I also wanted to see London. Being wise enough to throw most of the responsibility on the person who suggested such a change in my life and work, I answered the editor, saying that though I was a writer among navvies I might merely be a navvy among writers, and that journalistic work was somewhat out of my line. Still the editor persisted and enclosed the cost of my railway fare to London. To go I was not reluctant, to leave I was not eager. I accepted because the change promised new adventures, but there was no excitement in my heart, for now I took things almost as they came, unmoved and uncaring. Norah had gone out of my life, which, full of sorrow for losing her, was empty without her. The enthusiasm which once winged my way along the leading road to Strabane was now dead within me.

I washed the dirt of honest work from my hands and face, and the whole result of seven years' hard labour was dissipated in the wash-tub. Then I went out and bought two ready-made suits and several articles of attire which I felt would be necessary for my new situation. I packed these up, and with my little handbag for company I went out from Moran's model by Glasgow wharf, and caught the night express for London.

T

CHAPTER XXXIV

UNSKILLED LABOUR OF A NEW KIND

" A newspaper is as untruthful as an epitaph."
—BARWELL.

I HAD never seen an omnibus. I did not know that it was necessary to take off my hat when entering a dwelling. I had never used a fork when eating. I had never been introduced to a lady ; to me the approved form of introduction was a mystery. My boots had not been blackened for years. I wore my first collar when setting out for London. It nearly choked me. Since leaving Glenmornan I had rarely been inside an ordinary dwelling house. Most of the time I had lived under God's sky, the roof of a byre, and the tarred wooden covering of the navvies' shack at Kinlochleven. I had, it is true, seen the inside of a drawing-room and a dining-room— through the window. I lacked knowledge of most of the things which most people know and which really do not matter. I went to London a greenhorn gloriously green.

Outside Euston station I asked a man the way to Fleet Street. He inquired if I was going to walk or take an omnibus. Omnibus ! I had never heard of an omnibus ; he might have asked me if I intended to ride on a ptero- dactyl ! I said that I was going to walk, and the stranger gave me several hints as to the direction which I should follow. Even if I had understood what he was saying, I am certain that I could not have remembered the direc- tions. When he finished, he asked me for the price of his breakfast. This I understood, and gave him three-pence, which pleased the man mightily.

It was funny that the first man accosted by me in London should ask for the price of a meal. The prospects of making a fortune looked poor at the moment.

I walked to Fleet Street, making inquiries from police-men on the way. This was safest, and I hadn't to pay for a meal when my questions were answered. By ten o'clock I found myself at the office of the *Dawn*, and there I met the editor.

The editor was a Frenchman, short of stature and breath. His figure was ridiculously rotund, and his little legs were so straight that they looked as if they were jointless. He would not have made much of a show on a ten-hour shift in the cutting of Kinlochleven, and though Fleet Street knows that he is one of the ablest editors in London I had not much respect for the man when I first saw him. He was busily engaged in look-ing through sheets of flimsy when I entered, and for a few minutes he did not take much notice of me. He called me Pim, asked me several questions about the navvies, my politics and writings. He looked annoyed when I said I was a socialist.

" A writer among navvies, and a navvy among writers ; is that it ? " asked the news-editor when I entered his office, a stuffy little place full of tobacco smoke. " You see that we have heard of you here. Going to try your hand at journalism now, are you ? Feeling healthy and fit ? "

He plied me with several questions relating to my past life, took no heed of my answers and, fumbling amongst a pile of papers, he drew out a type-written slip.

" I have a story for you," he said. " A fire broke out early this morning in a warehouse in Holborn. Go out and get all the facts relating to it and work the whole affair up well. If you do not know where Holborn is, make enquiries."

I met a third man, a young, clean-shaven, alert youth, in the passage outside the news-editor's door.

" Are you Flynn ? " he asked, and when I answered in the affirmative he shook hands with me. " My name is Barwell," he continued. " I am a journalist like yourself. What the devil caused you to come here ? "

I had no excuses to offer.

" You might have stayed where you were," said Barwell. " You'll find that a navvies' office is much better than a newspaper office. Have you had lunch ? "

" No," I answered. It was now nearly one o'clock, but I had not had breakfast yet. I had never been inside a restaurant in my life, and the daintily-dressed waitresses and top-hatted feeders deterred me from entering that morning. I might have done something unbecoming and stupid, and in a strange place I am sensitive and shy.

" Come along then. We'll go out together and feed."

We entered a restaurant in the Strand, and my friend ordered lunch for two. During the course of the meal I suffered intense mental agony. The fork was a problem. the serviette a mystery, and I felt certain that everybody in the place was looking at me.

" The news-editor has asked me to write an account of a fire in Holborn," I said to Barwell when we had eaten, " Do you know where Holborn is ? "

" The whole account of the fire is given in the evening papers," said Barwell. " Therefore you do not require to go near the place."

" You mean——"

" Exactly what you are going to say," said the young man looking at the copy of the evening paper which he had bought at the door when entering. " You can write

your story now and get the facts from this.   Have you a
pencil and notebook ? "

"No."

"If you are going to take up journalism they are the
initial and principal requirements.   Beyond a little tact
and plenty of cheek you require nothing else.   A conscience
and a love of truth are great drawbacks.   Are you ready ? "

He handed me a pencil and notebook.

"Now begin.   The opening sentence must be crisp and
startling ; and never end your sentences with prepositions."

"But I know nothing about the fire," I expostulated.

"Oh ! I've forgotten."   He picked up the paper which
he had absent-mindedly kicked under the table.   "Now
you are all right.   Get your facts from this rag, but write
the story in your own way.   You'll find this good training
if ever you've got to weave out lies of your own.   Meanwhile I've three or four novels to review."

As he spoke he opened a parcel which he had brought
along with him, and took out several books which he
regarded critically for a moment.

"Are they worth reading ? " I asked.

"I do not know."

"You do not know and you're going to review them ! "

"It's bad policy to read a book before you review it,"
he answered.   "It is apt to give rise to prejudice.   This
volume," taking up one in his hand as he spoke, "*The
Woman who Fell*, is written by a personal friend of the
editor.   I must review it favourably.   This one, *In the
Teeth of the Tempest*, is written by a strong supporter
of the Liberal Government.   The *Dawn* is tory, the
author is liberal, therefore his work must be slated.   See ? "

"But your own opinion——"

"What the devil do I need with an opinion of my own ? "

Thereupon Barwell reviewed the books which he had
not read and I muddled through an account of the fire

which I had not seen, and when we had finished we took our way into the street again.

Although it was barely past three o'clock, the early December night had now fallen. Fleet Street was a blaze of light and a medley of taxi-cabs and omnibuses. Except for the down-at-heel mendicant, and the women who had more paint than modesty, everybody was in a great hurry.

" What do you think of it all, Flynn ? " asked Barwell suddenly. " Isn't it a great change from your past life ? London ! there's no place like it in all the world ! Light loves and light ladies, passion without soul, enjoyment without stint, and sin without scandal or compunction."

" Only those with some idea of virtue can sin with compunction," I said. This thought came to me suddenly, and Barwell looked surprised at my words.

" By Jove ! that's so," he answered, scribbling my remark down on his notebook. " Well, what is your opinion of London, all that you have seen of it ? "

" What the devil do I want with an opinion ? " I asked, quoting his own words.

" Quite so ; but we are now speaking in a confidential, not in a journalistic sense. Do you not think that it is a heavenly privilege to be allowed to write lies for a kingdom of fools within ninety-eight million miles of the sun ? You'll fall in love with London directly, old man, for it is the centre of the universe. The world radiates outwards from Charing Cross and revolves around the Nelson column. London is the world, journalism is the midden of creation."

" Do you really think that men are acting in a straightforward manner by writing unfair and untruthful articles for the public ? " I asked.

" The public is a crowd of asses and you must interest it. You are paid to interest it with plausible lies or unsavoury truths. An unsavoury truth is always palatable to those whom it does not harm. Our readers gloat over scandal, revel in scandal, and pay us for writing it. Learn what the public requires and give it that. Think one thing in the morning and another at night ; preach what is suitable to the mob and study the principle of the paper for which you write. That's how you have to do it, Flynn. A paper's principle is a very subtle thing, and it must be studied. Every measure passed in Parliament affects it, it oscillates to the breezes of public opinion and it is very intangible. The principle of a daily paper is elusive, old man, damned elusive. Come in and have a whisky and soda."

" Not elusive but changeable, I suppose," I said, alluding to his penultimate remark as we stood at the bar of the wine shop. " The principles of the *Dawn* are rather consistent, are they not ? "

" The principles oscillate, old man. Your health, and may you live until newspapers are trustworthy ! Consistent, eh ? Some day you'll learn of the inconsistencies of Fleet Street, Flynn. Here the Jew is an advocate of Christianity, the American of Protection, the poet a compiler of statistics, the penny-a-liner a defender of the idle rich, and the reporter with anarchistic ideas a defender of social law and order. Here charlatans, false as they are clever, play games in which the pawns are religion and atheism, and make, as suits their purpose, material advantages of the former or a religion of the latter. Fleet Street is the home of chicanery, of fraud, of versatile vices and unnumbered sins. It is an outcome of the civilisation which it rules, a framer of the laws which it afterwards destroys or protects at caprice ; without conscience or soul it dominates the world. Only in its falseness is it consistent. Truth is further removed from its jostling rookeries than the first painted savage who stoned the wild boar in the sterile wastes of Ludgate Circus."

Barwell's gestures were as astonishing as his eloquence.

One hand clutched the lapel of his coat ; in the other he held the glass of liquor which he shook violently when reaching the zenith of his harangue. The whisky splashed and sparkled and kept spurting over the rim of the glass until most of the contents were emptied on the floor. He hardly drank a quarter of the liquor. We went out, and once in the street he continued his vehement utterances.

" Take the *Dawn* for example," he said. " The editor is a Frenchman, the leader-writer a German, the American special correspondent an Irishman who came to England on a cattle boat and who has never ventured on the sea since. The *Dawn* advocates Tariff Reform, and most of the reporters are socialists. The leader-writer points out the danger of a German menace daily. What influences one of the Kaiser's subjects to sit down and, for the special benefit of the British nation, write a thrilling warning against the German menace ? Salary or conscience, eh ? The *Dawn* knows the opinions of Germany before Germany has formed an opinion, and gives particulars of the grave situation in the Far East before the chimerical situation has evolved from its embryological stages. Consistent, my dear fellow ? It is only consistent in its inconsistencies. The reviewers seldom read the books which they review in its pages, and the quack suffers from the ills which through its columns he professes to cure. The bald man who sells a wonderful hair restorer, the cripple who can help the lame, and the anæmic pill-maker who professes ability to cure any disease, all advertise in the *Dawn*. A newspaper is as untruthful as an epitaph, Flynn."

" If you dislike the work so much why do you remain on the staff ? " I asked.

" I do not dislike it. Being by nature a literary Philistine and vagabond journalist, I love the work. Anyhow, there is nothing else which I can do. If I happened to be placed on a square acre of earth fresh from the hands of the

Creator, and given a spade and shovel to work with, what use could I make of those tools of labour ? I could not earn my living with a spade and shovel. It was for the like of us that London and journalism were created."

For a while I was very much out of my place at my quarters in Bloomsbury, for it was in that locality that I obtained rooms along with Barwell. Everything in the place was a fresh experience to me ; at the dinner-table I did not know the names of the dishes. The table napkins were problems which were new to me, and the frilled and collared maid-servant was a phenomena, disconcerting and unavoidable.

I who had cooked my own chops for the best part of seven years, I who had dined in moleskin and rags for such a long while, felt the handicap of dining inside four walls, hemmed with restraint, and almost choked with the horrible starched abomination which decency decreed that I should wear around my neck. It was very wearisome. Barwell was utterly careless and outraged custom with impunity, but I, who feared to do the wrong thing, always remained on the tenter-hooks of suspense. Barwell knew what should be done and seldom did it, while I, who was only learning the very rudimentary affectations of civilised society, took care to follow out the most stringent commands of etiquette whenever I became aware of those commands.

At the office of the *Dawn* I was reticent and backward. I lacked the cleverness, the smartness and readiness of expression with which other members of the staff were gifted. I had come into a new world, utterly foreign to me, and often I longed to be back again with Moleskin Joe on some long road leading to nowhere.

For a while my stories were not successful, although I made a point of seeing the things of which I wrote. I came back to the office every evening full of my subject, whether a florist's exhibition, a cat show, or a police court case, and sat down seriously to write my story. When half-written I tore it up seriously and began again. When satisfied with the whole completed account I took it to the sub-editor, who read it seriously and seriously threw it into the waste-paper basket. At the end of the first week I found that only two articles of mine had appeared in the *Dawn.* I had written eight.

" You write in too serious a vein for a modern paper," said the sub-editor.

When the spring came round I could feel, even in Fleet Street, the spell of the old roving days come over me ; those days when Moleskin and I tramped along the roads of Scotland, thanking God for the little scraps of tobacco which we found in our pockets, while wondering where the next pipeful could be obtained ! My heart went out to the old mates and the old places. I had a longing for the little fire in the darkness, the smell of the wet earth, the first glimpse of the bend in the road, and the dream about the world of mystery lying round the corner. When I went across Blackfriars Bridge, or along the Strand, on a cold, bracing morning, I wanted to walk on ever so far, away—away. Where to—it didn't matter. The office choked me, smothered me ; it felt so like a prison. I wanted to be with Moleskin Joe, and often I asked myself, " Where is he now ? what is my old comrade doing at this moment ? Is the old vagabond still happy in his wanderings and his hopes of a good time coming, or has he finished up his last shift and handed in his final check for good and all ? " Often I longed to see him again and travel with him to new and strange places.

Of my salary, now three pounds a week, I sent a guinea home to my own people every Saturday. Of course, now, getting so much, they wanted more. Journalism to them implied some hazy kind of work where money was stint-less and to be had for the asking. My other brothers were going out into the world now, and my eldest sister had gone to America. " I wish that I could keep *them* at home," wrote my mother. " *You* are so long away now that we do not miss you."

" Will you go down to Cyfladd, Flynn, and write some ' stories ' about the coal strike ? " asked the news editor one morning. " I think that you have a natural bent for these labour affairs. Your navvy stories were undoubtedly good, and even a spicy bit of socialism added to their charm."

" Spicy bit of socialism, indeed ! " broke in the irrepressible Barwell. " The day will come when the working men of England shall invade London and decorate Fleet Street with the gibbeted bodies of hireling editors. Have you a cigarette to spare, Manwell ? "

" You go down to Cyfladd, Flynn," said the news editor, handing his cigarette-case to Barwell. " See what is doing there and write up good human stories dealing with the discontent of the workers. Do not be afraid to state things bluntly. Tell about their drinking and quarrelling, and if you come across miners who are in good circumstance don't fail to write about it."

" But suppose for a moment that he comes across men who are really poor, men who may not have had enough wages to make both ends meet, what is he to do ? " asked loquacious Barwell, the socialistic Philistine, who played with ideas for the mere sake of the ideas. " For myself, I do not believe in the right to strike, and I admire the man who starves to death without making a fuss. Why should uncultured and uneducated miners create a fuss if they are starved to death in order to satisfy the needs of honourable and learned gentlemen ? What right has a common worker to ask for higher wages ? What right has he to take a wife and bring up children ? The children of the poor should be fattened and served up on the tables of the rich, as advocated by Dean Swift in an age prior to the existence of the *Dawn*. The children of the poor who cannot become workers become wastrels; the rich wastrels wear eye-glasses and spats. We have no place in the scheme of things for the wastrels who wear neither eye-glasses nor spats, therefore I believe that it would be good for the nation if many of the children of the poor were fattened, killed, and eaten. But I am wandering from the point. Let us look at the highly improbable supposition of which I have spoken. It is highly improbable, of course, that there are poor people amongst the miners, for they have little time to spend the money which they take so long to earn. Now and again they die, leaving a week's wages lying at the pay-office. I have heard of cases like that several times. These men, who are out on strike, may leave a whole week's pay to their wives and children when they die, and for all that they grumble and go out on strike! But we cannot expect anything else from un-educated workmen. I am wandering from the point again, and the point is this: Suppose, for an instant, that Flynn doesn't find a rich, quarrelsome, and drunken miner in Cyfladd, what is he to do? Return again?"

" You're a fool, Barwell!" said the news editor.

" Manwell, you're a confirmed fool," Barwell replied.

I put on my coat and hat, stuffed my gloves, which I hated, into my pocket, and went out into the street. The morning was dry and cold, the air was exhilarating and good to breathe. I gulped it down in mighty mouthfuls. It was good to be in the open street and feel the little winds whipping by in mad haste. Up in the office, steaming with cigarette smoke, it was so stuffy, so dead. Everything there was so artificial, so unreal, and I was altogether out of sympathy with all the individuals on the *Dawn*. " Do I like the *Dawn*?" I asked myself. I wanted to face things frankly at that moment. " Do I like journalism, or merely feel that I should like it ? " But I made no effort to answer the question ; it was not very important, and now I was walking hurriedly, trying to keep myself warm. Two things occurred to me at the same instant : I was short of money and I had not asked for my railway fare to Wales at the office. Where did the train start from ? Was it Euston ? I did not exactly know, and somehow it didn't seem to matter.

I would not go to Wales ; I did not want to analyse my reasons for not going, but I was determined not to go. I felt that in going I would be betraying my own class, the workers. Moleskin Joe would never dream of doing a thing like that ; why should I ? I must make some excuse at the office, I thought, but asked myself the next instant why should I make any excuses ? Besides, the office was like a prison ; it choked me. I wanted to leave, but somehow felt that I ought not.

I found myself going along Gray's Inn Road towards my lodging-house. A girl opened a window and looked at me with a vacant stare. She was speaking to somebody in the room behind her and her voice trailed before me like a thin mist. She somewhat resembled Norah Ryan : the same white brow, the red lips, only that this girl had a sorrowful look in her eyes, as if too many weary thoughts had found expression there.

How often during the last four months had I thought of Norah Ryan. I longed for her with a mighty longing, and now that she was alone and in great trouble it was my duty to help her. I felt angry with myself for going up to London when I should have followed up my holier mission in Glasgow. What was fortune and fame to me if I did not make the girl whom I really loved happy ? Daily it became clearer to me that I was earnestly and madly in love with Norah. We were meant for one another from childhood, although destiny played against us for a while. I would find her again and we would be happy, very happy, together, and the past would be blotted out in the great happiness which would be ours in the future. To me Norah was always pure and always good. In her I saw no wrong, no sin, and no evil. I would look for her until I found her, and finding her would do my best to make her happy.

The girl closed the window as I passed. I came to my lodgings, paid the landlady, and wrote to the *Dawn* saying that I was leaving London. I intended to tramp to the north, but a story of mine had just been published in ———— and the money came to hand while I was settling with the landlady.

I learned later that Barwell went down to Wales. That night I set off by rail for Glasgow.

CHAPTER XXXV

THE SEARCH

"When I go back to the old pals,
  'Tis a glad, glad boy I'll be;
  With them will I share the doss-house bunk
  And join their revels with glee,
  And the lean men of the lone shacks
  Will share their tucker with me."

—From *Songs of the Dead End.*

I PAWNED my good clothes, my overcoat, and hand-bag in Glasgow, took a bed in Moran's model by the wharf, and once again recommenced my search for Norah.

The search was both fruitless and tiring. Day after day I prowled through the streets, and each succeeding midnight found me on the spot where I had met Norah on the evening of my wrestling encounter. For hours I would stand motionless at the street corner and scrutinise every woman who passed me by. Sometimes in these children of the night I fancied that I detected a resemblance to her whom I loved. With a flutter in my heart I would hurry forward, only to find that I was mistaken. Disappointed, I would once again resume my vigil, and sometimes the grey smoky dawn was slanting across the dull roofs of the houses before I sought my model and bed. It is a weary job, looking for a friend in a great big city. One street is more perplexing than a hundred miles of open country. A window or a wall separates you from her whom you seek. You pass day after day, perhaps, within speaking distance of her whom you love, and never know that she is near you. Every door is a puzzle, every lighted window an enigma. The great city is a Sahara, in which you look for one special grain of sand; and doubt, perplexity, and heart yearning accompany you on your mission. I could not write, neither could I turn my attention to manual labour. My whole being was centred on my search, and the thought of anything else was repugnant to me. My desire for Norah grew and grew, it filled my soul, leaving no room for anything else.

To Moran's, where I stayed, the navvies came daily when out on their eternal wanderings, and here I met many of my old mates. They came, stopped for a night, and then padded out for Rosyth, where the big naval base, still in process of construction, was then in its first stages of building. Most of the men had heard of my visit to London, and none seemed surprised at my return. None of them thought that the job had done me much good, for now my hands were as white as a woman's. Carroty Dan, who came in drunk one night, examined me critically and allowed that he could knock me out easily in my present condition, but being too drunk to follow up any train of reasoning he dropped, in the midst of his utterances, on the sawdust of the floor and fell asleep. Hell-fire Gahey, Clancy of the Cross, Ben the Moocher, and Red Billy Davis all passed through Moran's, one of their stages on the road to Rosyth. Most of them wanted me to accompany the big stampede, but I had no ear for their proposals. I had a mission of my own, and until it was completed no man could persuade me to leave Glasgow.

I made enquiries about Moleskin Joe. Most of the men had met Moleskin lately, but they did not know where he was at the moment. Some said that he was in gaol, one that he was dead, and another that he was married. But I knew that if he was alive, and that if I stopped long enough in Moran's, I would meet him there, for

most navvies pass that way more than once in their lives.
I had, however, lost a great deal of interest in Moleskin's
doings. There was only one thing for which I now lived,
and that was the search for the girl whom I loved.

One morning about four o'clock I returned to my lodgings
and stole upstairs to the bedroom, which contained three
other beds in addition to mine. The three were occupied,
and as I turned on the gas I took a glimpse of the sleepers.
Two of them I did not know, but I gave a start of surprise
when I caught a glimpse of the unshaven face showing
over the blankets of the bed next to mine. I was looking
at Moleskin Joe. I approached the bed. The man was
snoring loudly and his breath was heavy with the fumes
of alcohol. I clutched the blankets and shook the sleeper.

" Moleskin ! " I shouted.

He grumbled out some incoherent words and turned
over on his side.

" Moleskin ! " I called again, and gave him a more
vigorous shake.

" Lemme alone, damn you ! " he growled. " There's a
good time comin'—— "

The sentence ended in a snore and Joe fell asleep again.
I troubled him no further, but turned off the light and
slipped into bed.

In the morning I woke with a start to find Joe shaking
me with all his might. He was standing beside my bed,
undressed, save for his trousers.

" Flynn ! " he yelled, when I opened my eyes. " My
great unsanctified Pontius Pilate, it's Flynn ! Hurrah !
May the walls of hell fall on me if I'm not glad to see
you. May I get a job shoein' geese and drivin' swine to
clover if this is not the greatest day of my life ! Dermod
Flynn, I am glad to see—— Great blazes, your hands are
like the hands of a brothel slut ! "

Joe left off his wild discourses and prodded the hand

U

which I placed over the blankets with his knuckles. He was still half intoxicated, and a bottle three-quarters full of spirits was lying against the pillow of his bed.

"White as a mushroom, but hard as steel," he said when he finished prodding.

"How are you, Moleskin?" I asked. They were the first words that I had spoken.

"Nine pounds to the good!" he roared. "I'll paint Moran's red with it. I'll raise Cain and flamin' fiery hell until ev'ry penny's spent. Then Rosyth, muck barrows, hard labour, and growlin' gangers again. But who'd have thought of seein' you here!" he went on in a quieter tone. "Man! I've often been thinkin' of you. I heard that you went up to Lon'on, then I found the name of the paper where you were workin' your shifts and I bought it ev'ry day. By God! I did, Flynn. I read all them great pieces about the East Lon'on workin' people. I read some of your writin's to the men in Burn's at Greenock, and some of the lodgers said that you were stuck up and priggish. I knew what you'd do if you were there yourself. You would knock red and blue blazes out of ev'ry man of them. Well, you weren't there and I done the job for you. Talk about skin and hair! It was flyin' all over the place between the hot-plate and the door for two hours and longer. I'm damned eternal if it wasn't a fight! Never seen the like of it. . . . Man! your hands are like a woman's, Flynn! . . . Come and have a drink, one good long, gulpin' drink, and it will make a man of you! . . . Did you like the ways of London?"

"No," I replied. "The pen was not in my line."

"I knew that," said Joe solemnly, as he lifted the bottle from the pillow. "Finger doctorin' doesn't suit a man like you. When you work you must get your shoulder at the job and all the strength of your spine into the graft. Have some blasted booze?"

" I've given up the booze, Moleskin," I answered.

He glanced at me with a look of frosty contempt and his eyes were fixed for a long while on my white hands.

" Lon'on has done for you, man, and it is a pity indeed," he said at last, but I understood Moleskin and knew that his compassion was given more in jest than in earnest. " What are you goin' to do ? Are you for Rosyth ? "

" No."

" Then why the devil aren't you ? "

" Are you going there ? " I asked, forgetting that he had already told me of his design.

" When I burst the last tanner in my pocket," he answered. " I've nine quid clear, so I'll get drunk nine hundred times and more. What caused you to give up the booze ? A woman, was it ? "

Suddenly the impulse came to me and I told Joe my story, my second meeting with Norah Ryan, and my desire to see her again. There in the ragged bed, with Joe stripped naked to the buff, and half drunk, sitting beside me, I told the story of my love for Norah, our parting, her shame, and my weary searching for her through the streets of Glasgow. Much of the story he knew, for I had told it to him in Kinlochleven long before. But I wanted to unburden myself of my sorrow, I wanted sympathy, I wanted the consolation of a fellow-man in my hours of worry. When I had finished my mate remained silent for a long while and I expected his usual tirades against women when he began to speak. On the contrary, the story seemed to have sobered him and his voice was full of feeling when he spoke.

" I'm goin' to help you to find your wench, Dermod," he said. " That's better than gettin' drunk, though I'd prefer gettin' drunk to gettin' married."

" But——"

"Don't but me!" roared Joe. "I'm goin' to give you a hand. Do you like that or do you not?"

"I'll be more than glad to have your help," I answered; "but——"

"No more damned buts, but let's get to business. Here, Judas Iscariot, are you feelin' sour this mornin'?"

Joe spoke to one of the lodgers, a hairy and deformed fellow who was just emerging in all his nakedness from the blankets.

"Hellish sour, Moleskin!" answered the man. "Anything to spare?"

"Take this and get drunk out of sight," said Moleskin, handing him the bottle.

"You mean it?" exclaimed the man. "You are goin' to give me the whole bottle?"

"Take it and get out of my sight," was all that Joe said and the old man left the room, hugging the bottle under his naked arm.

"He was a bank clerk did you say?" asked Moleskin. "Them sort of fellows that wear white collars and are always washing themselves. I never could trust them, Flynn, never in all my natural. Now give me the farmer cully's address; maybe he knows where your wench is."

In my heart of hearts I knew that the mission proposed by Joe would have no beneficial results, but I could not for the life of me say a word to restrain him from going. In my mind there was a blind trust in some unshapen chance and I allowed Joe to have his way.

The farmhouse where Alec Morrison lived being twenty miles distant from Glasgow, I offered Joe his railway fare, and for a moment I was overwhelmed by his Rabelaisian abuse. He would see me fried on the red-hot ovens and spits of hell if ever I offered him money again.

Morrison maybe was not at home; perhaps he had gone to London, to Canada. But Joe would find him out,

I thought; and it was with a certain amount of satisfaction that I remembered having heard how Joe once fought a man twenty-six times, and getting knocked out every time challenged his opponent to a twenty-seventh contest. In the last fight my mate was victorious.

During his absence I moped about, unable to work, unable to think, and hoping against hope that the mission would be successful. Late in the afternoon he returned with a sprained thumb and without any tidings of my sweetheart. The clerk was at home, and the encounter with Joe was violent from the outset. Morrison said that my mate was a fool who had nothing better to do than meddle with the morals of young women; and refused to answer any questions. Joe took the matter in hand in his usual fistic and persuasive way and learned that the farmer's son had not seen Norah for years and that he did not know where she was. Joe, angry at his failure, sprained his thumb on the young man's face before coming back to Glasgow.

"And what was the good of this?" said Moleskin, holding up his sprained thumb and looking at it. "It didn't give one much satisfaction to knock him down. He is a fellow with no thoughts in his head; one of them kind that thinks three shillings a week paid to a woman will wipe out any sin or shame. By God! I'm a bad one, Flynn, damned bad, but I hope that I've been worse to myself than anybody on this or the other side of the grave. Look at these young women who come over from Ireland! I'd rather have the halter of Judas Iscariot round my neck than be the cause of sendin' one of them to the streets, and all for the woman's sake, Flynn. There should be something done for these women. If we find a tanner lying in the mud we lift and rub it on our coats to clean it; but if we find a woman down we throw more mud over her. . . . I like you, Flynn, for the way you stand up for that wench of yours. Gold rings, collars, and clean boots, and under it all a coward. That's what Morrison is."

"What is to be done now?" I asked. Joe was silent, but his mind was at work. All that evening he sat by the bed, his mind deep in thought, while I paced up and down the room, a prey to agony and remorse.

"I have it, Flynn," he cried at length. "I have it, man!" He jumped up from his bed in great excitement.

"Your wench was Catholic and she would go to the chapel; a lot of them do. They steal into church just like thieves, almost afraid to ask pardon for their sins, Flynn. If there is anything good in them they hide it, just as another person would hide a fault; but maybe some priest knows her, some priest on the south side. We'll go and ask one of the clergy fellows thereabouts. Maybe one of them will have met the woman. I've never knew a——" He stopped suddenly and left the sentence unspoken.

"Go on," I said. "What were you going to say?"

"Most of the women that I know go to church."

His words spoke volumes. Well did I know the class of women who were friends of Moleskin Joe, and from personal experience I knew that his remarks were true.

It was now eight o'clock. We went out together and sought the priest who had charge of the chapel nearest the spot where many months before I had met Norah Ryan. The priest was a grey-haired and kindly old Irishman, and he welcomed us heartily. Joe, to whom a priest represented some kind of monster, was silent in the man's presence, but I, having been born and bred a Roman Catholic, was more at home with the old man.

I told my story, but he was unable to offer any assistance. His congregation was a large one and many of its members were personally unknown to him.

"But in the confessional, Father," I said. "Probably there you have heard a story similar to mine. Maybe the girl whom I seek has told you of her life when confessing her sins. Perhaps you may recollect hearing such a story in the confessional, Father."

"It may be, but in that case the affair rests between the penitent and God," said the old priest sadly, and a far-away look came into his kindly eyes.

"If the disclosure of a confessional secret brings happiness to one mortal at the expense of none, is it not best for a man to disclose it ? " I asked.

"I act under God's orders and He knows what is best," said the old man, and there was a touch of reproof in his voice.

Sick at heart, I rose to take my leave. Moleskin, glad to escape from the house, hurried towards the door which the priest opened. As I was passing out, the old man laid a detaining hand upon my arm.

"In a situation like this, one of God's servants hardly knows what is best to do," he said in a low whisper which Moleskin, already in the street, could not hear. "Perhaps it is not contrary to God's wishes that I should go against His commands and make two of His children happy even in this world. Three months ago, your sweetheart was in this very district, in this parish, and in this chapel. Do not ask me how I have learned this," he hurried on, as I made a movement to interrupt him. "If I mistake not she was then in good health and eager to give up a certain sin, which God has long since forgiven. Be clean of heart, my child, and God will aid you in your search and you'll surely find her."

He closed the door softly behind me and once again I found myself in the street along with Moleskin.

"What was the fellow sayin' to you ? " asked my mate.

" He says that he has seen her three months ago," I answered. " But goodness knows where she is now ! "

In the subsequent search Moleskin showed infinite resource. Torn by the emotions of love, I could not form correct judgments. No sooner had one expedient failed, however, than my mate suggested another. On the morning after our interview with the priest he suddenly rose from his seat in the bedroom, full of a new design.

" My great Jehovah, I have it, Flynn ! " he roared enthusiastically.

" What is it ? " I asked. Every new outburst of Moleskin gave me renewed hope.

" Gourock Ellen, that's the woman ! " he cried. " She knows ev'rything and she lives in the south side, where you saw your wench for the last time. I'm goin' to see Gourock Ellen, for she's the woman that knows ev'rything, by God ! she does. You can stop here and I'll be back in next to no time."

About seven o'clock in the evening Joe returned. There was a strained look on his face and he gazed at me furtively when he entered. Instantly I realised that the search had not gone well. He was nervous and agitated, and his voice was low and subdued. It was not Moleskin's voice at all. Something had happened, something discouraging, awful.

" I'm back again," he said.

" Have you seen her, Joe ? " I asked hoarsely. I had been waiting his return for hours and I was on the tenterhooks of suspense.

" I've seen Gourock Ellen," said Joe.

" Does she know anything about Norah ? "

" She does." I waited for further information, but my mate relapsed into a silence which irritated me.

" Where is Norah, Moleskin ? " I cried. " Tell me what

that woman said. I'm sick of waiting day after day. What did Gourock Ellen tell you, Joe?"

"I saw Norah Ryan, too," was Moleskin's answer.

"Thank you, Moleskin!" I cried impetuously. "You're a real good sort——"

A look at Joe's face damped my enthusiasm. Why the agitation and faltering voice? Presentiments of bad tidings filled my mind and my voice trembled as I put the next question.

"Where did you see her, Joe?" I asked.

"In Gourock Ellen's house."

"In that woman's house!" I gasped involuntarily, for I had not rid myself of the fugitive disgust with which I had regarded that woman when first I met her. "That's not the house for Norah! What took her there?"

"Gourock Ellen found Norah lyin' on the streets hurted because some hooligans treated her shameful," said Joe, in a low and almost inaudible voice. "For the last six weeks she has watched over your girl, day and night, when there was not another friend to help her in all the world. And now Norah Ryan is for death. She'll not live another twenty-four hours!"

To me existence has meant succeeding reconciliations to new misfortunes, and now the greatest misfortune had happened. Moleskin's words cut through my heart as a whiplash cuts through the naked flesh. Fate, chance, and the gods were against me, and the spine of life was almost broken.

CHAPTER XXXVI

THE END OF THE STORY

" Our years pass like a tale that is told badly."
—Moleskin Joe.

THE darkness had long since fallen over the tumbledown rookeries of the Glasgow alley wherein this story is to end, but the ragged children still played in the gutters and the old withered women still gossiped on the pavements. Two drunken men fought outside a public-house and another lay asleep on the dirty kerbstone. When Moleskin and I came to the close which was well known to my mate we had to step over the drunken man in making an entrance.

We passed through a long arched passage and made our way up a flight of rickety wooden stairs, which were cracked at every step, while each crack was filled with the undisturbed dirt of months.

" In there," said Joe, pointing to a splintered door when we gained the top landing. " I'm goin' to stop outside and wait till you come back again."

I rapped on the door, but there was no response. I pushed against the handle and it opened inwards. An open door is a sure sign of poverty. It is a waste of time to lock a door on an empty house. Here where the wealth of men was not kept, the purity of women could not be stolen. Probably Death had effected his entrance before me, but he is one whom no door can hold. I looked into the room.

How bare it looked ! A guttering candle threw a dim light over the place and showed up the nakedness of the apartment. The paper on the walls was greasy to the height of a man's head and there was no picture or ornament in the place to bring out one reviving thought. The floor was dirty, worn, and uncarpeted ; a pile of dead ashes was in the fireplace and a frying-pan without a handle lay in one corner of the room. No chair was to be seen. A pile of rags lay on the floor and these looked as if they had been used for a bed. The window was open, probably to let the air into the room, but instead of the pure fresh air, the smoke of a neighbouring chimney stole into the chamber.

This much did my eyes take in vaguely before I saw the truckle bed which was placed along the wall near the window. On the bed a woman lay asleep—or maybe dead ! I approached quietly and stood by the bedside. I was again looking at Norah, my sweetheart, grown fairer yet through sin and sorrow. The face was white as the petals of some water flower, and the shadow of the long wavy hair about it seemed to make it whiter still. She was asleep and I stood there lost in contemplation of her, a spirit which the first breeze might waft away. Her sleep was sound. I could see her bosom rising and falling under the ragged coverlet and could hear the even breath drawn softly in between the white lips now despoiled of all the cherry redness of six years ago. Instinctively I knew that the life of her was already broken in the grip of sorrow and death.

Suddenly she opened her soft grey eyes. In their calm and tragic depths a strange lustre resembling nothing earthly shone for a moment. There was in them the peace which had taken the place of vanished hopes and the calm and sorrowful acceptance of an end far different from her childish dreams.

She started up in the bed and a startled look stole into

her face. A bright colour glowed faintly in her cheeks, and about her face there was still the girlish grace of the Norah whom I had met years before on the leading road to Greenanore.

"I was dreamin' of ye, Dermod," she said in a low silvery voice. "Ye were long in comin'."

Sitting up with one elbow buried in the pillow, her chemise slipped from her shoulders and her skin looked very pink and delicate under the scattered locks of brown hair. I went down on my knees by the bedside and clasped both her hands in mine. She was expecting me—waiting for me.

"Ellen told me that ye were lookin' for meself," she continued. "A man came this mornin'."

"I sent him, Norah," I said. "'Tis good to see you again, darling. I have been looking for you such a long time."

"Have ye ? " was all her answer, and gripping my two big hands tightly with her little ones she began to sob like a child.

"It's the kindly way that ye have with ye, Dermod," she went on, sinking back into the bed. Her tearless sobs were almost choking her and she gazed up at the roof with sad, blank eyes. "Ye don't know what I am and the kind of life I have been leadin' for a good lot of years, to come and speak to me again. It's not for a decent man like ye to speak to the likes of my kind ! It's meself that has suffered a big lot, too, Dermod, and I deserve pity more than hate. Me sufferin's would have broke the heart of a cold mountainy stone."

"Poor Norah ! well do I know what you have suffered," I said. "I have been looking for you for a long while and I want to make you happy now that I have found you."

"Make me happy ! " she exclaimed, withdrawing her hands from mine. "What would ye be doin' wantin' to make me happy ? I'm dead to ev'rybody, to the people at home, and to me own very mother ! What would she want with me now, me, her daughter, and the mother of a child that never had a priest's blessin' on its head? A child without a lawful father ! Think of it, Dermod ! What would the Glenmornan people say if they met me on the streets ? It was a dear child to me, it was. And ye are wantin' to make me happy. Ev'ry time ye come ye say that ye are goin' to make me happy. D'ye mind seein' me on the streets, Dermod ? "

"I remember it, Norah," I said. She had spoken of the times I came to see her and I did not understand. Perhaps I came to her in dreams.

"It was the child, Dermod," she rambled on ; "it was the little boy and he was dyin', both of a cough that was stickin' in his throat and of starvation. I hadn't seen bread or that what buys it for many's a long hour, even for days itself. I could not get work to do. I tried to beg, but the peelis was goin' to put me in prison, and then there was nothin' for me, Dermod, but to take to the streets. . . . There was long white boats goin' out and we were watchin' them from the strand of Trienna Bay, Dermod and me. I called him Dermod, but he never got the christenin' words said over him or a drop of holy water. . . . Where is Ellen ? Ellen, ye're a good friend to me, ye are. The people that are sib to meself do not care what happens to one of their own kind, but it's ye yerself that has the good heart, Ellen. And ye say that Dermod Flynn is comin' to see me ? I would like to see him again. . . . I called me little boy after him, too. . . . Little Dermod, I called him, and now he's dead without the priest's blessin' ever put over him."

"I'm here, Norah," I said, for I knew that her mind was wandering. "I am here, Norah. I am Dermod Flynn. Do you know me now ? "

The long lashes dropped over her eyes and hid them from my sight.

"Norah, do you remember me?" I repeated. "I am Dermod, Dermod Flynn. Say Dermod after me."

She opened her eyes again and looked at me with a puzzled glance.

"Is it ye, Dermod?" she cried. "I knew that ye were comin' to see me. I was thinkin' of ye often and many's the time that I thought ye were standin' be me bed quiet like and takin' a look at me. Ye're here now, are ye? Say true as death."

"True as death," I repeated after her. The phrase was a Glenmornan one.

"Then where is Ellen and where is the man that came here this mornin' and left a handful of money to help us along?" she asked. "He was a good kindly man, givin' us so much money and maybe needin' it himself, too. Joe was his name."

"Moleskin Joe," I said.

"There were three men on the street and they made fun of me when I was passin' them," said Norah, and her mind was wandering again. "And one of the men caught me and I tried to get away and I struggled and fought. For wasn't I forgiven for me sins at the chapel that day and I was goin' to be a good woman all the rest of me life? I told the men to let me alone and one of them kicked me and I fell on the cold street. No one came to help me. Who would care at all, at all, for a woman like me? The very peelis will not give me help. 'Twas Ellen that picked me up when the last gasp was almost in me mouth. And she has been the good friend to me ever since. Sittin' up at night be me side and workin' her fingers to the bone for me durin' the livelong day. Ellen, ye're very good to me."

"Ellen is not here, Norah," I said, and the tears were running down my cheek.

I placed my hand on Norah's forehead, which was cold as marble, and at that moment somebody entered the room. I was aware of the presence of the newcomer, but never looked round. Norah's face now wore a look of calm repose and her lashes falling slowly hid the far-away look in her grey eyes. For a moment I thought that she held silent council with the angels.

I was still aware of the presence. Somebody came forward, bent tenderly over the bed and softly brushed the stray tresses back from Norah's brow. It was the woman, Gourock Ellen. At that moment I felt myself an intruder, one who was looking on things too sacred for his eyes.

" Norah, are you asleep ? " Ellen asked, and there was no answer.

" Norah ! Norah ! " The woman of the streets bent closer to the girl in the bed and pressed her hand to Norah's heart.

" Have ye come back, Ellen ? " Norah asked, in a quiet voice without opening her eyes. " I was dreamin' in the same old way. I saw him comin' back again. He was standin' be me bed and he was very kind, like he always was."

" He's here, little lass," answered Ellen ; then to me, " Speak to her, man ! She's been wearin' her heart awa' thinkin' of you for a lang, lang, weary while. Speak to her and we'll save her yet. She's just wanderin' a bit in her heid."

" Then it's not dreamin' that I was ! " cried Norah. " It's Dermod himself that's in it and back again. Just comin' to see me ! It's himself that has the kindly Glenmornan heart and always had. Dermod, Dermod ! "

Her voice became low and strained and I bent closer to catch her words.

" It was ye that I was thinkin' of all the time and I

was foolish when we were workin' with Micky's Jim. It's all me fault and sorrow is on me because I made ye suffer. Maybe ye'll go home some day. If ye do, go to me mother's house and ask her to forgive me. Tell her that I died on the year I left Micky's Jim's squad. I was not me mother's child after that ; I was dead to all the world. My fault could not be undone—that's what made the blackness of it: Niver let yer own sisters go into a strange country, Dermod. Niver let them go to the potato-squad, for it's the place that is evil for a girl like me that hasn't much sense. Ye're not angry with me, Dermod, are ye ? "

"Norah, I was never angry with you," I said, and I kissed her lips. They were hot as fire. "Darling, you didn't think that I was angry with you ? "

"No, Dermod, for it's ye that has the kindly way ! " said the poor girl. "Would ye do something for me if iver ye go back to yer own place ? "

"Anything you ask, Norah," I answered, "and anything within my power to do."

"Will ye get a mass said for me in the chapel at home, a mass for the repose of me soul ? " she asked. "If ye do I'll be very happy."

When I raised my head, Moleskin was in the room. He had stolen in quietly, tired of waiting, and perhaps curious to see the end. He removed his cap and stood in the middle of the floor and looked curiously around. Norah sat up in bed and beckoned Ellen to approach.

She opened her mouth as if to speak, but there was a rattle in her throat, her teeth chattered, her hands opened and closed like those of a drowning man who clutches at floating sedge, and she dropped back to the pillow. Ellen and I hastened to help her, and laid her down quietly on the bed. Her eyes were open, her mouth wide apart showing two rows of white teeth. The spirit of the girl I loved had passed away. Without doubt, outside and over the smoke of the large city, a great angel with out-spread wings was waiting for her soul.

I was conscious of a great relief. Death, the universal comforter, had smoothed out things in a way that was best for the little girl, who knew the deep sorrows of an erring woman when only a child.

Joe looked awkwardly around. There was something weighing on his mind. Presently he touched me on the arm.

" Would there be any harm in me goin' down on my knees and sayin' a prayer ? " he asked.

" No harm, Joe," I said, as I knelt again by the bedside.

Ellen and Joe went down on their knees beside me. Outside the sounds of the city were loud in the air. An organ-grinder played his organ on the pavement ; a crowd of youngsters passed by, roaring out a comic song. Norah lay peacefully in the Great Sleep. I could neither think nor pray. My eyes were riveted on the dead woman.

The candle made a final splutter and went out. Inside the room there was complete darkness. Joe hardly breathed, and not knowing a prayer, he was silent. From time to time I could hear loud sobs, the words of a great prayer—the heart prayer of a stricken woman. Gourock Ellen was weeping.

THE END

CPSIA information can be obtained
at www.ICGtesting.com
Printed in the USA
LVHW080044220821
695831LV00008B/583